Tinkercad Basics
An Easy Approach

K Prathima

Table of Contents

Chapter 1: Getting Started

Tinkercad is a free and easy-to-use app for 3D design, electronics, and coding, used by various individuals to create different projects. It offers a learning center with starter projects for beginners and requires no downloads, making it accessible to everyone. With over 50 million users, Tinkercad helps bring designs to life, from 3D models to electronic circuits. The platform provides resources like guides, tutorial videos, and a quickstart guide to assist users in learning and exploring various design concepts.

Log in to Tinkercad

When you first log into Tinkercad, you will see the dashboard. The dashboard is the central hub of your Tinkercad experience. It's where you can access your designs, learn from tutorials, and explore designs shared by other users.

To log in, navigate to the Tinkercad website on your web browser. Click on the "**Log In**" button located at the top right corner of the homepage. You will be redirected to the login page. On the **Login** page, you can select anyone of the four options available. These options are explained next.

1. Educators Login:
- Click the **Educators** button.
- Click the **Email or Username** button.
- Enter your email address and password associated with your educator account.
- Click on **Sign In** to access your educator dashboard where you can manage your classes and view student work.

2. Student Accounts Login:
- Click the **Student Accounts** button.
- Click the **Email or Username** button.
- Enter your email address and password associated with your student account.
- Click on **Sign In** to access your personal workspace where you can create and manage your designs.

3. Student with Class Code Login:
- Click the **Student with Class Code** button.
- Enter the class code provided by your teacher.
- Click the **Go to my Class** button to start creating 3D designs. Your designs will be saved under your nickname and can be viewed by your teacher.

4. Personal Account Login:
- Click the **Personal accounts** button.
- Click the **Email or Username** button.
- Enter your email address and password associated with your personal account.
- Click on **Sign In** to access your personal workspace where you can create and manage your designs.

If you do not have an account, you can create one by clicking on "**Sign Up**".

Once you've logged in, you'll be taken to your personal dashboard. This is where you can see all your projects, drafts, and shared designs. You can also access Tinkercad's learning resources and community from the dashboard.

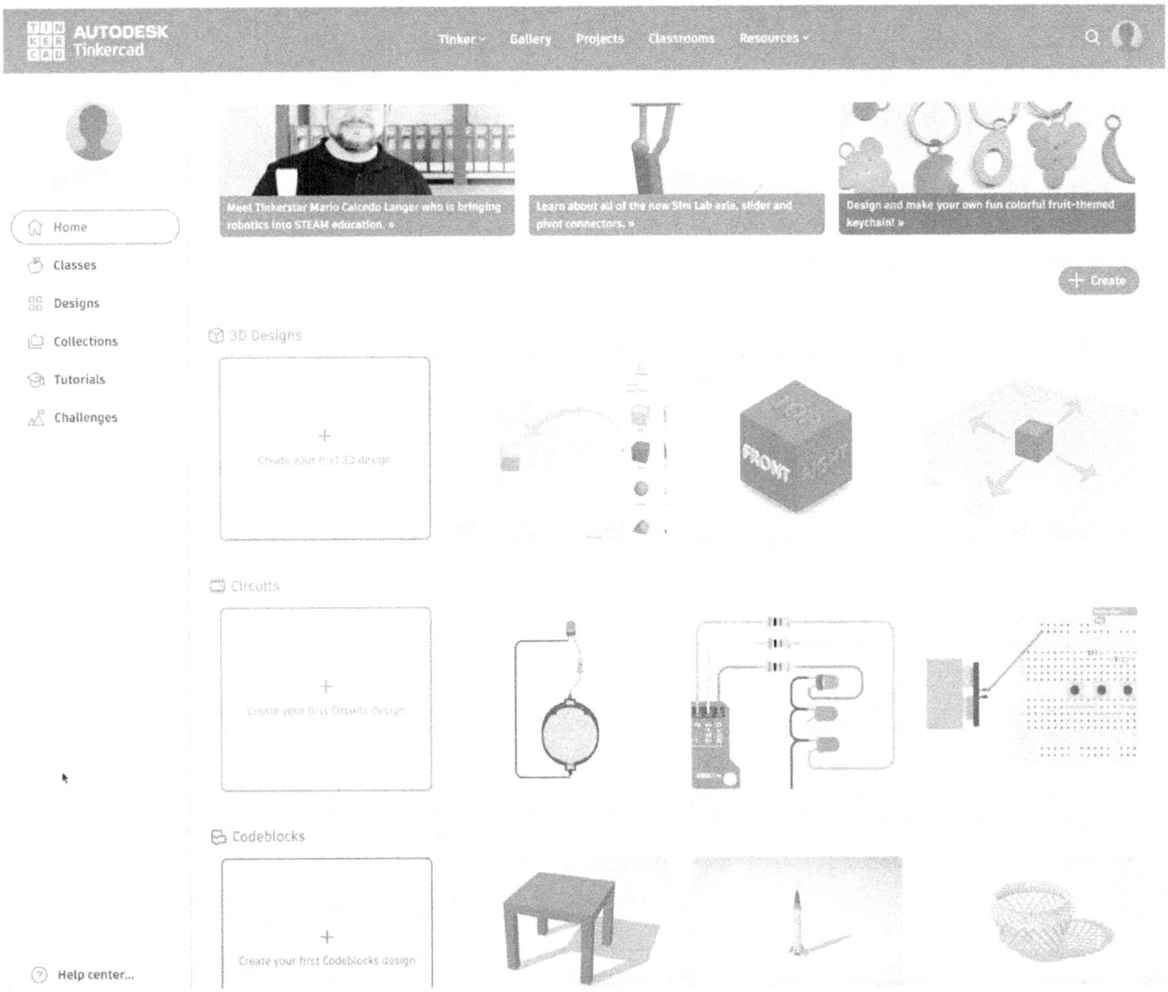

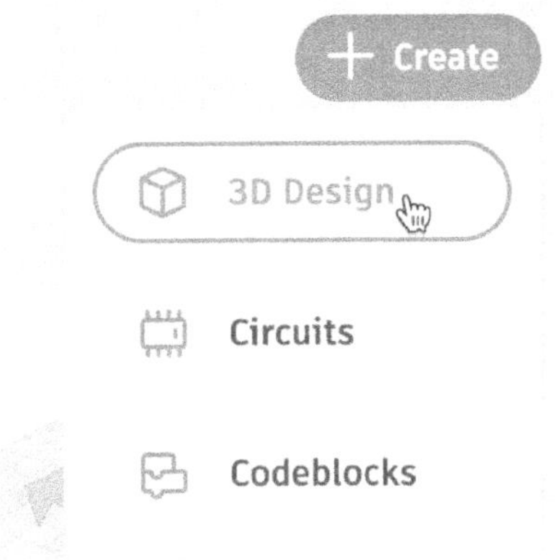

Create a New Design

To start a new project, click on the "**Create**" button, which is located in the middle of the dashboard. Next, select the **3D Design** option from the drop-down displayed; this will open up a new workspace for you to start designing in 3D.

The workspace is where you'll do all your designing. It's a grid that you can add shapes to, modify them, and arrange them to create your design. At the top of the workspace, you'll find the toolbar, which contains all the tools you'll need to manipulate your design.

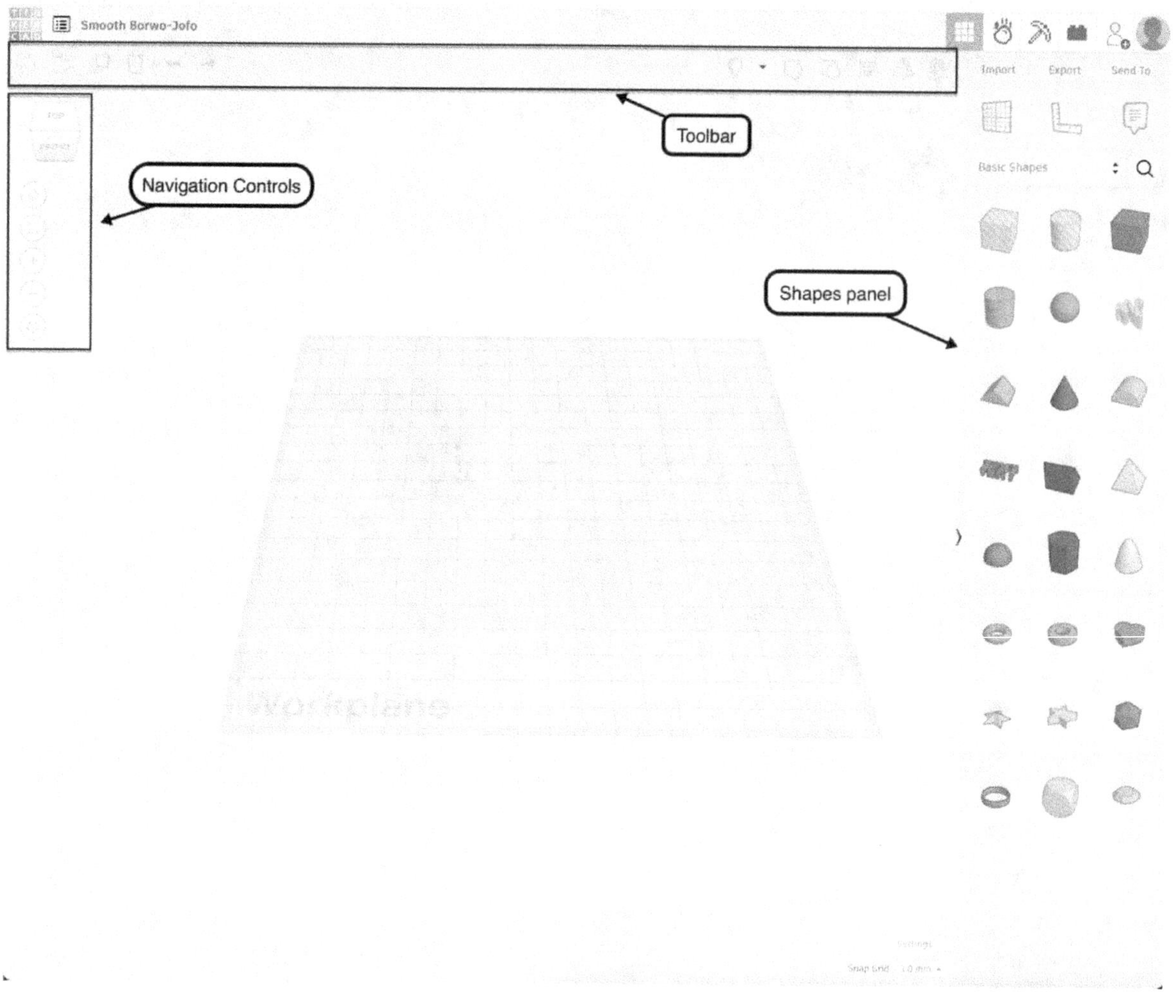

When you click **Create > 3D Design**, a new tab will open with a blank workspace. The name of your design will be automatically generated, but you can change it by clicking on the name at the top of the page and typing in your desired name.

User Interface

The Tinkercad interface is designed for simplicity and ease of use, suitable for all user levels. It consists of several sections, each dedicated to specific functions.

In the upper left-hand corner, you'll find a header with icons, each representing different Tinkercad features:

Tinkercad Logo

Clicking the Tinkercad logo returns you to the dashboard. Use this to quickly access your main page, where you can manage other designs or explore additional features.

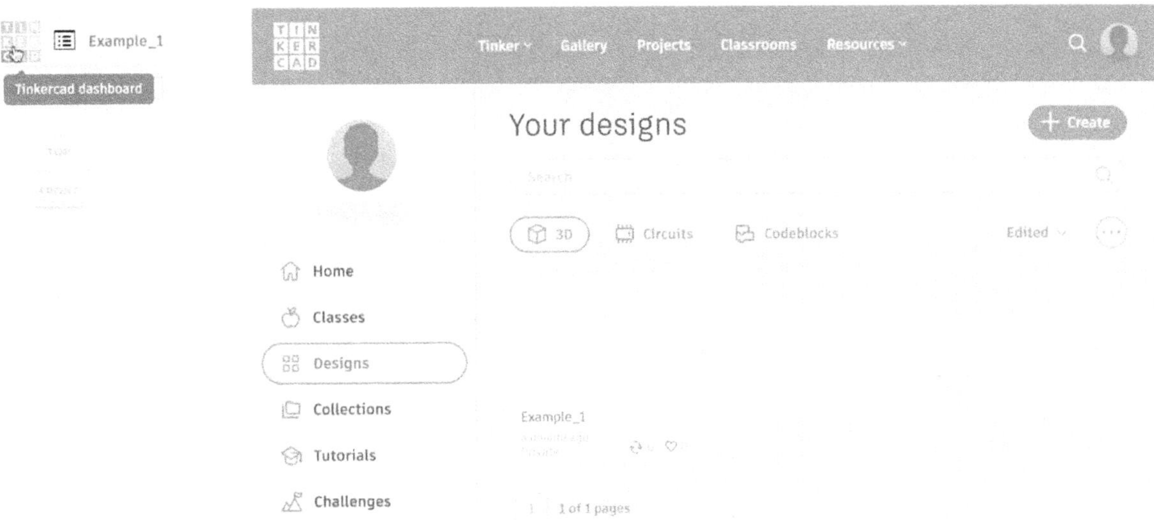

Box with Bullets Icon

This icon opens a gallery displaying your recent designs. Click any design to open it, or click " New Design" at the top of the menu to start a new deesign. Close the menu by clicking the 'X' in the top right corner of the gallery.

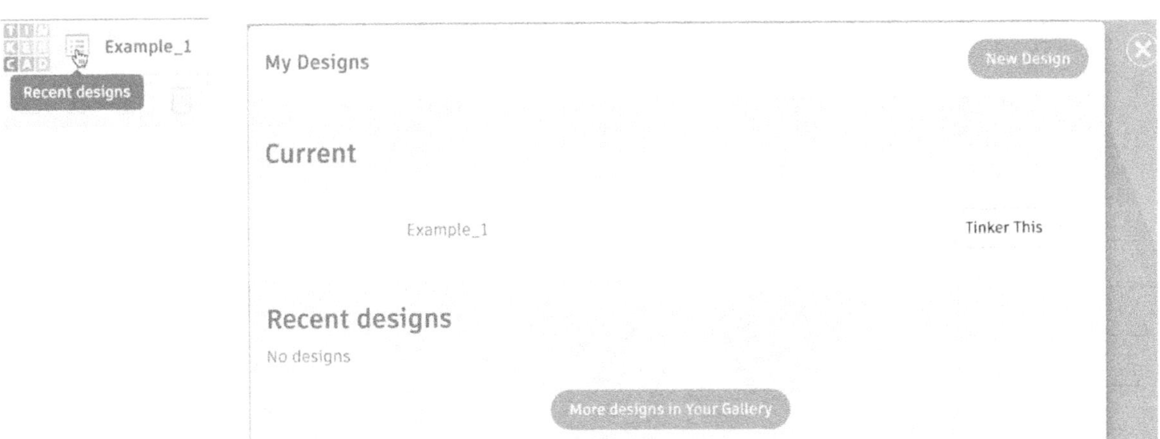

Workspace Icons

On the top-right corner of the Tinkercad user-interface, you will find four distinct workspace icons. Each icon is designed to represent a different mode of operation within Tinkercad, allowing for various styles of design work:

3D Design Workspace

This is the primary workspace where most design activities occur. In this mode, you can create and modify three-dimensional designs. It is set as the default workspace.

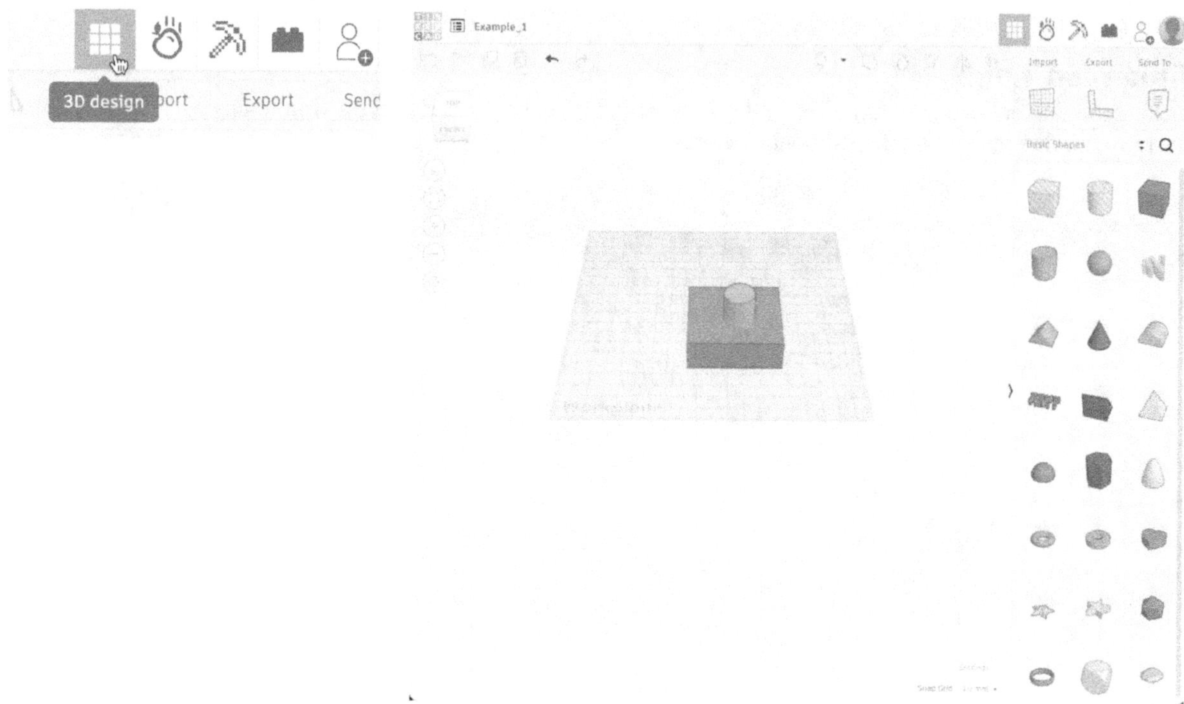

Block Mode

This mode allows you to use Minecraft-like blocks for creating pixel-style structures or objects. It's ideal for building architectural models or objects with a pixelated look.

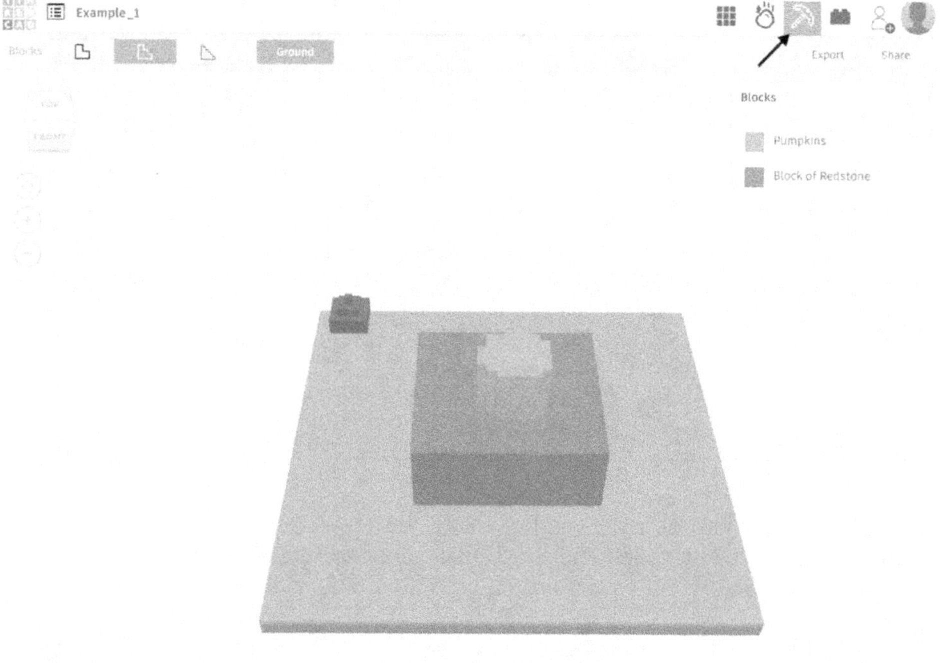

Brick Mode

This mode, like using LEGO bricks, lets you build structured models by assembling designs with interlocking elements.

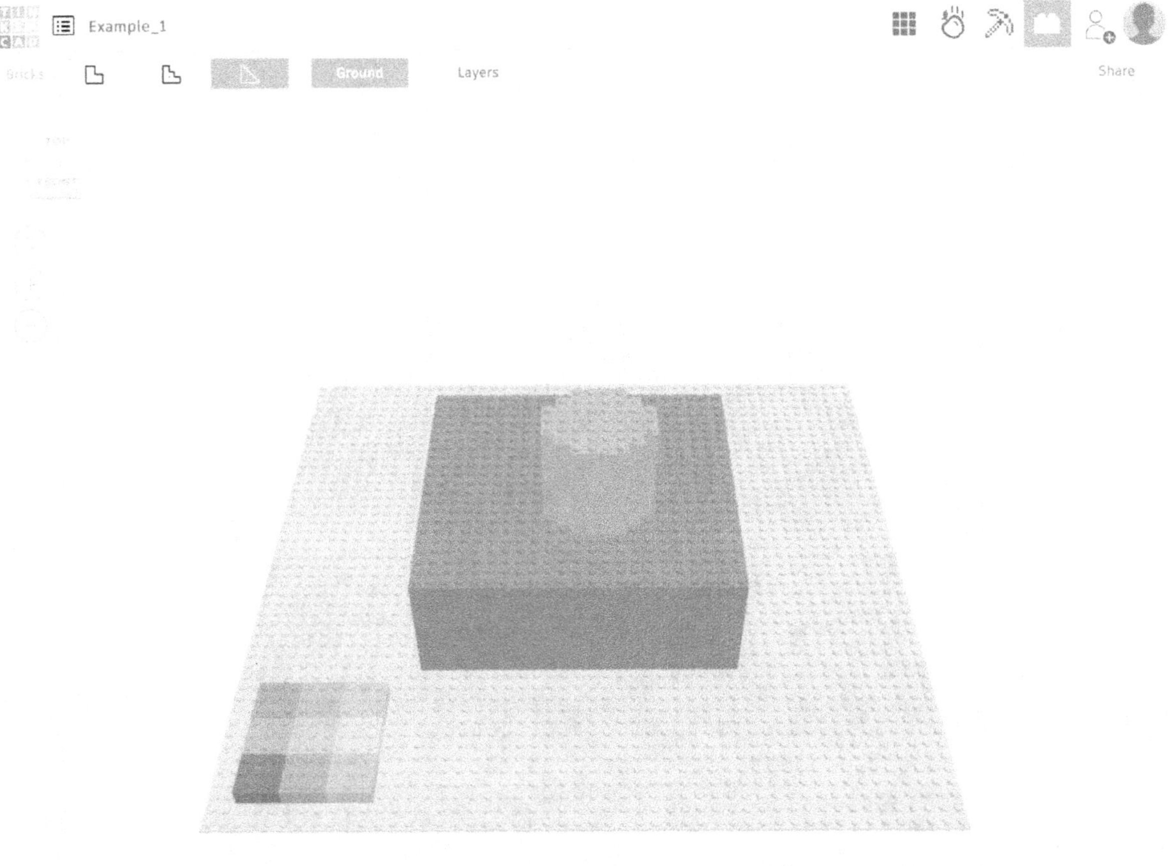

Sim Lab

The Sim Lab workspace simulates real-world physics. It allows you to simulate gravity, assign materials, build simple machines, and share their simulations. You can also set shapes as dynamic(movable) or static(immovable). While running simulations, you can 'throw' new objects into your design, which interact with existing shapes based on simulated physics.

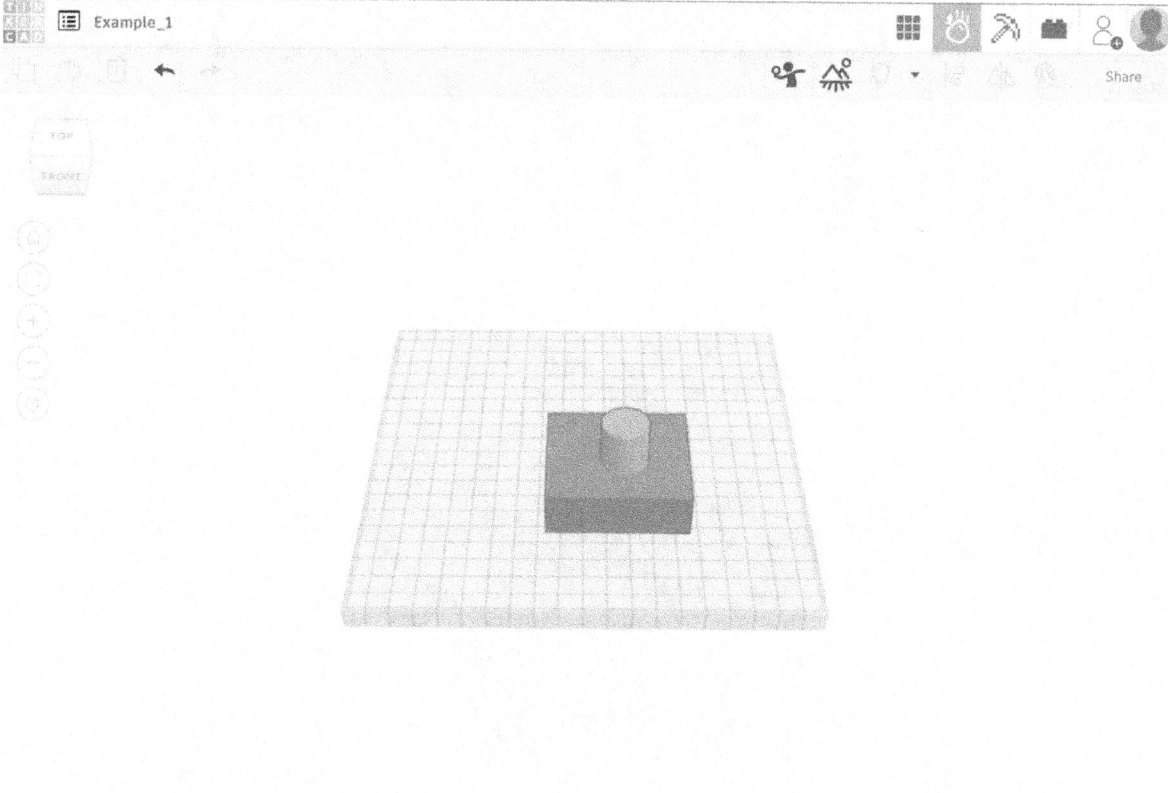

Each mode is accessible by clicking on the corresponding icon, which switches the workspace to your selected mode, enabling you to utilize the specific tools and features associated with that mode.

Invite people to design with you

Tinkercad facilitates collaborative design by offering a dedicated feature represented by the **Invite people to design with you** icon. This option enables you to invite others to view and edit their designs, fostering teamwork and shared creativity. To utilize this feature, follow these steps:

1. In the upper-right corner of the Tinkercad interface, click the **Invite people to design with you** icon; the **Collaborate** dialog appears.
2. On the **Collaborate** dialog, click the **Generate new link** button.
3. Click **Copy Link** to copy the generated link.
4. Share the copied link through email or other messaging platforms.

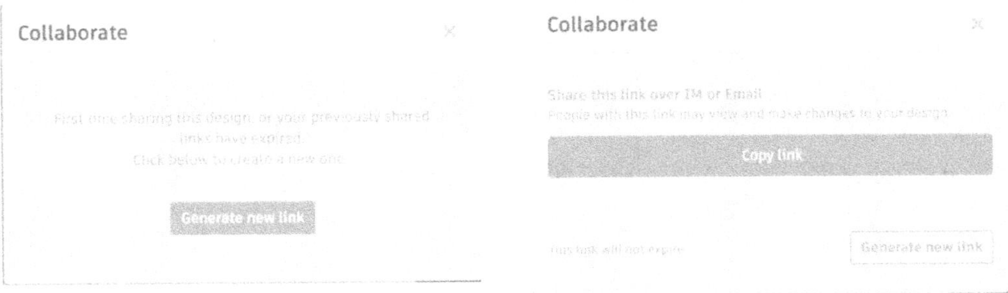

Toolbar

The toolbar is located at the top of your work area. It has many tools like **Copy**, **Paste**, **Duplicate**, etc. These tools help you change your design..

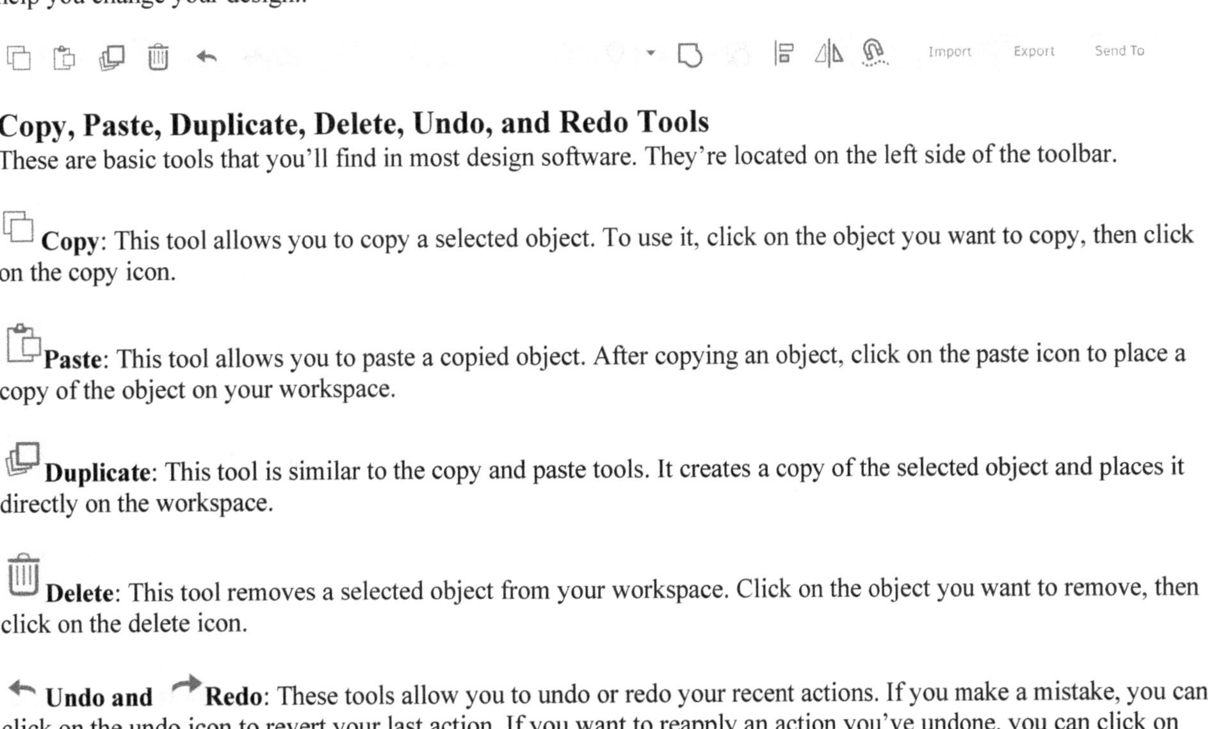

Copy, Paste, Duplicate, Delete, Undo, and Redo Tools

These are basic tools that you'll find in most design software. They're located on the left side of the toolbar.

Copy: This tool allows you to copy a selected object. To use it, click on the object you want to copy, then click on the copy icon.

Paste: This tool allows you to paste a copied object. After copying an object, click on the paste icon to place a copy of the object on your workspace.

Duplicate: This tool is similar to the copy and paste tools. It creates a copy of the selected object and places it directly on the workspace.

Delete: This tool removes a selected object from your workspace. Click on the object you want to remove, then click on the delete icon.

Undo and Redo: These tools allow you to undo or redo your recent actions. If you make a mistake, you can click on the undo icon to revert your last action. If you want to reapply an action you've undone, you can click on the redo icon.

Modification Tools

Next to the basic tools, you'll find the modification tools. These tools allow you to manipulate the shapes and objects in your design.

Group: This tool allows you to group multiple objects together so that they can be moved or modified as a single unit.

Ungroup: This tool allows you to ungroup a group of objects, enabling you to move or modify them individually.

Show Hidden Shapes: This option enables you to display shapes or objects that have been previously hidden from view.

Hide Notes: This option allows you to hide any text-based notes or annotations that you have added to your design.

Hide Connectors: This option enables you to hide the visual representation of any connectors or joints between objects in your design.

Align: Helps position your objects precisely.

Mirror: Flips your object along a chosen axis.

Cruise: Allows you to place shapes onto any surface in your workspace by simply clicking and dragging.

Import/Export Options

These options allow you to import designs from your computer or export your designs to be used in other software or to be 3D printed.

Import: This option allows you to import a design from your computer into Tinkercad. You can import designs in various formats, including STL, OBJ, and SVG.

Export: This option allows you to export your design in a format that can be used by other software or 3D printers. You can export designs in STL, OBJ, SVG, and other formats.

Send To: This option allows you to export your 3D designs to other platforms or software for further modification or 3D printing

Shapes Panel

The Shapes Panel is a key feature located on the right-hand side of the screen. It contains a variety of shapes and tools that you can use in your designs.

Collapsing and Expanding the Shapes Panel

You can collapse the Shapes Panel to give yourself more workspace. To do this, locate the arrow on the edge of the panel. Clicking on this arrow will collapse the panel, hiding it from view and giving you more space to work on your design. If you want to bring the panel back, simply click on the arrow again. The panel will expand, and you can access all the shapes and tools again.

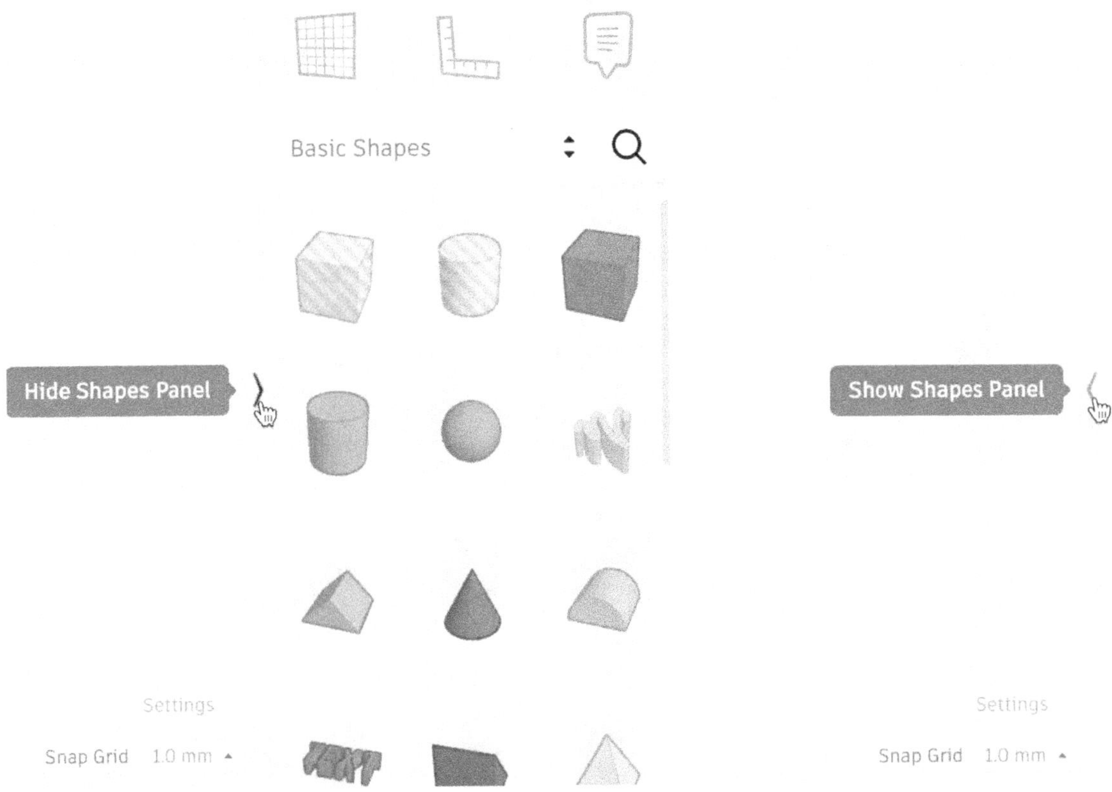

At the top of the Shapes Panel, you'll find three important tools: the Work Plane, the Ruler, and the Notes.

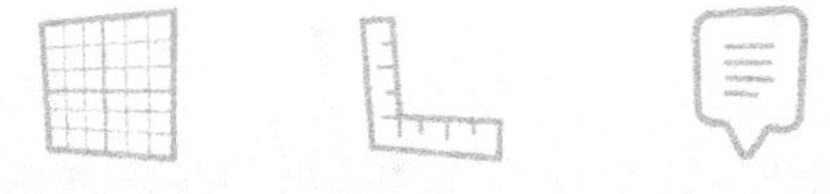

Work Plane: This tool allows you to add a work plane to your design. A work plane is like a surface that you can place shapes on. You can add multiple work planes to your design, allowing you to work on different parts of your design at the same time.

Ruler: This tool allows you to measure distances and angles in your design. To use it, click on the ruler icon and then click on the point in your design that you want to measure from. A line will appear that you can drag to the point you want to measure to. The distance or angle between the two points will be displayed.

Notes: This tool lets you add comments to your designs. This is helpful for adding extra information or instructions about specific parts of your design.

Accessing and Utilizing Shape Sets in Tinkercad

In Tinkercad, beneath the Work Plane and Ruler tools on the interface, there is a dropdown menu. This menu provides access to a variety of shape sets that can be used to enhance your 3D designs.

Types of Shape Sets

Shape sets are categorized into different types based on the nature of the shapes they contain. These categories include:

1. **Basic Shapes**: This set comprises fundamental shapes such as cylinder, sphere, cube, cone, text and so on.

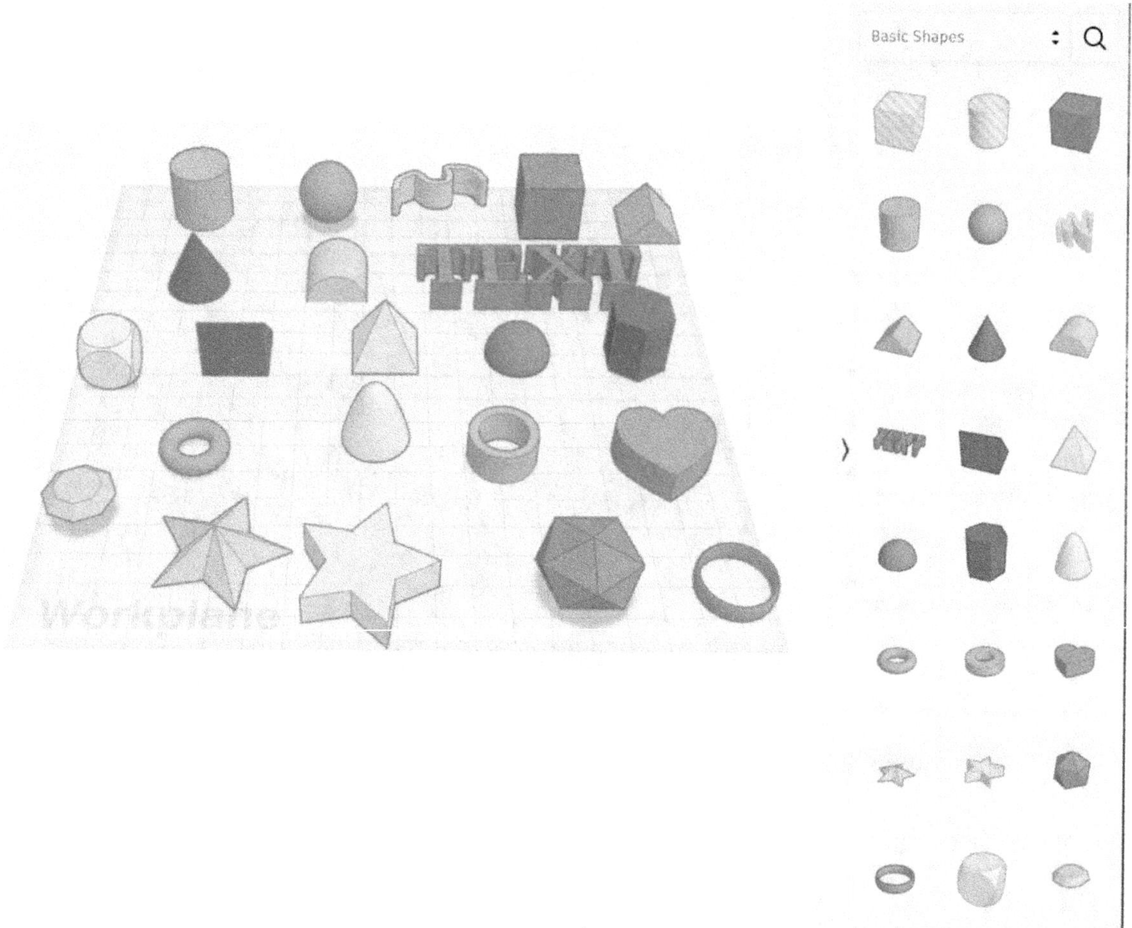

2. **Design Starters**: Predefined shapes that you can use as a starting point for your designs, including basic geometric shapes, letters, numbers, symbols, and decorative elements.

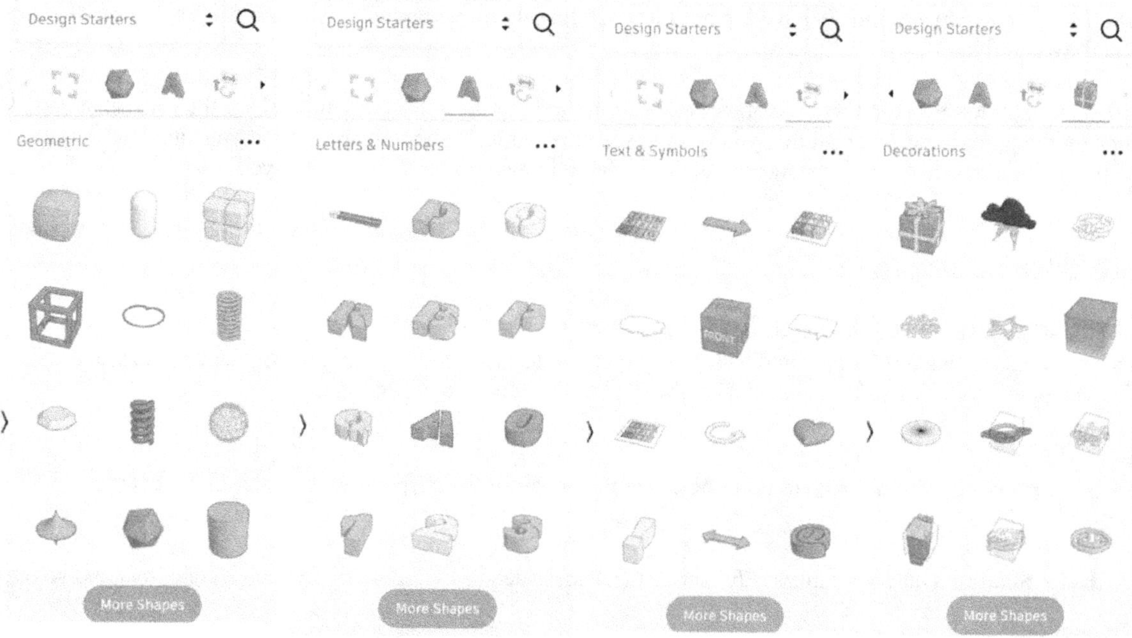

3. **Creatures & Characters**: This set includes various shapes such as bodies, faces, accessories, people, and animals. These shapes helps you to create new characters and creatures.

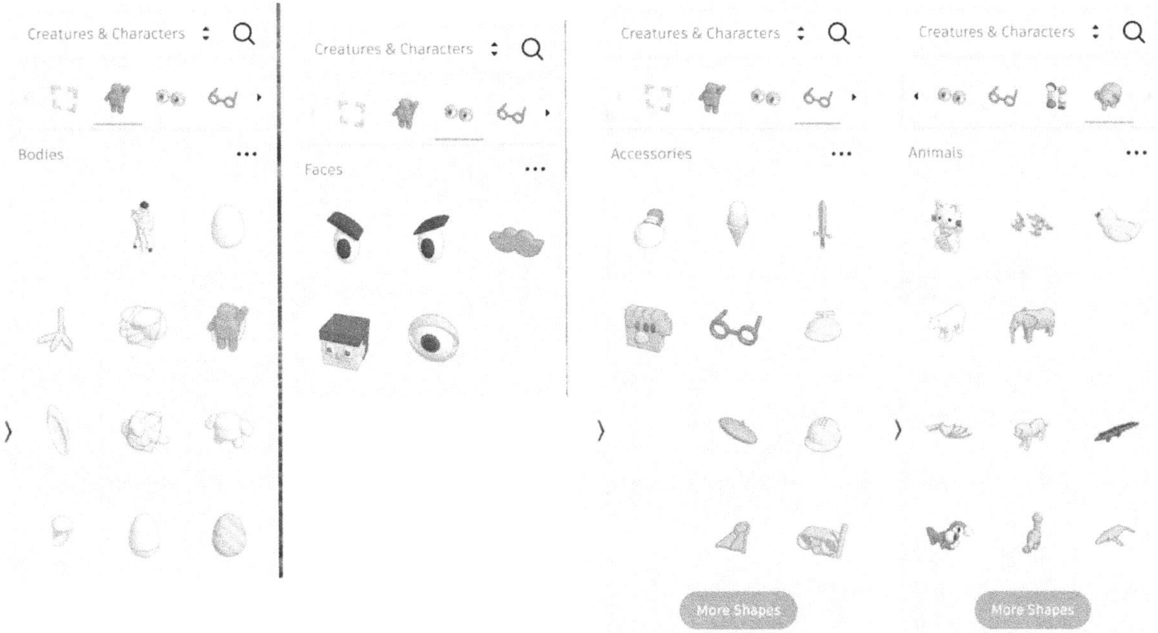

4. **Vehicles & Machines**: This set includes shapes of different vehicles and machines such as wheels, space, and robots.

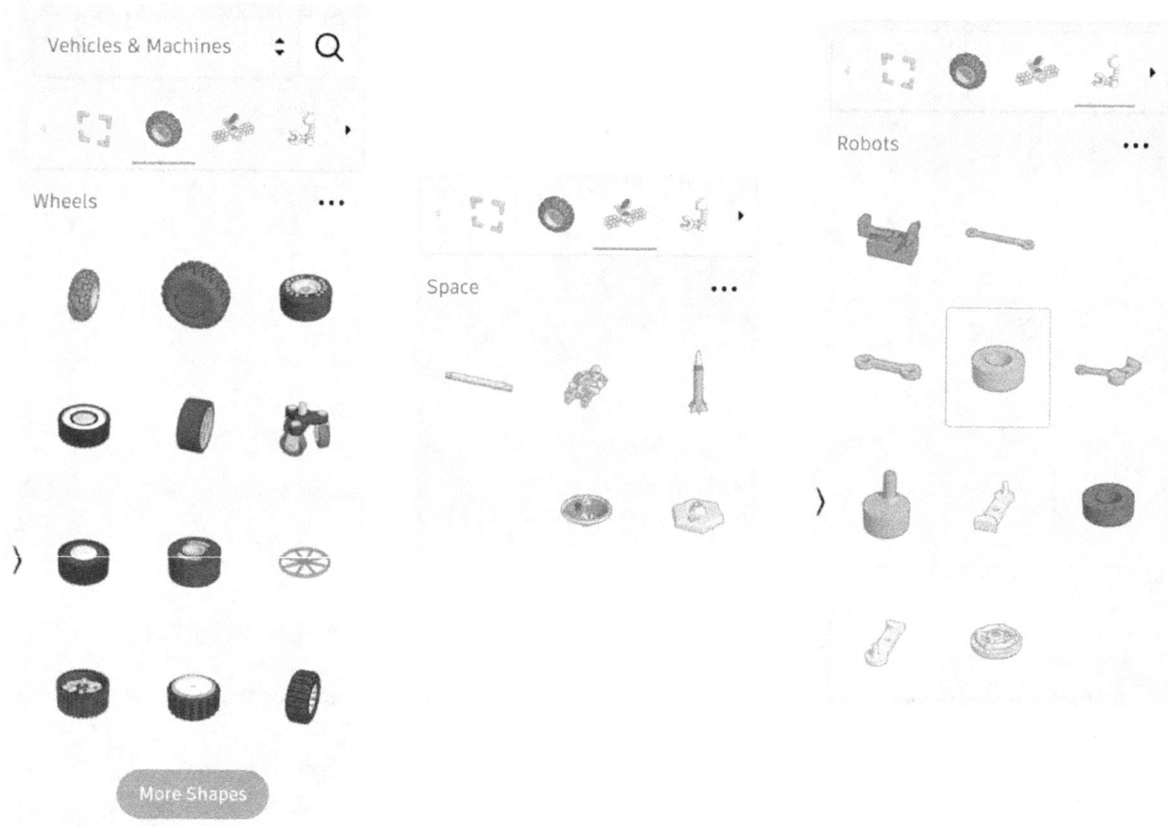

5. **Structures & Scenery**: This set includes shapes of different structures and scenery items such as buildings, structures, landscapes, and furniture.

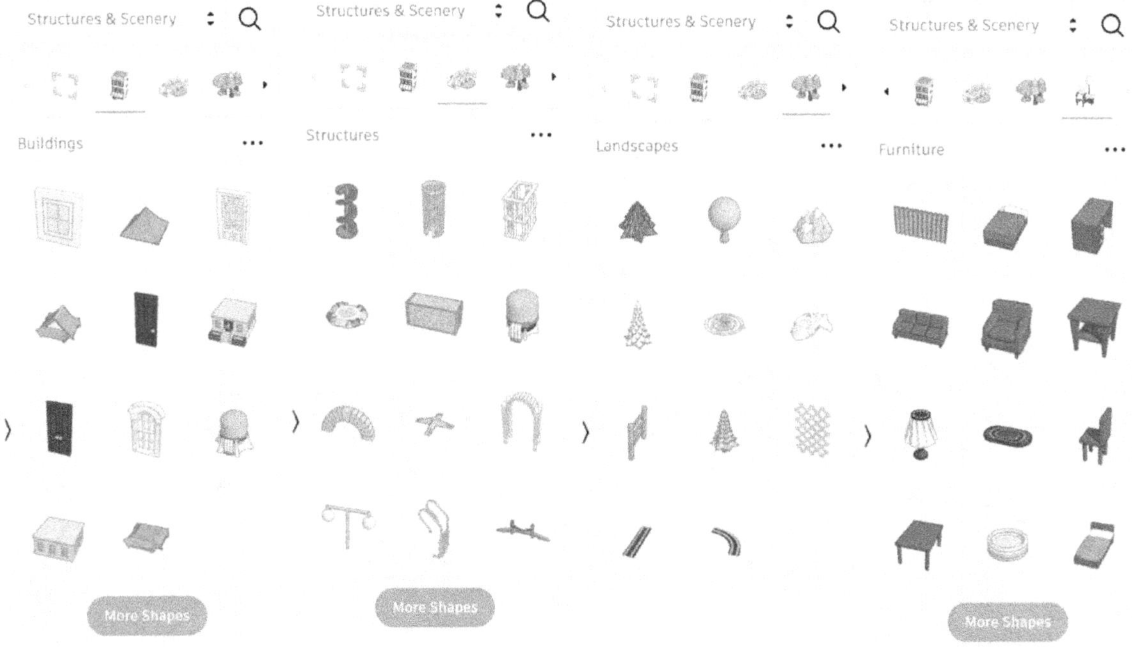

6. **Hardware**: This set includes various hardware components such as gears/axles, connectors, and fittings.

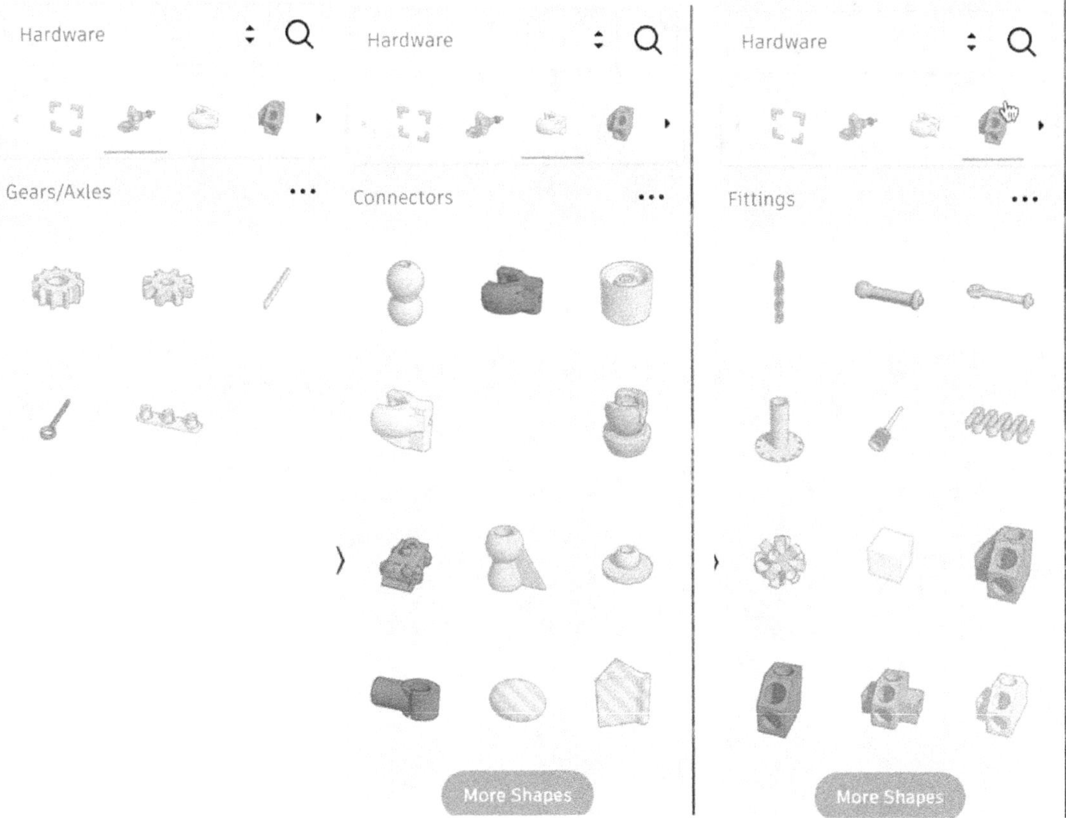

7. **Electronics**: This set includes various electronic components for creating and simulating circuits in your designs.

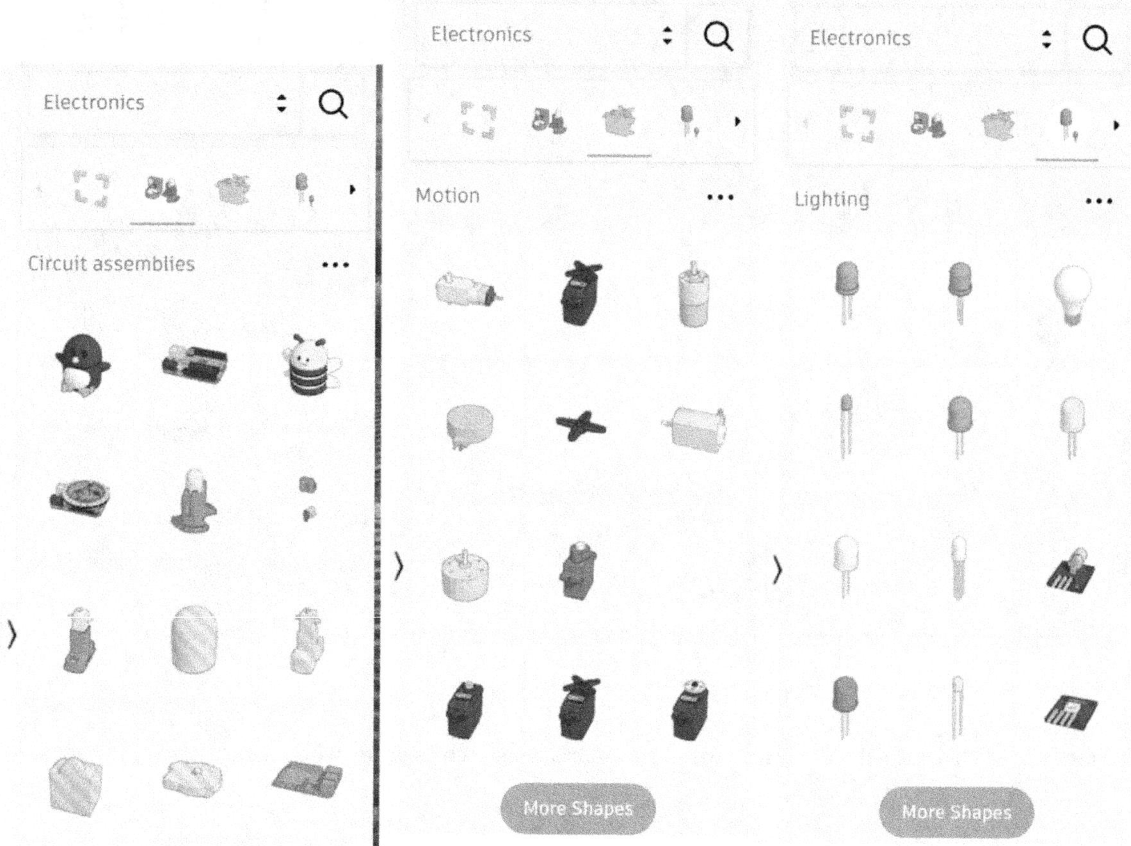
Electronics
Circuit assemblies
Electronics
Motion
Electronics
Lighting
More Shapes
More Shapes

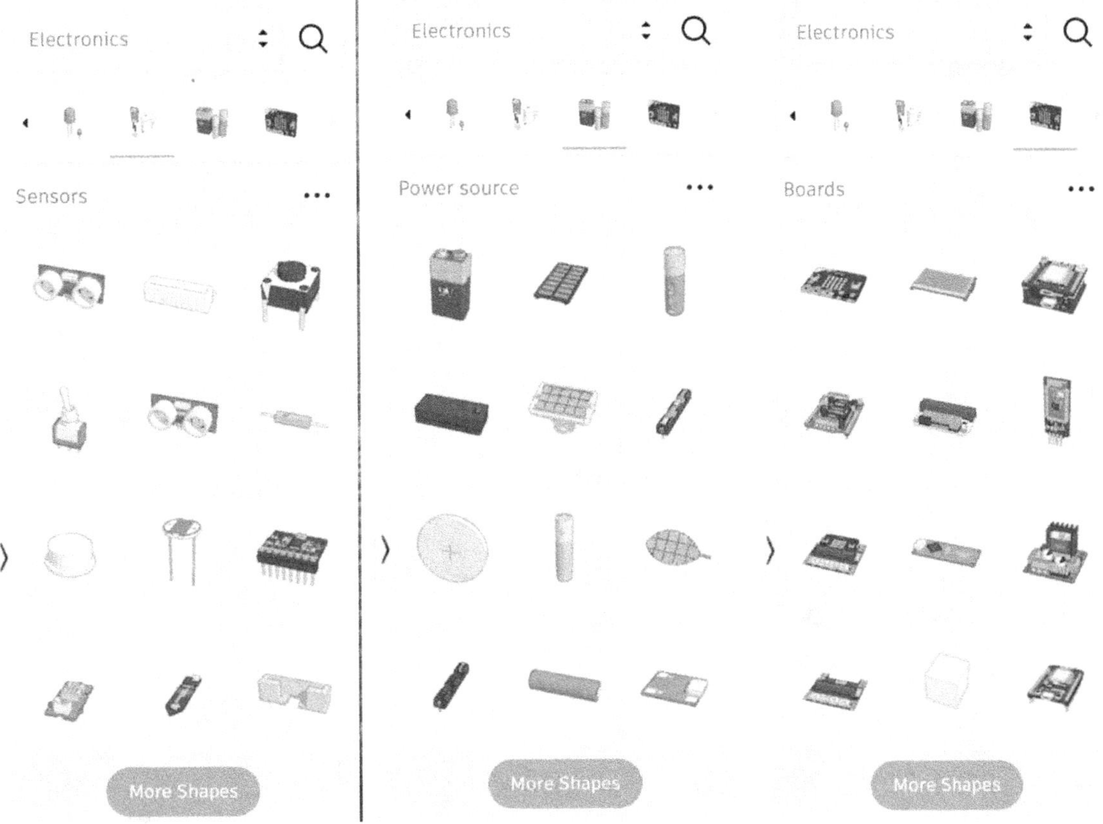

8. **Fun & Games**: This set includes various game-related shapes and components such as toys, sports, playground, music, holiday, and building toys.

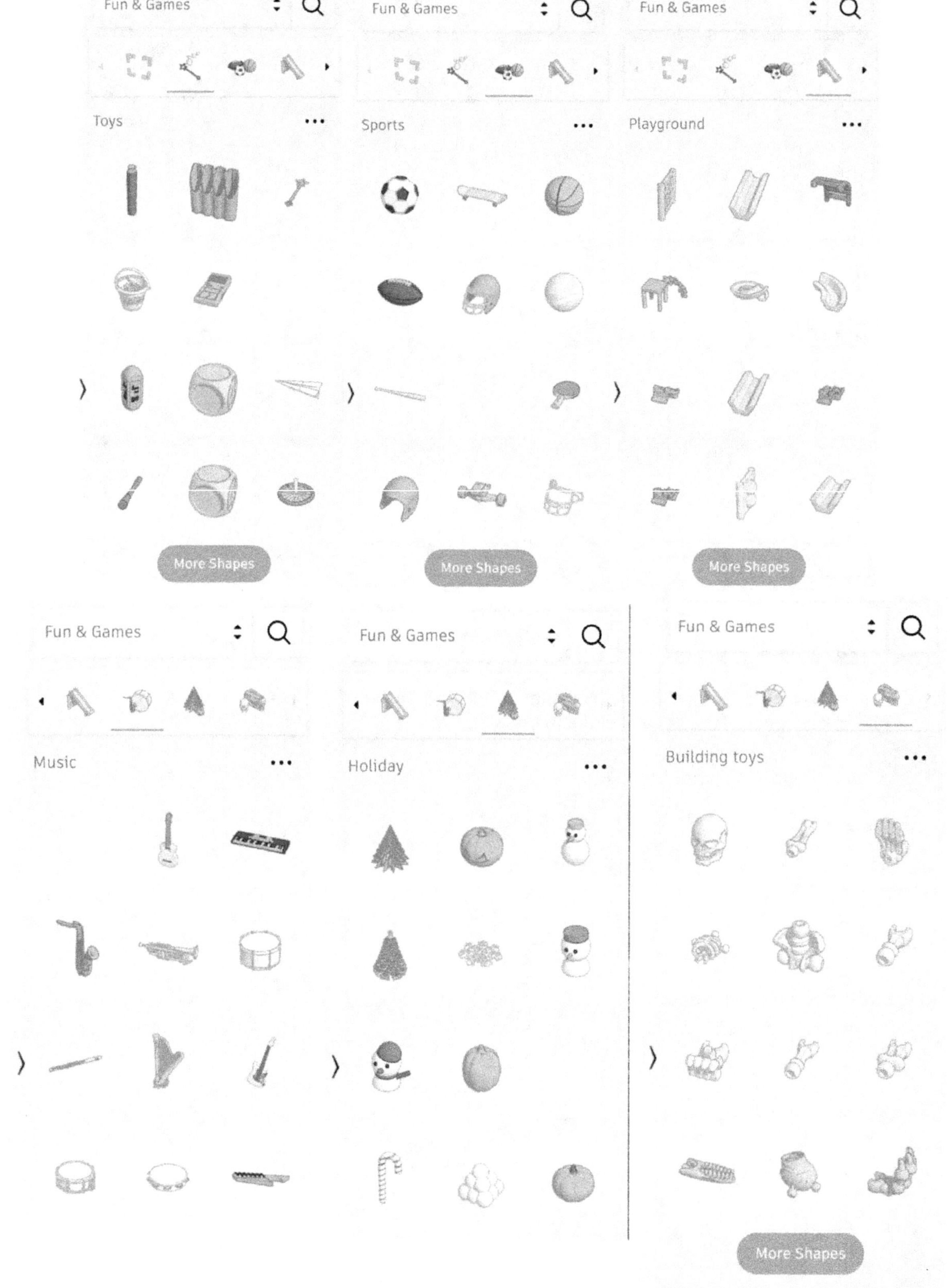

Fun & Games
Toys
More Shapes
Fun & Games
Sports
More Shapes
Fun & Games
Playground
More Shapes
Fun & Games
Music
Fun & Games
Holiday
Fun & Games
Building toys
More Shapes

9. **Everyday Objects**: This set includes shapes of everyday objects such as office supplies, wood stock, gadgets, recyclables, art supplies, and tools.

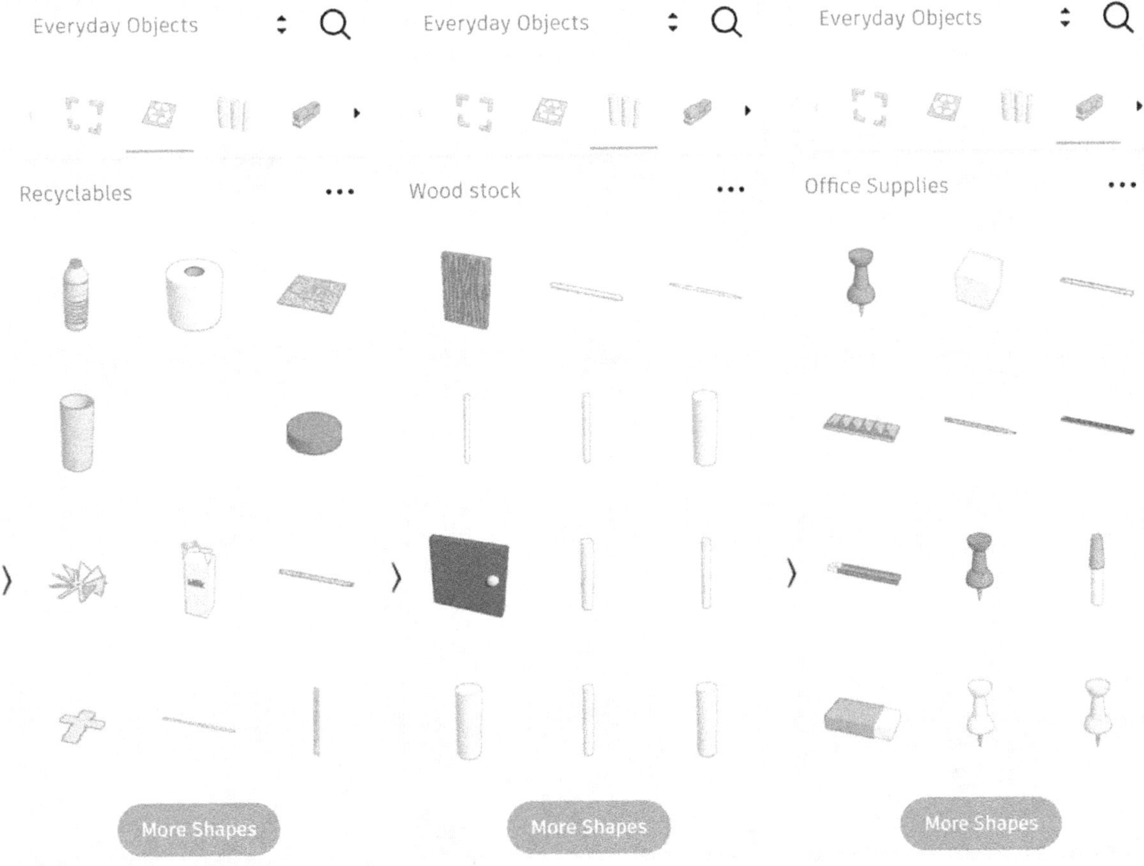

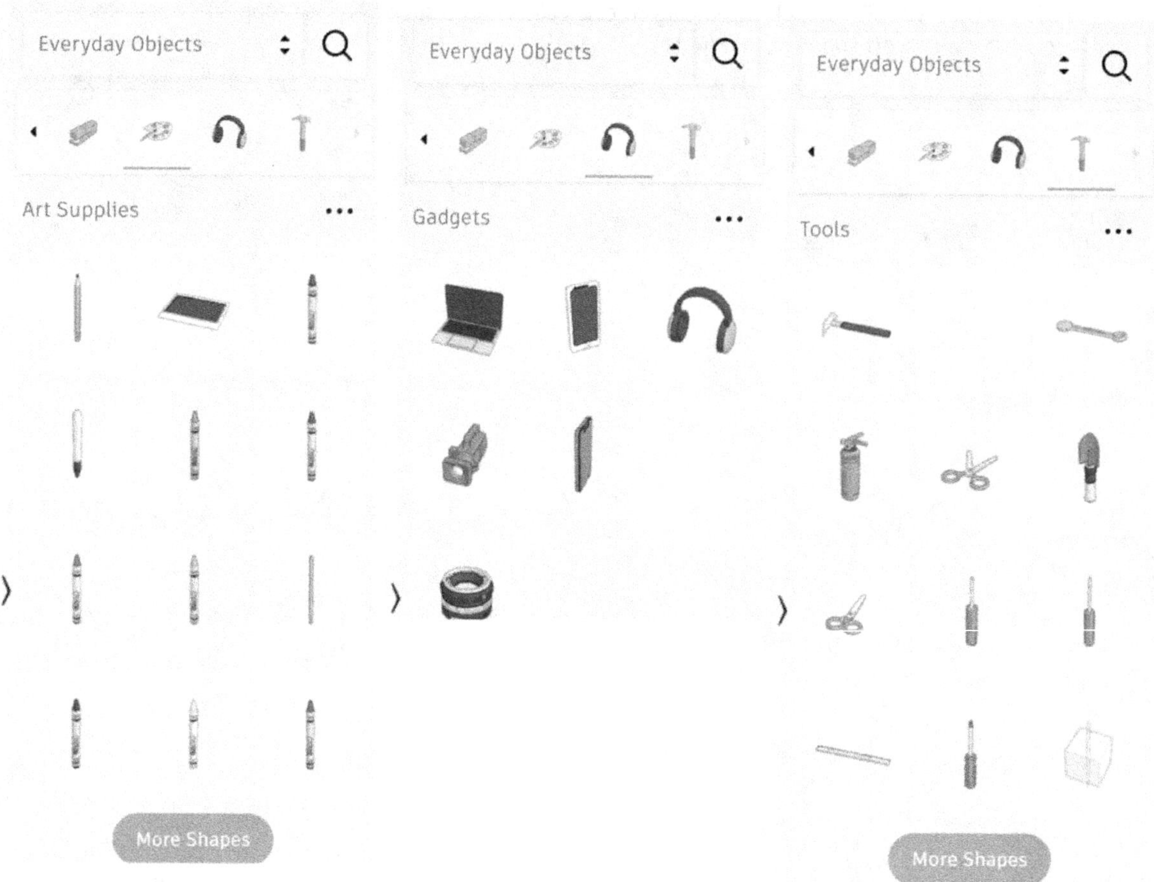

10. **Featured Collections**: This set includes featured collections of shapes from Oregon Museum of Science and Industry, Smithsonian, STEMFIE, and XRP Battery Cover for regular chassis.

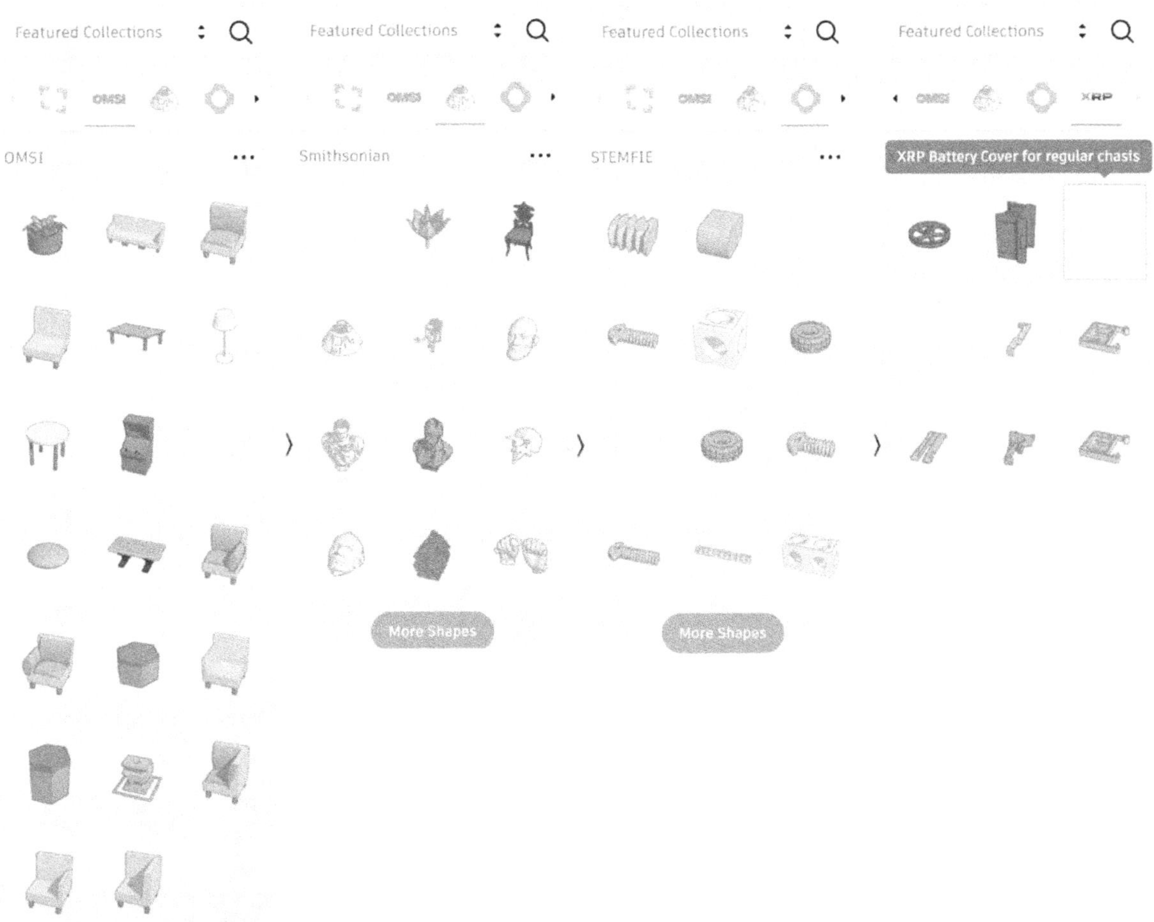

11. **Sim Lab**: This set includes various connectors and objects that simulate the real-world physics.

12. **Shape Generators**: Scripts that generate 3D shapes in Tinkercad, allowing you to create complex shapes using simple parameters.

Work Plane

The work plane is the primary area in the Tinkercad interface where you construct your design. It's a flat, grid-like surface that acts as your virtual tabletop. Building your design in Tinkercad involves adding and manipulating shapes on this work plane.

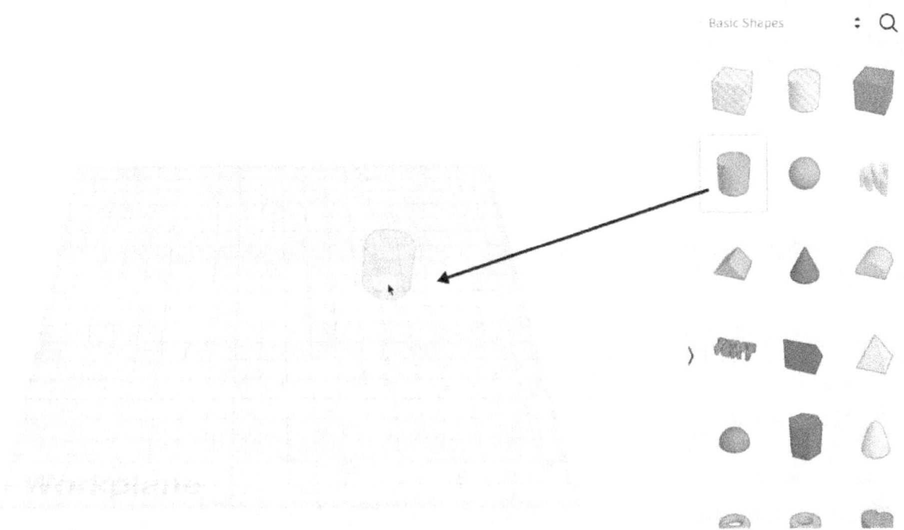

Navigation Controls

The navigation controls are located to the left of the work plane. These offer several options for adjusting your view of the work plane. These controls enable you to view your design from various angles and perspectives.

- **Zoom in**: Click this icon to zoom in and get a closer look at your design.
- **Zoom out**: Click this icon to zoom out and see your design from a distance.
- **Home**: The home icon resets your view to the default orientation. Click on this icon if you ever get lost while navigating and want to quickly return to the default view.
- **Fit in All View**: This option fits the model in the current size of the graphics window so that it will be visible completely.

Viewcube

The ViewCube is a cube-shaped navigation tool that appears at the upper-left corner. It provides visual feedback about the current viewpoint of the model as view changes occur. By clicking on different faces of the ViewCube, you can quickly switch to standard views such as top, front, right, and isometric views.

Orbiting

To rotate your view around the work plane, you can use the orbiting feature. Press and hold the right mouse button and drag to spin the work plane around.

Panning

You can also pan your view, moving it horizontally or vertically without changing the orientation. To do this, press and hold the middle mouse button and drag to shift your view.

Switching between Two View Modes

In Tinkercad, there are two different view modes that you can use to visualize your designs: Orthographic and Perspective.

Orthographic Mode

Orthographic mode is a type of projection in which objects are displayed with parallel edges and the same size, regardless of their distance from the viewer. This means that objects further away from the viewer do not appear smaller, as they would in real life or in perspective mode.

In orthographic mode, the size of an object on the screen is solely determined by its actual size, not its distance from the viewer. This can make it easier to accurately measure and align objects, as their size and shape are not distorted by perspective.

To switch to orthographic mode, click the **Switch to flat view** icon located at the bottom of the Navigation controls.

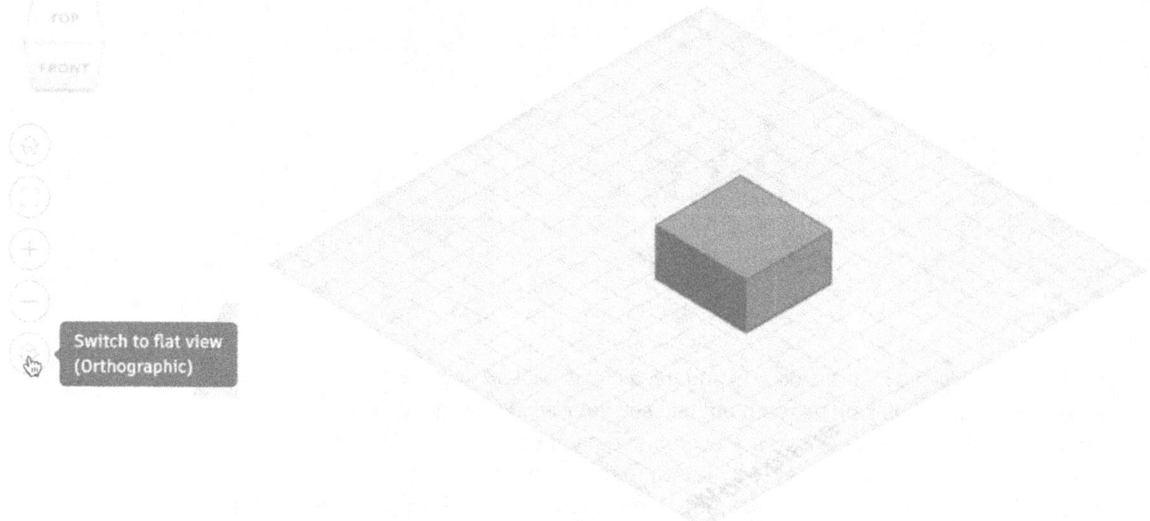

Perspective Mode

Perspective mode, on the other hand, shows objects with receding edges and varying sizes based on distance. This means that objects further away from the viewer appear smaller, while objects closer to the viewer appear larger, mimicking the way we see things in real life.

In perspective mode, the size of an object on the screen is determined by both its actual size and its distance from the viewer. This can make designs appear more realistic and three-dimensional, but it can also make precise measurements and alignments more challenging.

To switch to perspective mode, click the **Switch to Perspective view** icon located at the bottom of the Navigation controls.

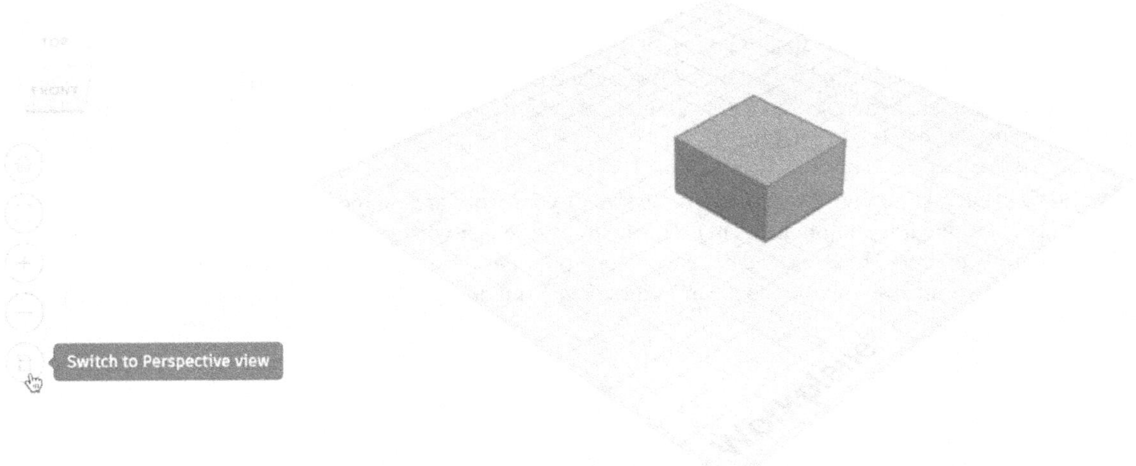

Adjusting the Workspace Settings

In this section, you will go through the process of changing the units, width, height, and snap grid of the work plane.

Step 1: Access the Grid Settings

The grid settings are located in the lower right-hand corner of your workspace. To access these settings, look for the "**Settings**" button and click on it. This will open a dialog box with various options for adjusting the grid settings.

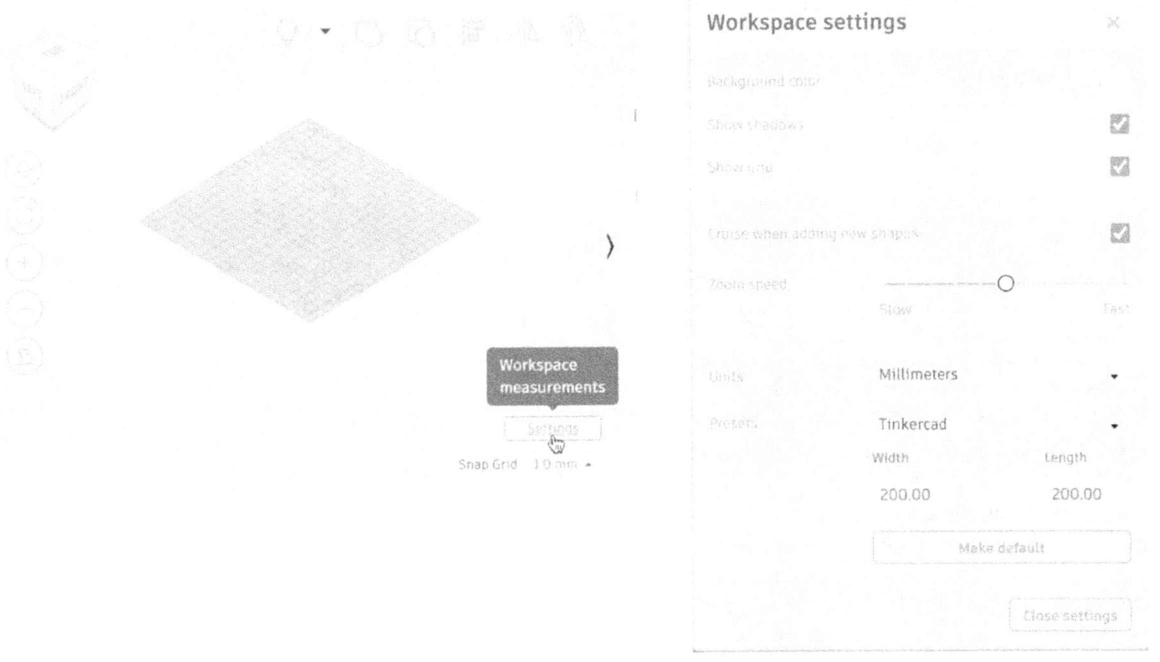

Step 2: Change the Units

The first setting you'll see in the dialog box is the units. Tinkercad gives you the option to choose between millimeters, inches, and bricks. For the purpose of this book, you will be using millimeters. To change the units, click on the dropdown menu next to "**Units**" and select "**Millimeters**".

Step 3: Change the Width and Height

Imagine you're working on a project that's very small. If the work plane is too big, it can be difficult to work with. That's where adjusting the width and height of the work plane comes in. By changing the size of the work plane, you can make it fit your project better, so you can work more efficiently. You can do this by simply entering the desired values in the "**Width**" and "**Height**" fields.

If you own a 3D printer, you might need to adjust the size of your work area in the software to match the size of your printer's base (where the printing happens). This helps ensure that what you design can fit and be printed correctly on your 3D printer. The **Presets** drop-down menu provides a list of pre-set options that represent popular 3D printer brands. This means you can choose from these ready-made settings that are tailored to fit specific brands.

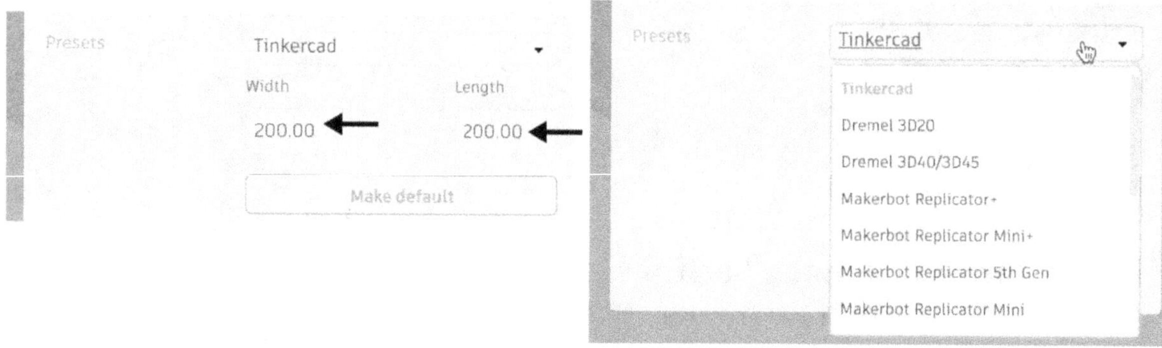

Step 4: Change the Background color

To modify the background color of your workspace, follow these steps:

1. Click on the **Background color** swatch.
2. Choose a color from the **Presets** gallery.

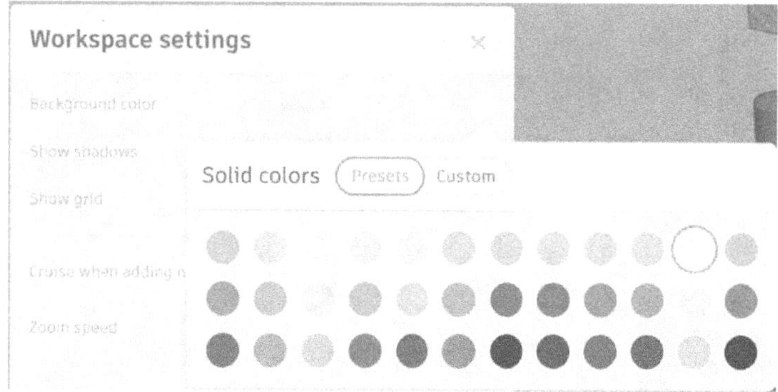

If you want to set a custom color, you can do so by:

1. Clicking on the **Custom** tab.
2. Selecting a color from the color wheel.

Alternatively, you can specify the color using RGB (Red, Green, Blue) values, HSB (Hue, Saturation, Brightness) values, or a **Hex** code. This allows for precise color selection to customize your workspace according to your preferences.

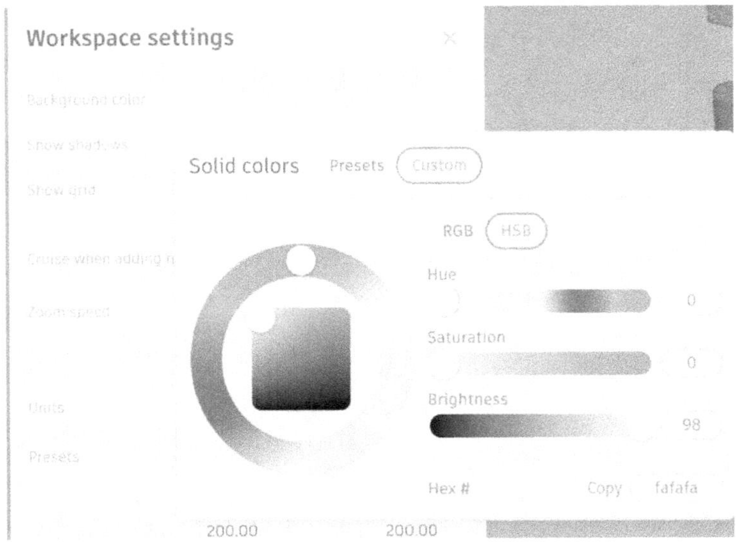

Step 6: Enabling and Disabling Grid and Shadows

To turn the grid and shadows ON or OFF, select or deselect the 'Show Grid' and 'Show Shadows' options respectively.

Step 7: Using the Cruise Feature When Adding New Shapes

The '**Cruise when adding new shapes**' option is usually turned on by default. This means when you drag a new shape from the Shapes panel onto your workspace, it will automatically move or 'cruise' onto other shapes that are already there. This can make it easier to add and position new shapes in your design.

Step 8: Adjusting Zoom Speed with the Slider

The '**Zoom speed**' slider is a lets you control how fast or slow you zoom in or out. When you move this slider, it changes how quickly the view gets closer or farther away when you click the '**Zoom in**' or '**Zoom out**' buttons. This can help you get a better look at your work.

Click the **Close Settings** button after adjusting the workspace settings.

Step 9: Change the Snap Grid

The snap grid is a setting in Tinkercad that controls how objects and dimensions align or "snap" into place when you move or resize them. It's like having invisible lines on your workspace that help you place your objects accurately.

By default, the snap grid is set to one millimeter. This means that when you move or resize an object, it will align to the nearest millimeter.

However, you can adjust the snap grid to fit your needs. To do this, click on the dropdown menu next to "Snap grid" and choose a different measurement. For instance, if you're working on a project that requires more precision, you might change the snap grid to 0.5 or 0.1 millimeters.

Off
0.1 mm
0.25 mm
0.5 mm
1.0 mm
2.0 mm
5.0 mm
Brick
Snap Grid   1.0 mm ▲

Chapter 2: Working with Shapes

Adding and Moving Shapes

Adding shapes is a straightforward process that involves selecting from a variety of basic forms such as cubes, spheres, cylinders, and more. Each shape can be customized in terms of size, color, and position, allowing you to build complex structures piece by piece.

Step 1: Adding Shapes

In Tinkercad, adding shapes to your workspace is a simple process. To begin, locate the Shapes Panel on the right side of your screen. Click on the desired shape, such as a box, and drag it to the center of your workspace while holding down the mouse button. Release the button to place the shape, ready for customization.

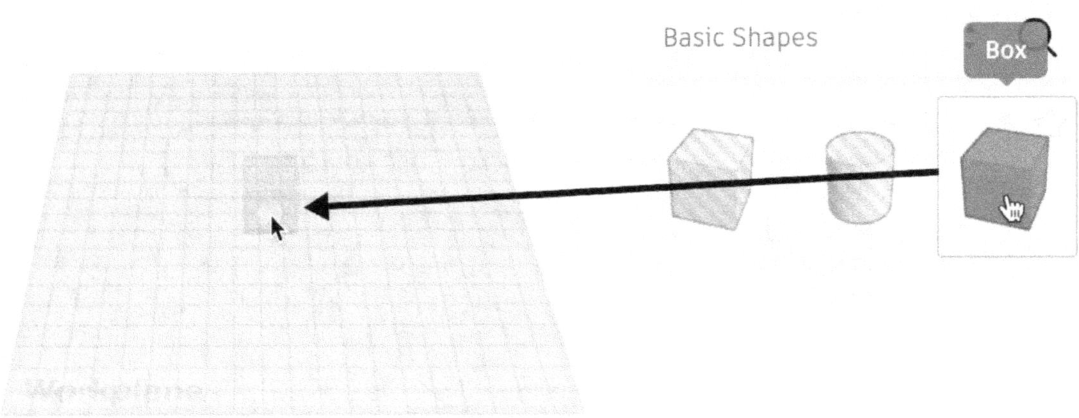

Step 2: Change the settings in the Inspection Window

The Inspection Window allows you to modify various parameters of the box shape. Click anywhere in the workspace to close the Inspection Window.

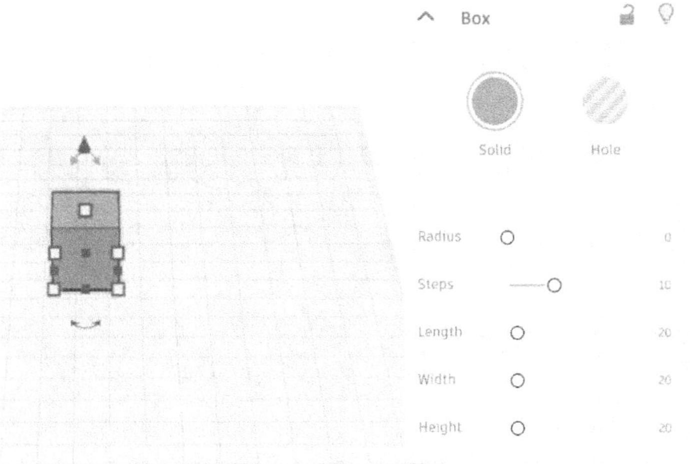

Step 3: Moving Shapes

Moving shapes in Tinkercad is easy. Click on the shape you want to move with your mouse button. Keep the button pressed and drag the shape to where you want it. The gridlines on your workspace can help you see where to place your shape. The smaller gridlines are one millimeter apart, and the larger ones are ten millimeters apart.

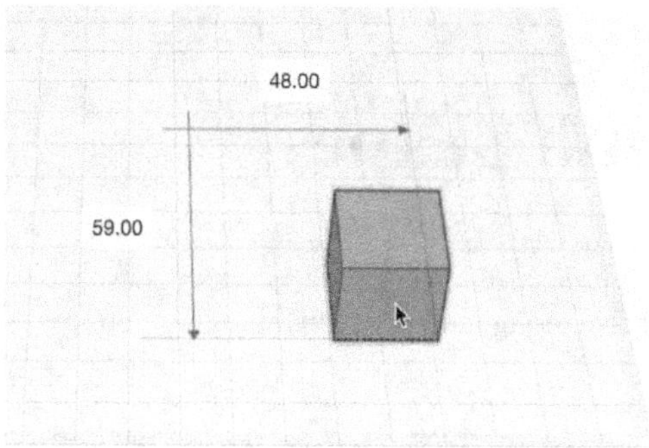

Step 4: Constrained Movement

If you want to move your shape in a straight line, either horizontally or vertically, you can use the Shift key. Hold down the Shift key while you click and drag your shape. This will keep your shape moving in a straight line, which can help you line up your shapes exactly how you want them.

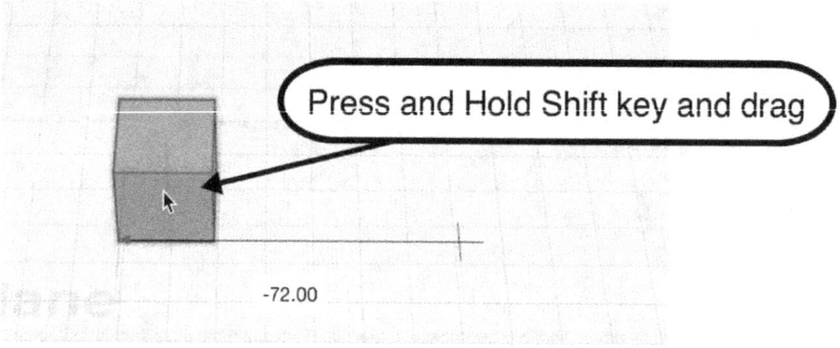

Step 5: Moving with Arrow Keys

Select the shape and use the arrow keys on your keyboard to move it. This allows you to move the object horizontally (left or right) and vertically (forward or backward).

Step 6: Moving on the Z-Axis

To elevate an object, hover over the black cone at the top of the object until it turns red. Click and drag this cone upwards to move the object along the Z-axis, which gives it height.

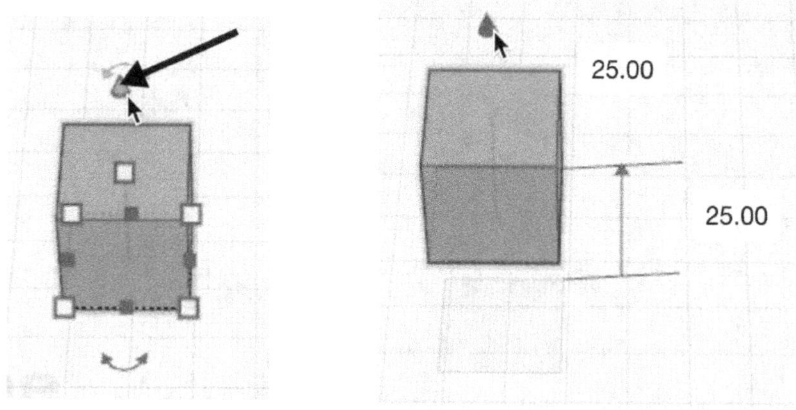

Step 7: Adjusting Dimensional Values

As you move an object, you'll see dimensional values appear. These values indicate how far the object has moved from its original position. You can click on these values and enter a new number to change the distance the object has moved.

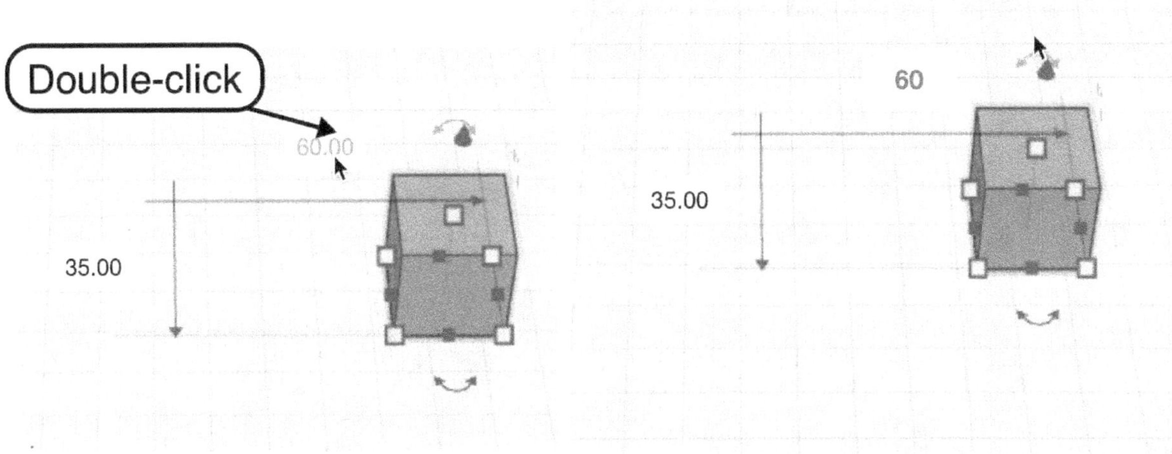

Step 8: Moving in Larger Increments

To move an object a greater distance more quickly, hold down the Shift key and press the arrow keys. This will move the object ten times the normal distance with each keystroke.

Step 9: Resetting Snap Grid Measurement

To reset the snap grid measurement, navigate to the Edit Grid settings in the lower right-hand corner of your workspace. Change the snap grid back to one millimeter to ensure that your objects snap to the grid at one millimeter increments.

Step 10: Moving on the X-Axis and Y-Axis

You can move an object side to side (along the X-axis) and forward and backward (along the Y-axis). This is useful for precisely positioning your objects on the work plane.

Step 11: Moving on the Z-Axis with Arrow Keys

You can also use the arrow keys to move an object along the Z-axis. Select your object, hold down the CTRL key, and use the up and down arrows. This will move your object up and down along the Z-axis.

Step 12: Dropping a Shape Back to the Work Plane

To place an object back on the work plane, use the keyboard shortcut 'D'. This will align the base of the object with the surface of the work plane.

Modifying 3D Shapes

In this section, you will modify shapes by using the grips and dimensions.

Modifying a Cylinder

Step 1: Drag the Cylinder

Start by dragging a cylinder onto the work plane.

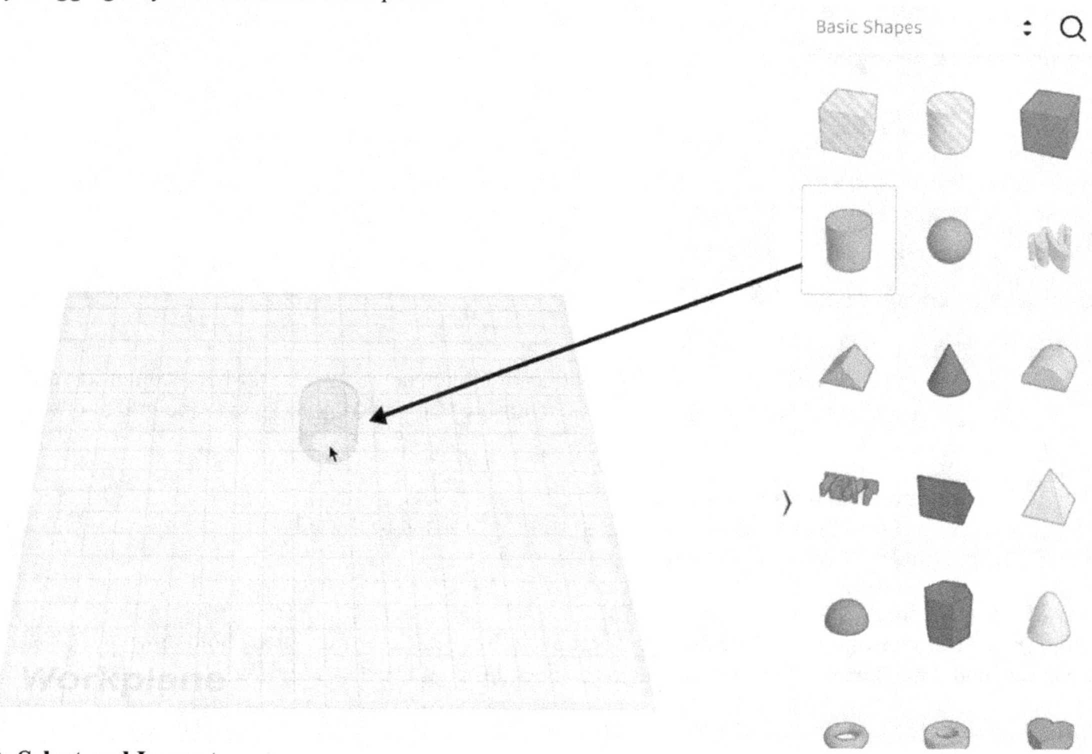

Step 2: Select and Inspect

Hover over the white or black grips of the selected cylinder to view its dimensions. This helps you understand its current size before making modifications.

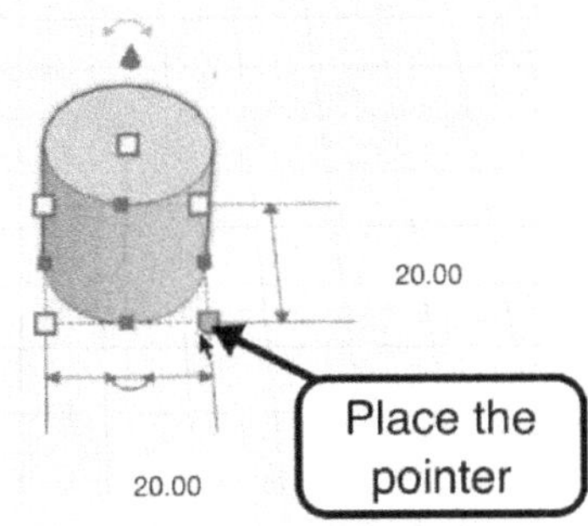

Step 3: Change Dimensions

Click any grip of the cylinder to display the dimensions. Click on the desired dimension and type-in a new value. Press Enter to apply changes. Alternatively, drag the grips to adjust the dimensions dynamically.

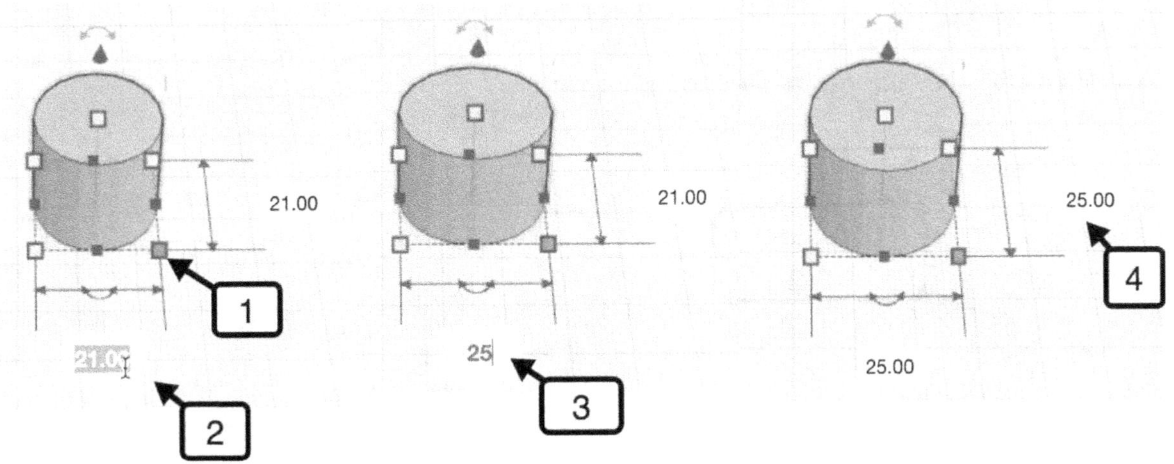

Step 4: Use Grip Types

Click and drag the black grips at the midpoints to change the dimensions in one direction.

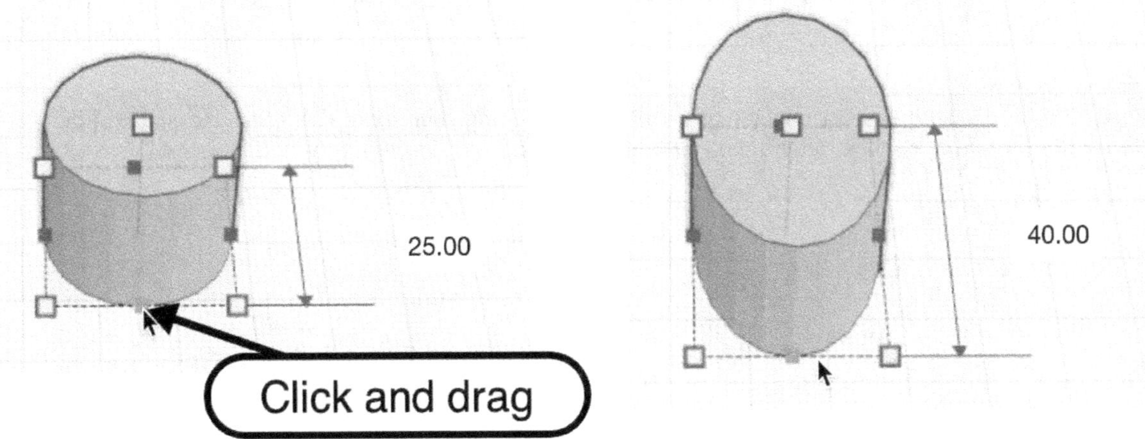

Click and drag the white corner grips to change two dimensions at once.

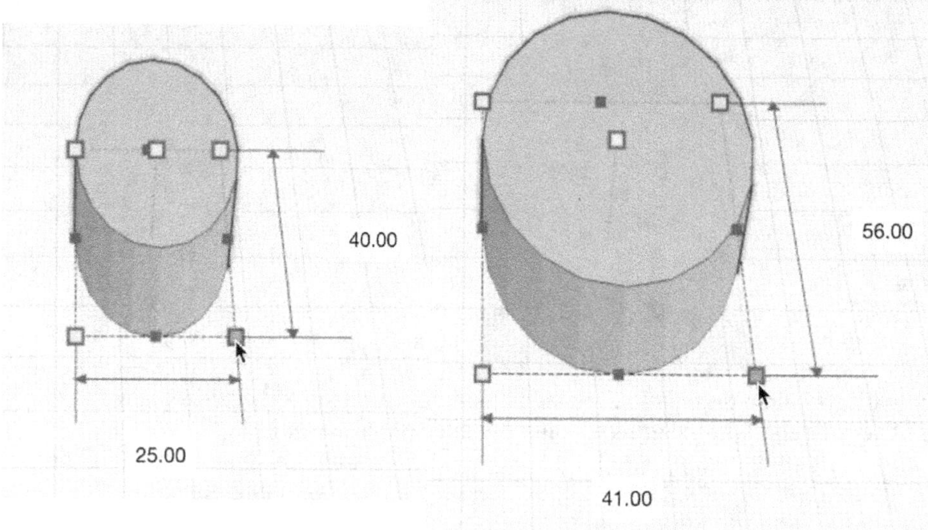

Click and drag the top white grip to adjust the height of the cylinder.

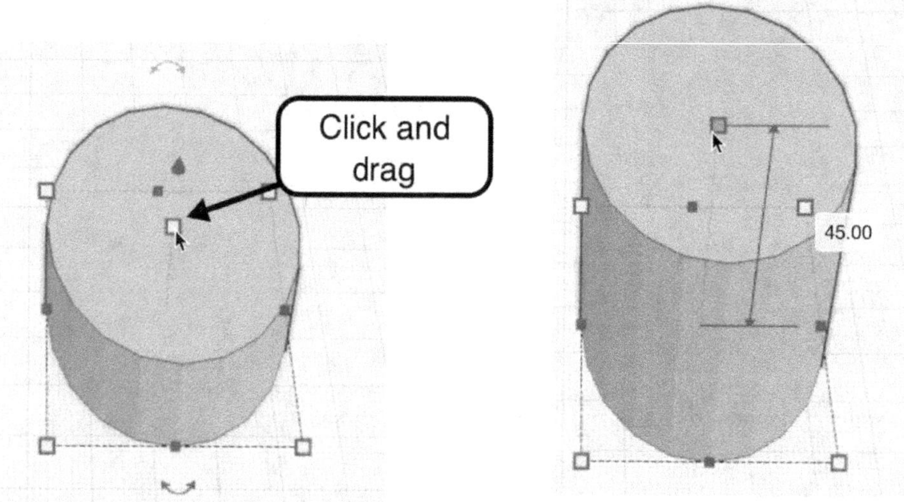

Step 5: Use ALT Keys
Press and hold the Alt or Option key on your keyboard while dragging your grips. This keeps the center of the cylinder stationary while you make adjustments to its dimensions.

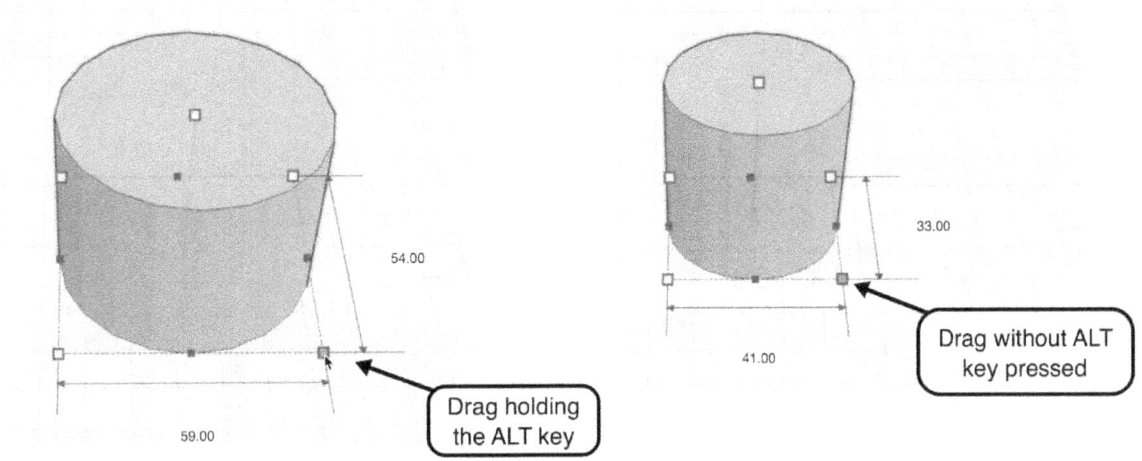

Step 6: Uniform Scaling

To uniformly scale your cylinder, you must ensure that the proportions on all three axes (height, width, and depth) are maintained while altering the size of the entire shape. This process is known as uniform scaling. To achieve this, you are required to hold down the Shift key on your keyboard. Simultaneously, utilize any grip to adjust the size by dragging it out.

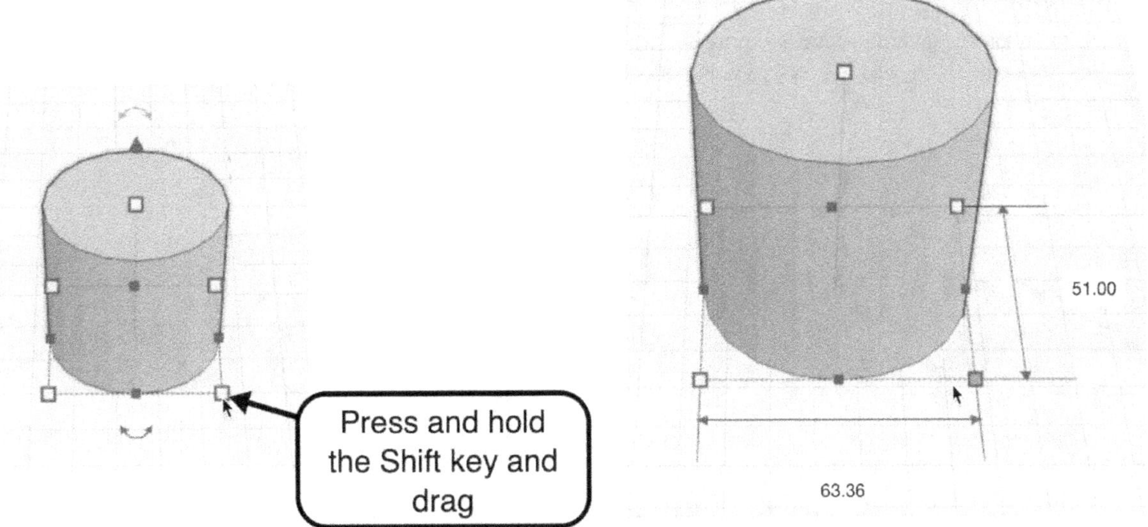

Step 7: Scale from the Center

In order to scale the cylinder from its center, you must hold down both the Alt or Option key in conjunction with the Shift key. Once these keys are depressed, you can proceed to drag a grip. This action will enable the cylinder to scale uniformly from its center.

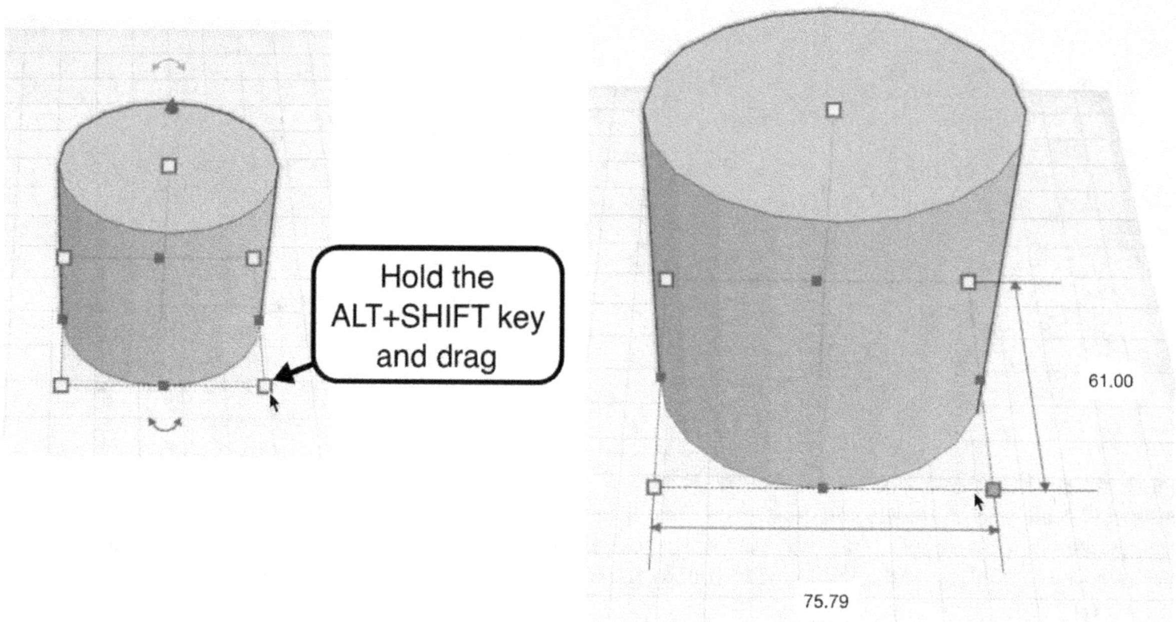

Step 8: Enter Exact Values

If you want to enter an exact value for the dimensions, first scale the shape approximately using the Shift key. Next, click into the value box and type the exact value you want. Press Enter to apply the value, and you will see the other values scale uniformly.

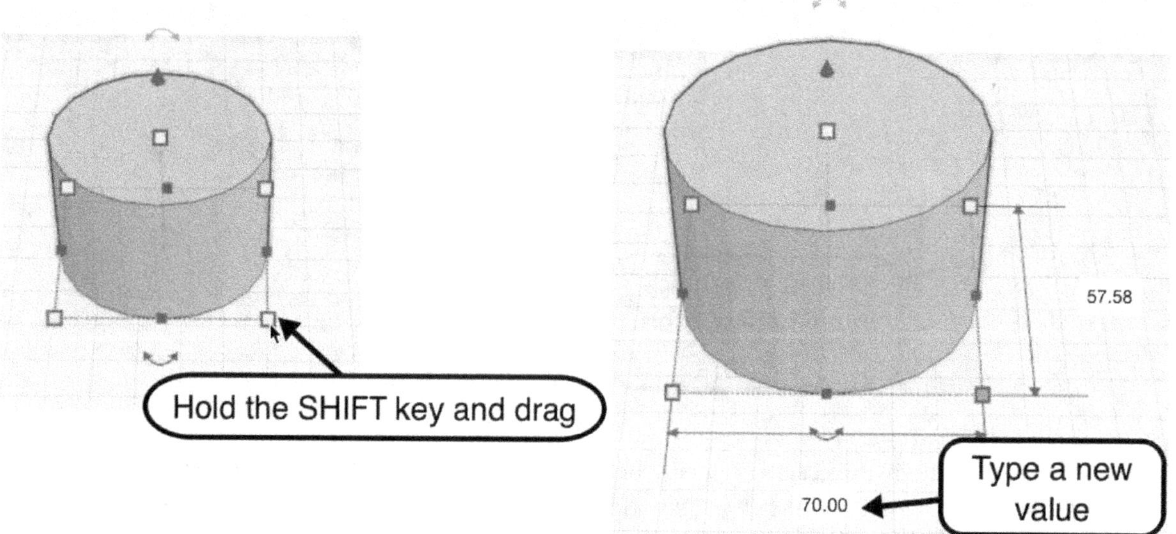

Modifying a Box

Step 1: Bringing a Box into the Workplane

Drag and place a Box shape from the Shapes panel onto the workplane.

Step 2: Modifying the Length, Width, and Height

In this step, you will change the size of your box Inspector window. This window pops up when you click on an object. It has various controls that let you modify the object.

Inside the Inspector Window, notice the sliders next to the labels **Length**, **Width**, and **Height**. These sliders allow you change the size of your box. Simply click and drag the slider to increase or decrease the size.

If you need your box to be a certain size, you can type that size directly into the fields next to the sliders. For example, if you want your box to be exactly 50 units long, you can type '50' into the **Length** field.

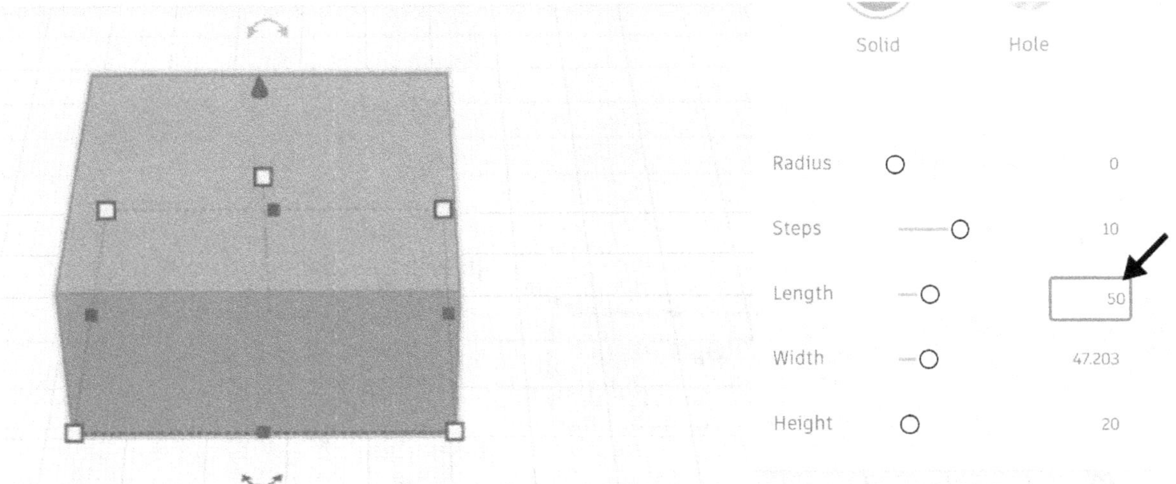

Step 3: Modifying the Radius and Steps

The 'Radius' refers to the degree of roundness of your box's corners. By increasing the **Radius** value on the Inspection window, you can make the corners more rounded. Conversely, decreasing the radius will make the corners more pointed.

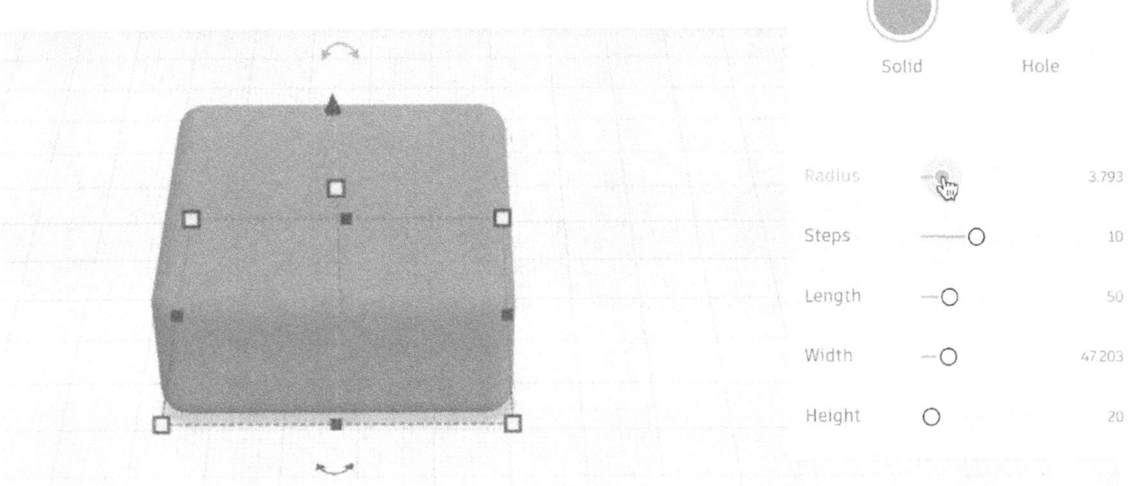

The '**Steps**' refer to the resolution or level of detail of your box. Increasing the Steps value on the Inspection window will enhance the detail of your box, making it appear smoother. On the other hand, decreasing the steps will reduce the detail, giving your box a more blocky appearance.

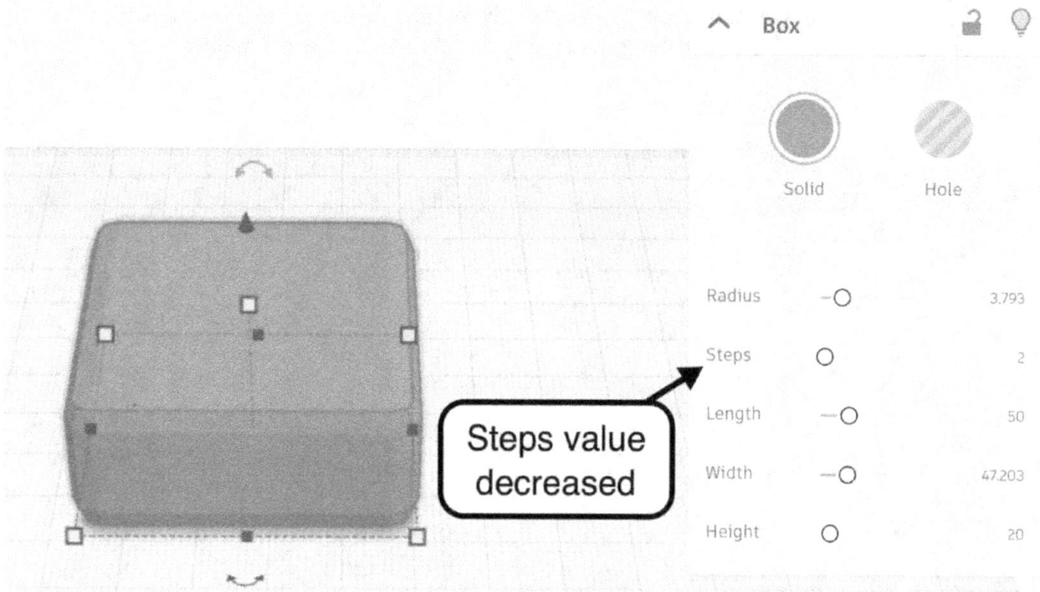

Step 4: Changing the Color

To change the color of the box, click the **Solid** color swatch on the Inspection window. Next, select a new color from the **Presets** tab (or) use the **Custom** tab to define a new color.

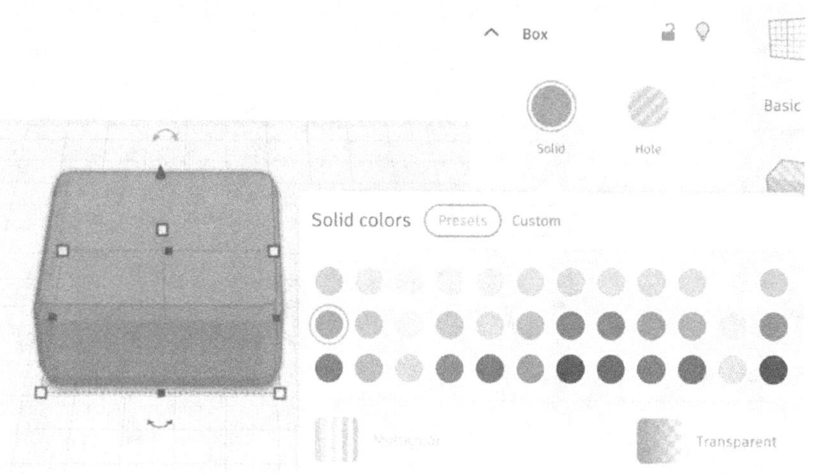

Step 5: Deleting the Box

If you want to remove the box from the workplane, simply select the box and hit the Delete key on your keyboard.

Modifying other shapes

1. **Add the Shapes**: Click and drag a Cone and Polygon from the shape library onto the workplane.
2. **Modify the Cone**:
    - **Select the Cone**: Click on the Cone on the workplane to select it. This will open the Cone Inspector window.
    - **Adjust the Base Radius**: Drag the Base Radius slider in the Inspector window to change the size of the cone's base.
    - **Modify the Top Radius**: Notice the Top Radius option in the Inspector window. By default, it's set to 0, meaning the cone comes to a point. You can change this value to add a flat face at the top of the cone.
    - **Change the Height**: Adjust the Height value to increase or decrease the height of the cone.

- **Alter the Sides**: Use the Sides slider to change the number of sides of the cone. Increasing this value will make the cone appear smoother.

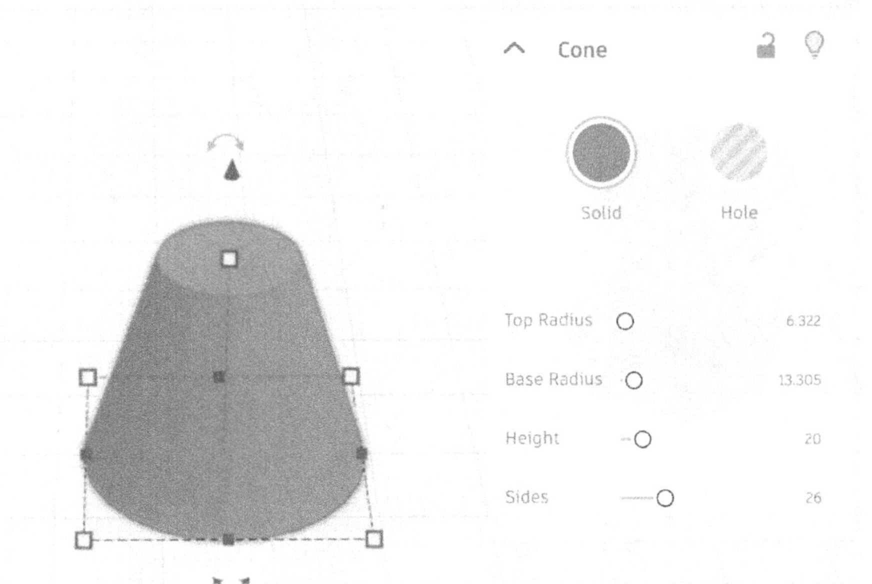

3. **Modify the Polygon**:
   - **Select the Polygon**: Click on the Polygon on the workplane to select it. This will open the Polygon Inspector window.
   - **Change the Sides**: Adjust the **Sides** value in the Inspector window to change the number of sides of the polygon.

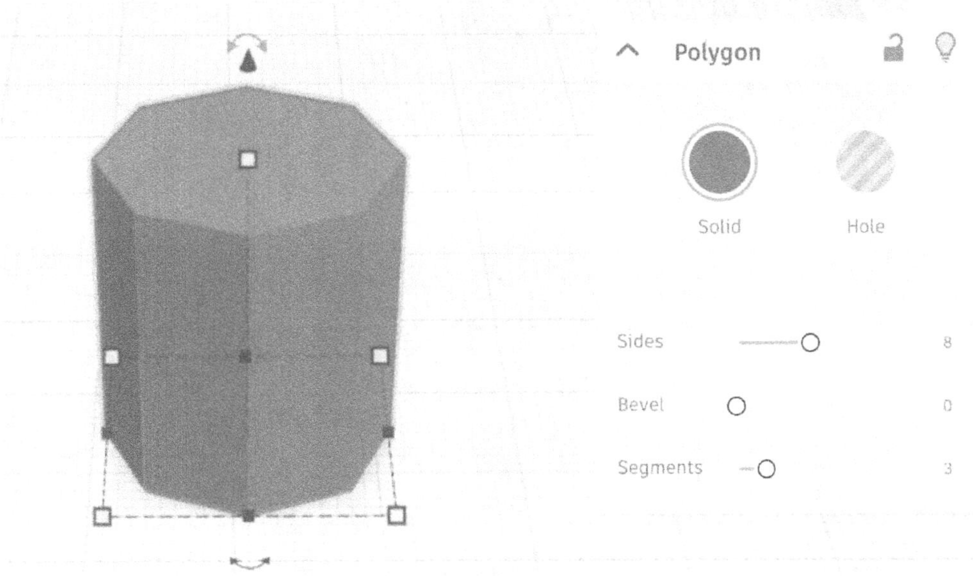

- **Add a Bevel**: Enter a value in the **Bevel** field to bevel the top and bottom edges of the polygon, giving it a more rounded appearance.

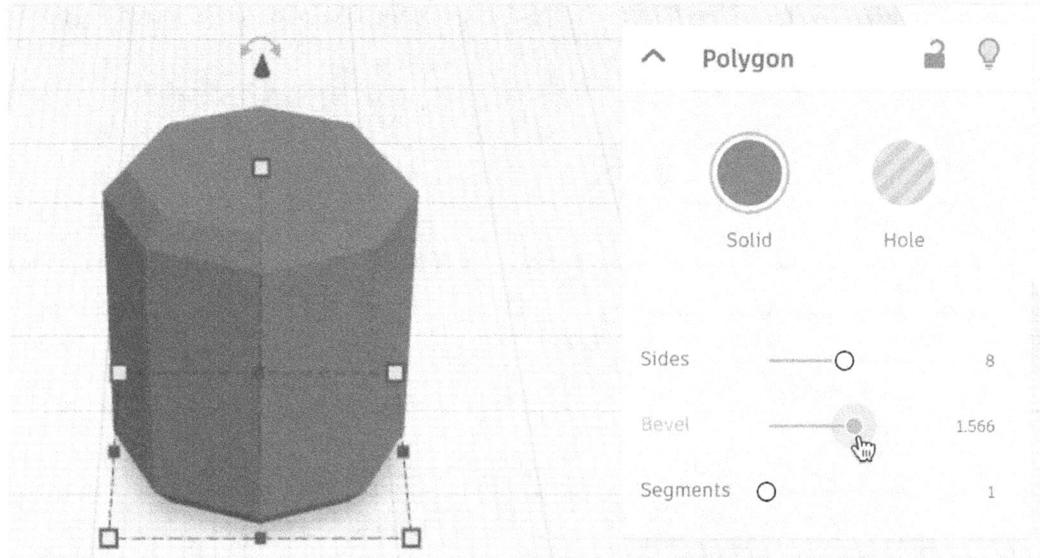

- **Smooth the Bevel**: Increase the **Segments** value to make the bevelled edges smoother.

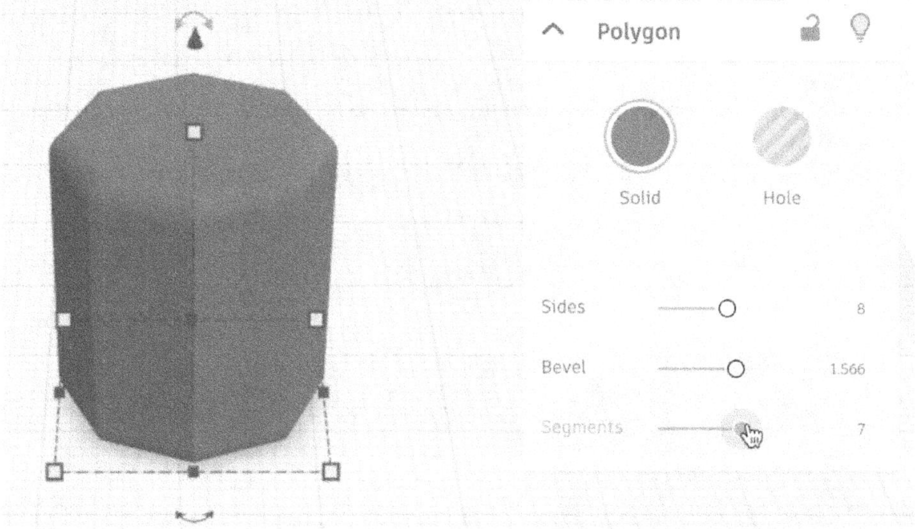

4. **Hiding Shapes**: Click on the Light bulb icon in the Inspector window to temporarily hide a shape from view.

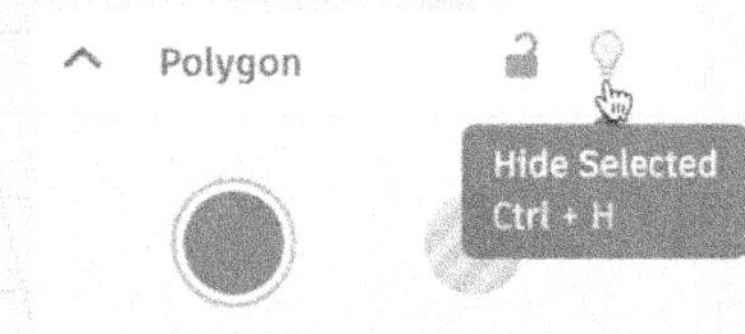

5. **Locking Shapes**: Click on the **Lock** icon in the Inspector window to prevent accidental modifications to a shape.

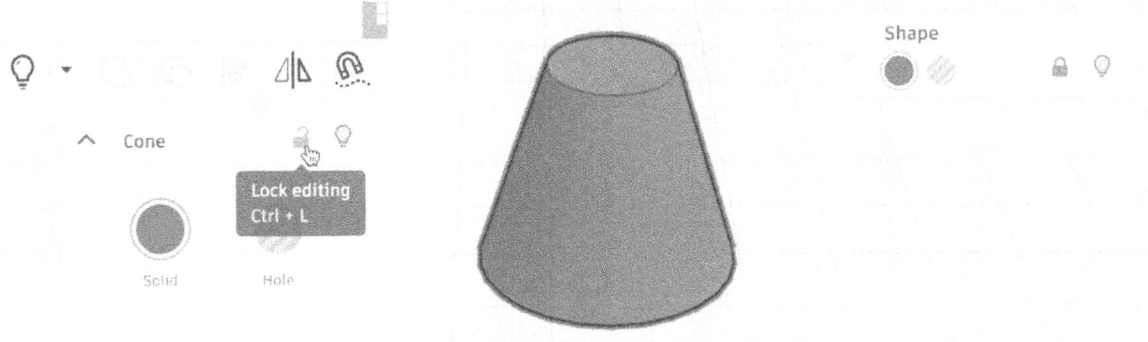

6. **Revealing Hidden Shapes**: Click on the light bulb icon in the Toolbar or use the keyboard shortcut Control or Command + Shift + H to reveal all hidden shapes.

Rotating 3D Shapes

1. **Drag Three shapes onto the Work Plane**: Drag a Roof shape onto the work plane. Align the edges of the roof with the grid lines, as shown.

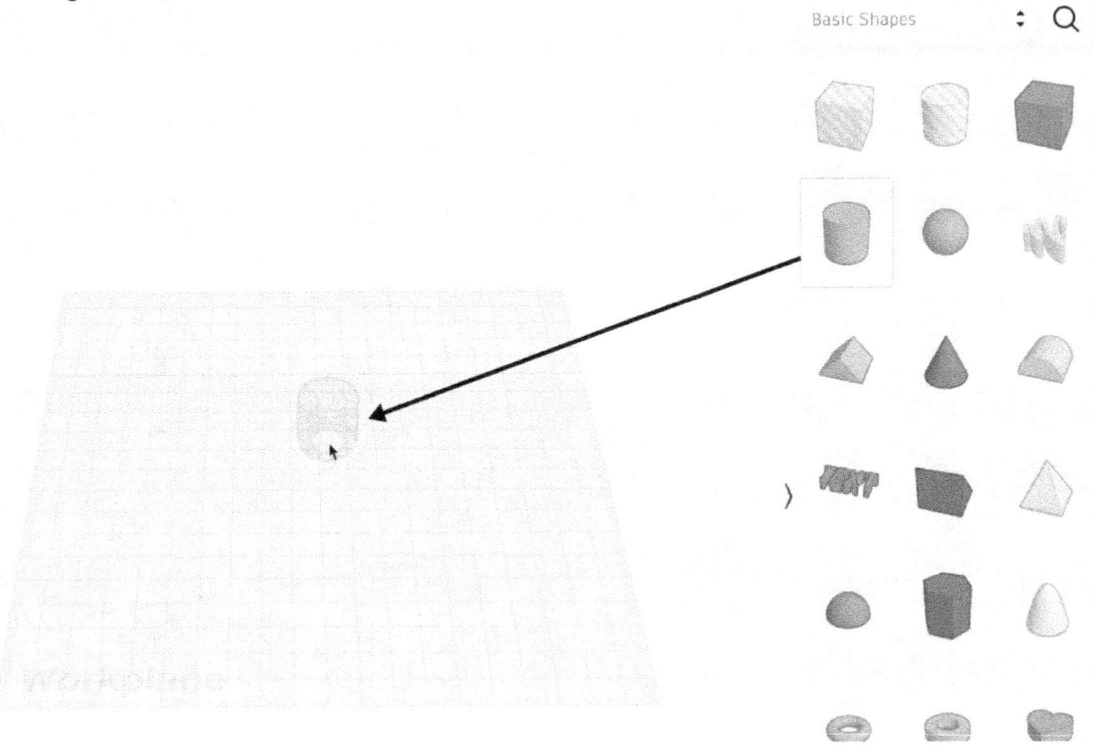

Select the **Wedge** shape from the **Shapes** panel. Click and hold to drag it onto the workplane. Position it three grid boxes to the right of the roof shape, then release your mouse button to place it.

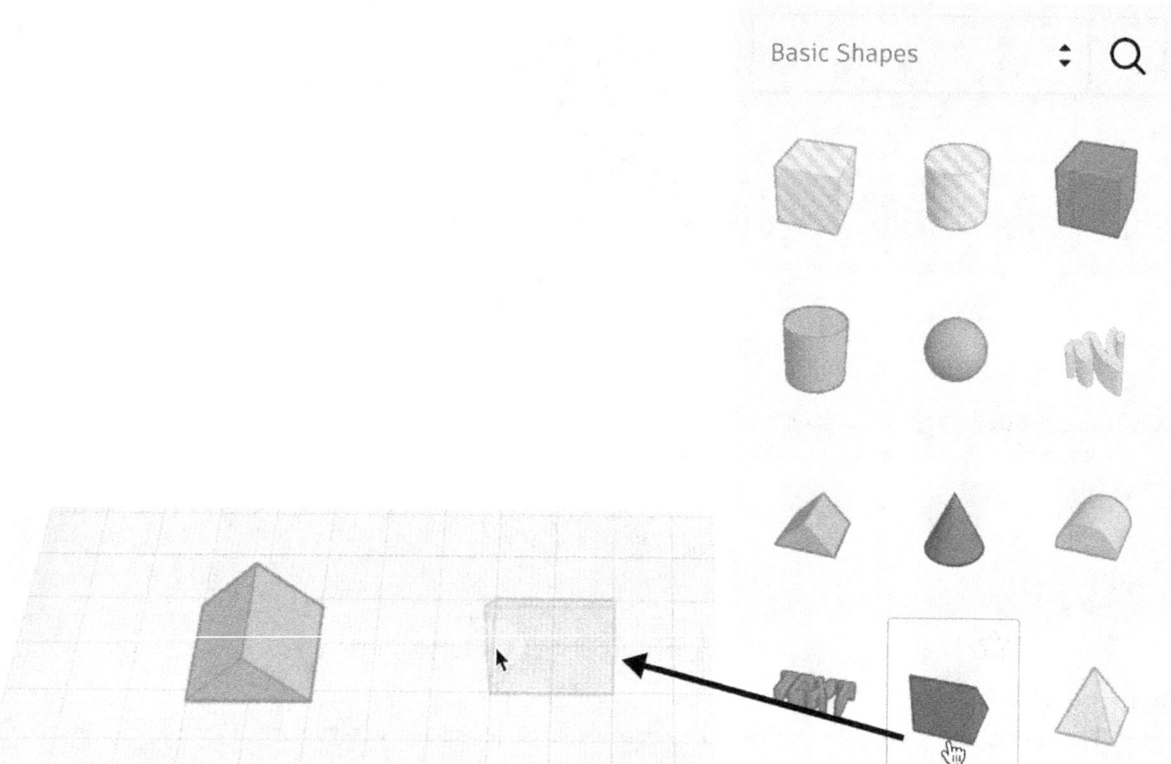

Select the **Pyramid** shape from the **Shapes** panel. Click and hold to drag it onto the workplane. Position it three grid boxes to the right of the wedge shape, then release your mouse button to place it.

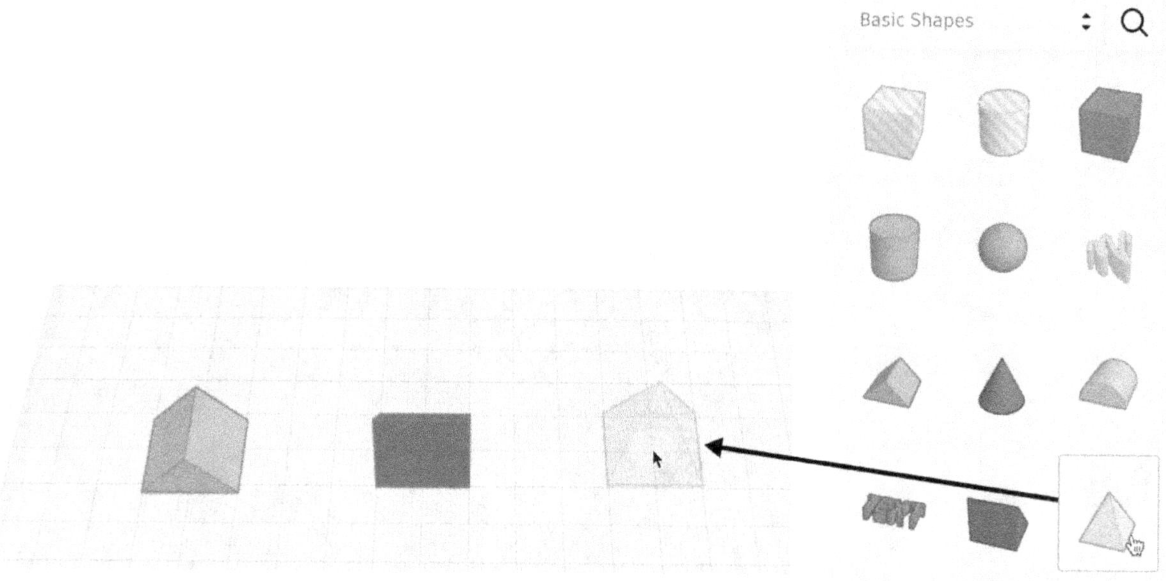

2. **Fit the Roof to View:** Click on the roof and press the '**F**' key to fit it to view. This will center the roof in your view. Notice the curvy arrow grips that appear around the pyramid. These grips allow you to rotate the shape. Press and hold the right mouse button and drag the mouse to orbit the view. Notice two more rotate grips.

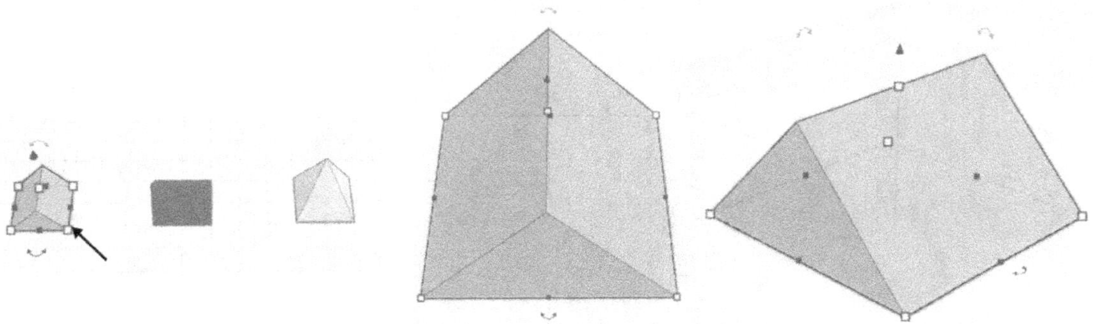

3. **Rotate the roof:** Hover your mouse over a rotation grip to display the compass. Click and hold on a grip to start rotating the roof. Notice the inner and outer rings of the rotation compass. Place the mouse pointer on the inner ring.

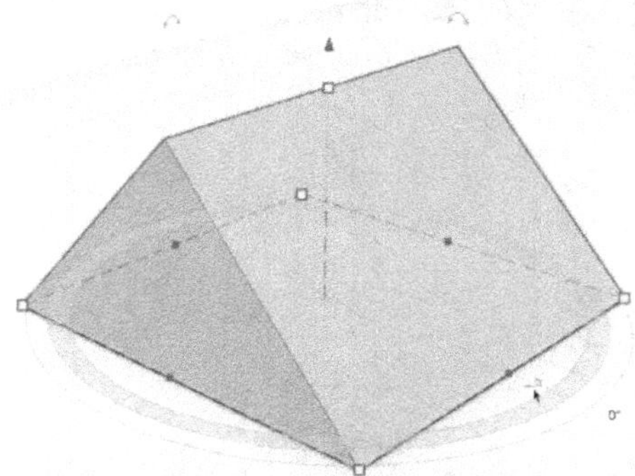

4. **Experiment with Rotation Increments:** Move your mouse around to see the roof rotate in 22.5-degree increments. To rotate the roof to a specific angle, locate the value box in the rotation tool. Click inside this box and type in your desired angle. You can specify the angle up to two decimal points for precision. This allows you to rotate the roof accurately to your preferred orientation.

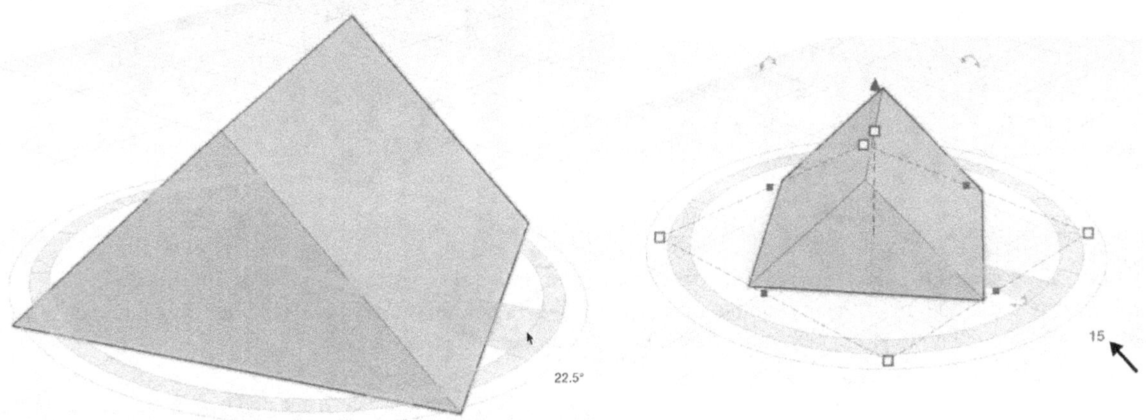

5. **Pan to the Wedge:** Press and hold the middle mouse button and drag the pointer toward left; the view is panned to the wedge, click on it, and press 'F' to fit it to view.

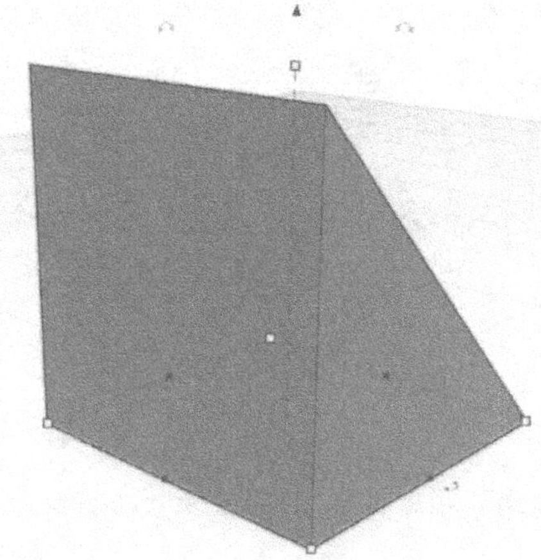

6. **Rotate the Wedge:** Locate the rotate grip at the top of the wedge and click on it. Keep the mouse button pressed and move your cursor into the outer ring of the compass that appears. Now, drag your cursor around the compass. As you do this, observe how the wedge rotates in increments of one degree.

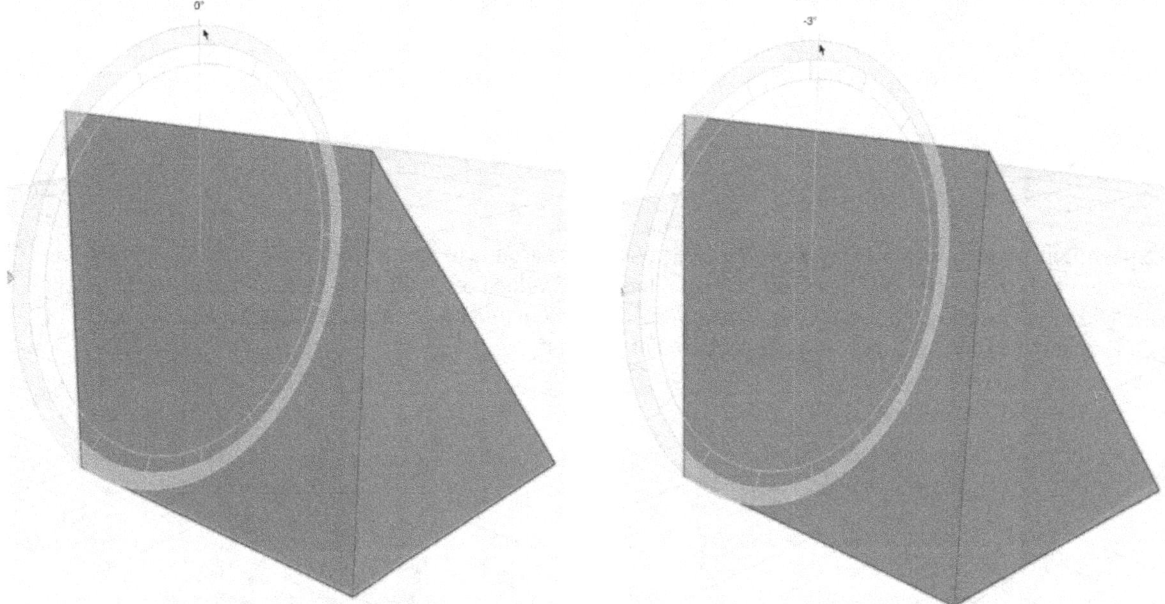

7. **Rotate the Pyramid:** Select the pyramid by clicking on it, then press 'F' to bring it into full view. Find the rotate grip at the bottom of the pyramid and click on it. While holding down the SHIFT key, click and drag the rotate grip. You'll notice that the pyramid rotates in increments of 45 degrees.

8. **Deselect and Fit All to View:** Click anywhere outside the pyramid to deselect it. Then, press 'F' to fit all objects within your view. Hover your mouse over the grips of the pyramid to display its dimensions.

Selecting and Deselecting Multiple Shapes

1. **Selecting Multiple Objects**: To select multiple objects simultaneously, use the shortcut Command or Ctrl + A. Deselect by clicking anywhere on the work plane.

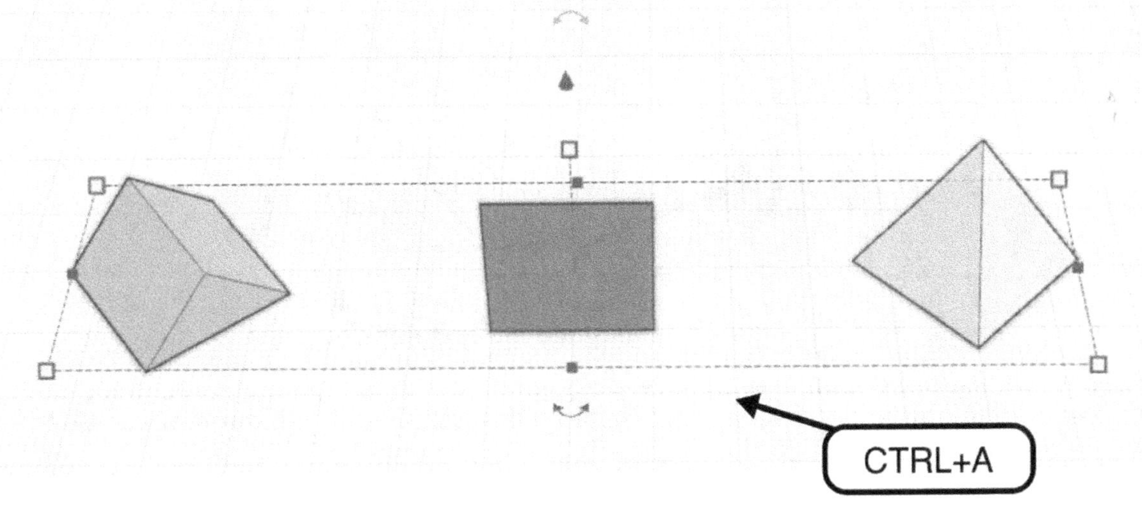

2. **Using the Bounding Box**: You can also select multiple objects by drawing a bounding box around them. Click in an empty space, drag to form a selection box around the objects, and release.

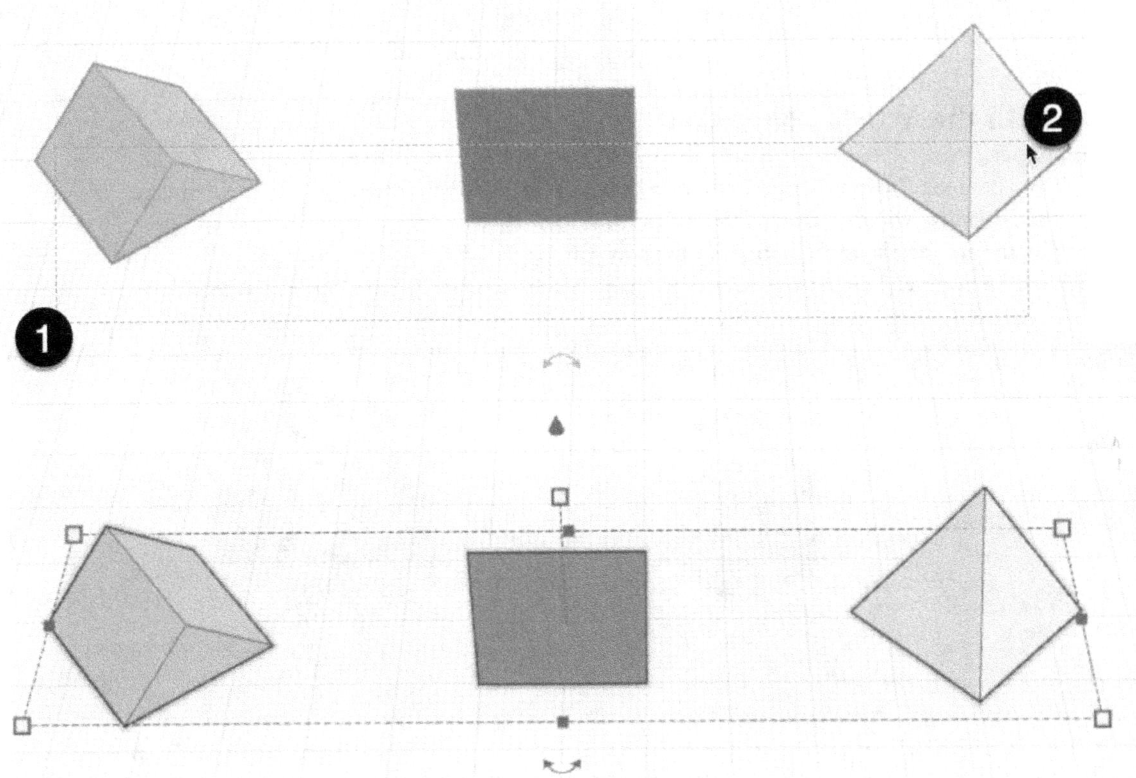

3. **Selecting Objects Individually**: Hold down the Shift key and click on each object to create a selection set. Click again on any selected object to deselect it.

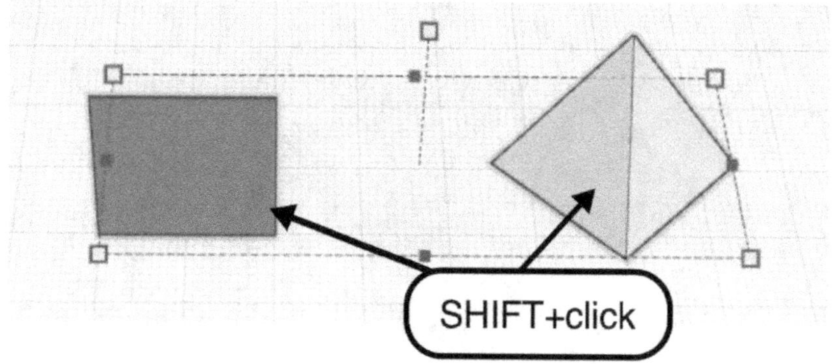

4. **Handling Overlapping Objects**: If objects are overlapping and you want to select an obscured object, select the obscuring object and click the Hide selected icon on the Inspection window. This will reveal the object underneath.

Working with the Work Plane Tool

1. **Adding Shapes**:
   - Click and drag the **Polygon** shape from the **Shapes** panel, and then release onto the work plane.
   - On the **Inspection** window, change the **Sides** value to 5.
   - Click on the corner grip at the bottom of the polygon.
   - Click on the displayed dimension value and change each value to 30 for a uniform shape.

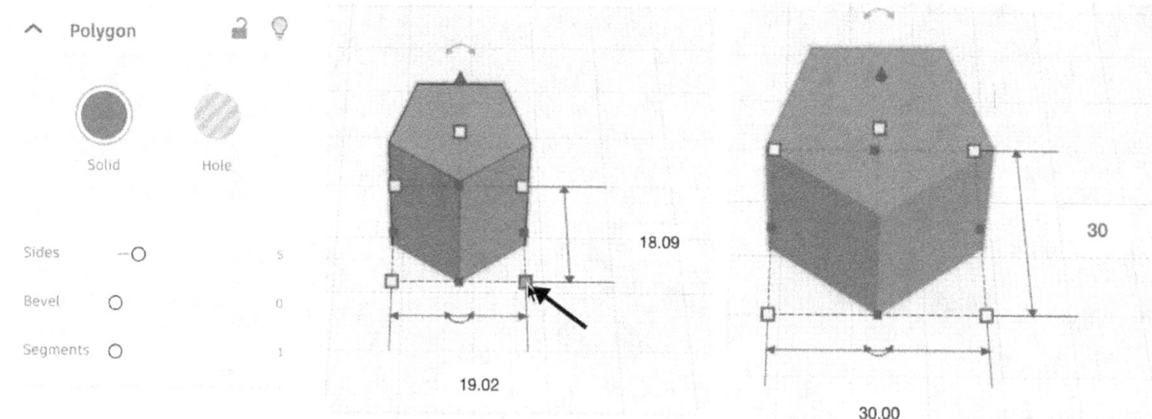

2. **Stacking Shapes**: Click and drag the **Cylinder** shape from the **Shapes** panel, and then release onto the top face of the polygon.

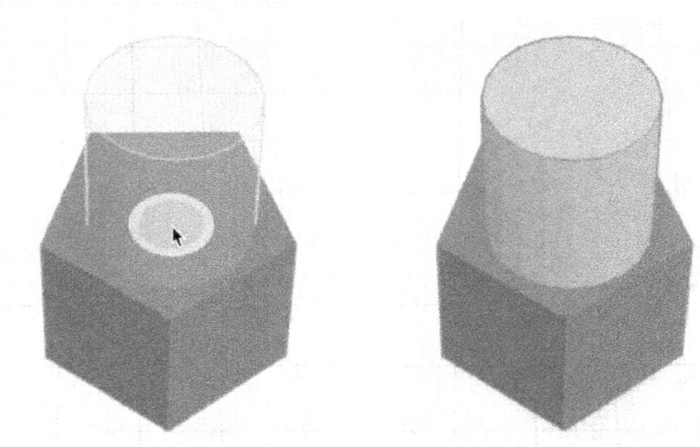

3. **Using the Work Plane Tool**: At the top of the shapes panel, click the Work plane tool. Click and drag it onto the side face of the polygon. The work plane will align to the poylgon's side face. Release it to create a temporary work plane.

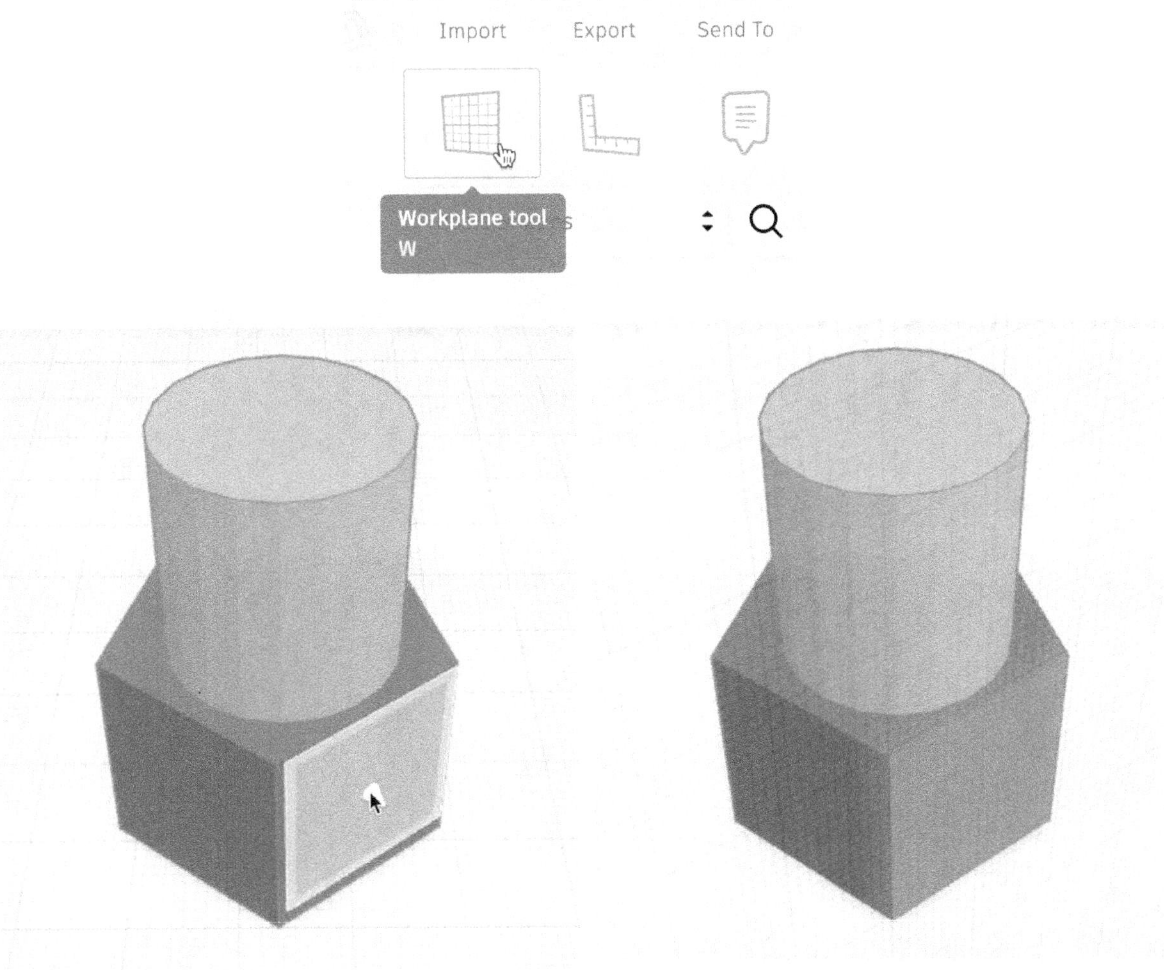

4. **Stacking Shapes Precisely**: Drag another cylinder onto the work plane. It will snap into place, perfectly stacked on the box.

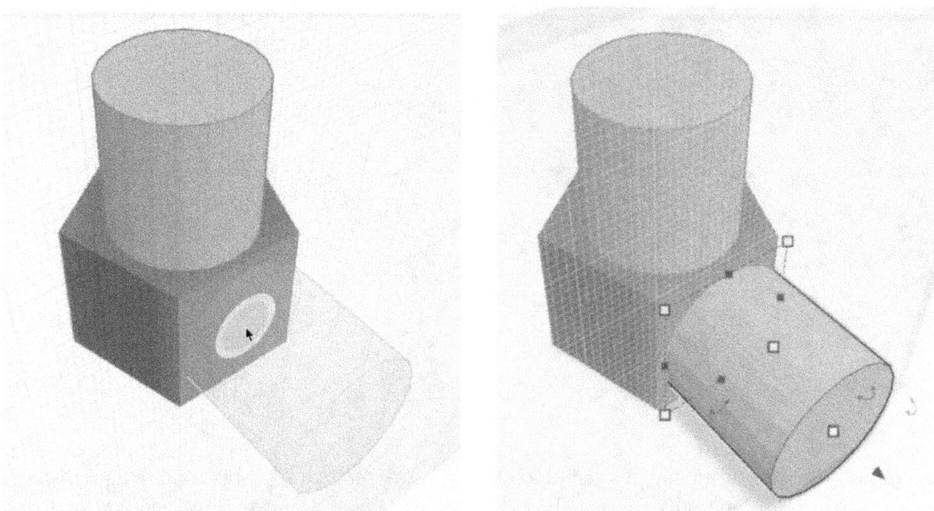

5. **Resetting the Work Plane**: To reset the work plane, press 'W' or select it from the shapes panel and click in an empty space.

Chapter 3: Advanced Shape Manipulation

The Ruler Tool

The Ruler tool in Tinkercad serves as a measurement instrument, enabling you to gauge the distances between objects and the point where you position the ruler. It provides two key measurements:

1. **Origin to Endpoint:** This measures the distance from the ruler's origin point (where you placed the ruler) to the endpoint of an object.
2. **Origin to Midpoint:** This measures the distance from the ruler's origin to the midpoint of an object.

These measurements are crucial for precise modeling and accurate alignment of objects within your design. By understanding the spatial relationships between objects, you can create more complex and detailed 3D models.

Measuring from Origin to Endpoint

1. Drag a Box, Roof, and Wedge onto the workplane.

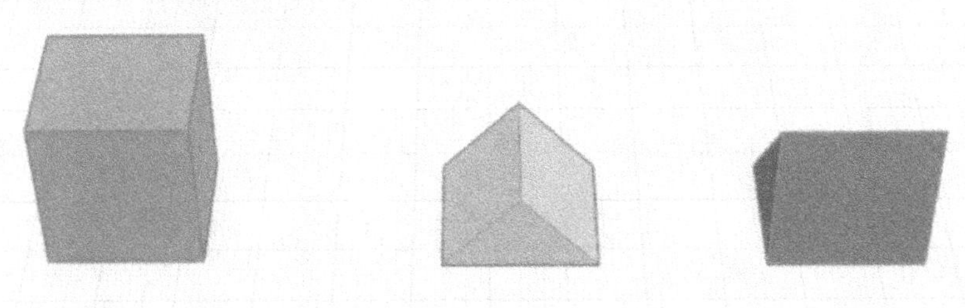

2. Right-click on the work plane and pan to zoom in on the upper right-hand corner of your grid.

3. Select the **Ruler** tool from the toolbar and place it onto the upper right-hand corner of the grid.

4. Click on the origin point of the ruler (where the horizontal and vertical lines intersect) to adjust its position until the ruler aligns with your grid lines.

5. Click on the icon with three dashes until the **Use endpoint** option is set. This ensures you are in endpoint mode, which measures distances from the corners of the shapes.

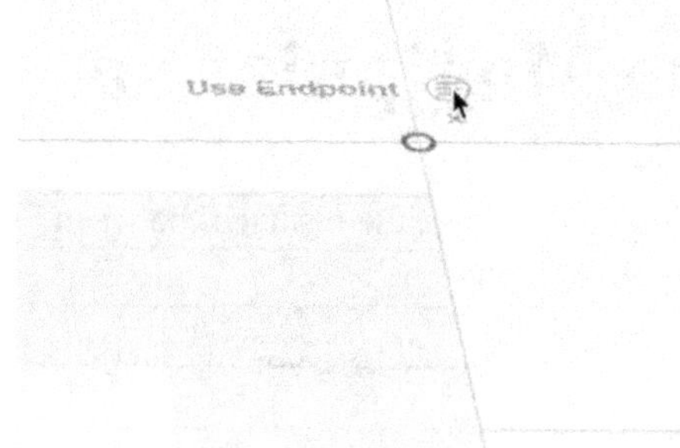

6. Select the wedge on your work plane. Then, adjust the green dimensions (which represent the distance from the origin to the box) to 30 by 30. This will move the box 30 units away from the origin in both the x and y directions.

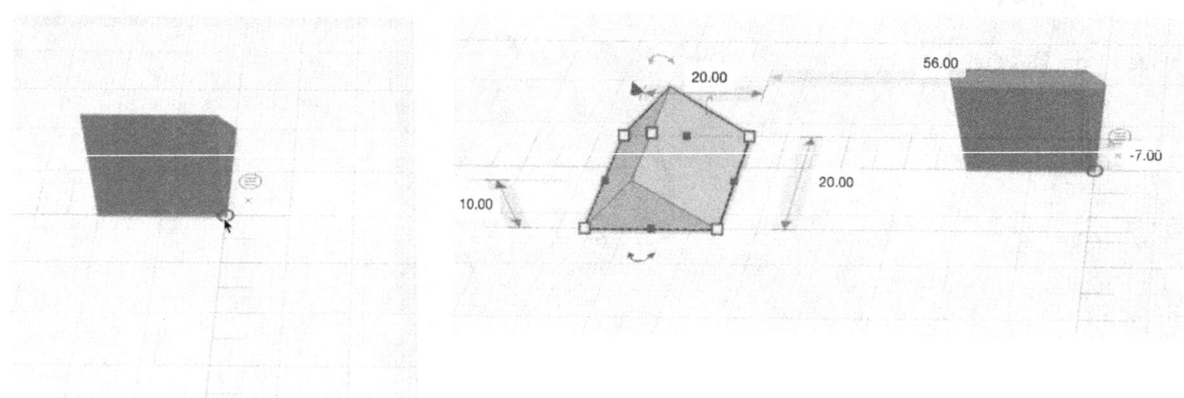

7. Drag the origin point of the ruler to the corner of the wedge.

8. Select the Roof shape and set the distances to 0 and 30 mm.

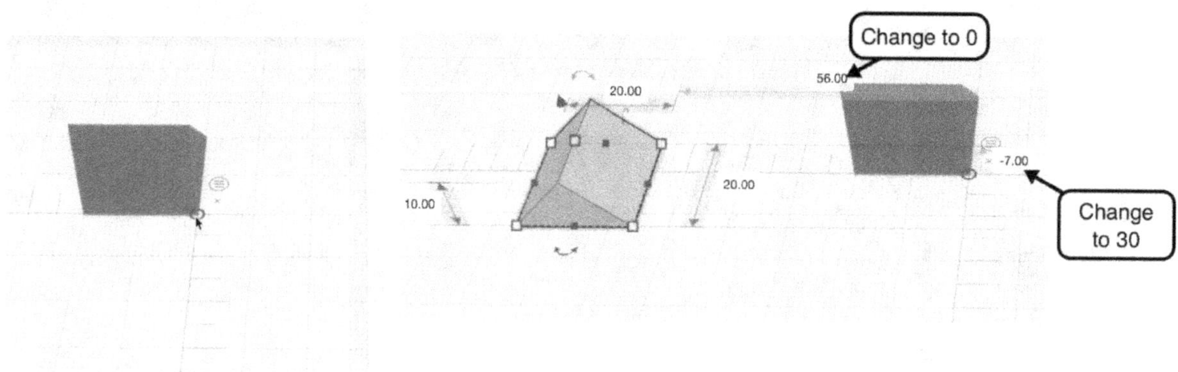

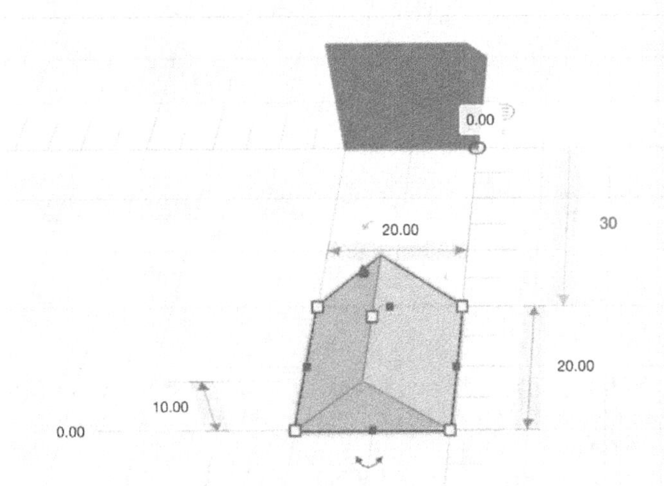

9. Repeat steps 7 and 8 for the Box on your work plane. Drag the origin point of the ruler, adjust it until you receive a confirmation that the offset is zero, and then change the offsets to 30 mm and 0 mm.

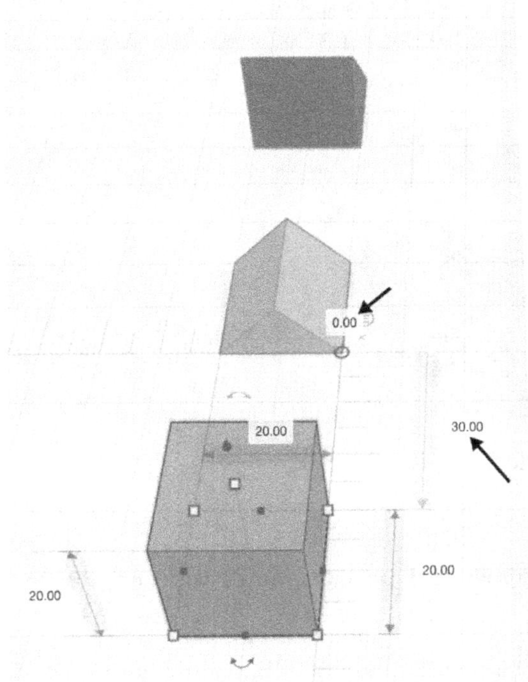

Measuring from Origin to Midpoint

1. Drag and drop Tube onto the work plane.

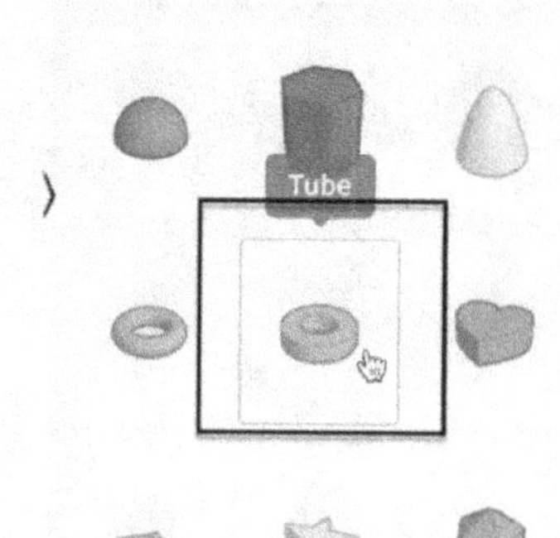

2. Select the **Ruler** tool from the toolbar and place it onto the upper left-hand corner of the grid.
3. Click on the origin point of the ruler (where the horizontal and vertical lines intersect) to adjust its position until the ruler aligns with your grid lines.
4. Click on the icon with three dashes until the **Use midpoint** option is set. This ensures you are in endpoint mode, which measures distances from the corners of the shapes.
5. Select the Tube and you will notice that measurements appear, indicating the distance between the origin of the ruler and the centerpoint of the Tube. These measurements provide valuable information about the Tube's position relative to the ruler's origin.
6. Modify the green measurements, which represent the distance from the ruler's origin to the centerpoint of the Tube. Set these measurements to 30 each. This action will move the centerpoint of the Tube to a position that is 30 units away from the ruler's origin in both the x and y directions.

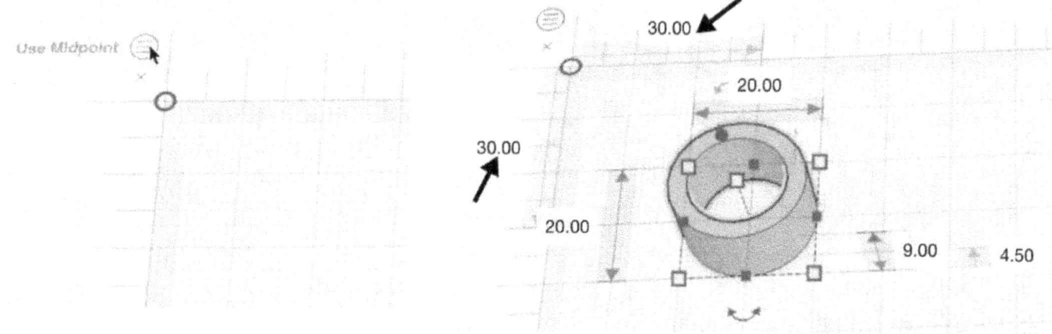

7. To turn off the ruler, click the X icon located on the ruler tool.

Tutorial 1

In this tutorial, you'll learn how to insert shapes onto the workplane, duplicate them, mirror them, and group them together.

1. Start by selecting the **Ruler** tool from the toolbar and placing it approximately at the center of the workplane.

2. Set the mode to **Use Midpoint** using the icon with three dashes next to the .
3. Drag the Cylinder shape on to the Workplane from the Shapes panel.

4. Modify the measurements of the cylinder shapes by clicking on them, as shown.

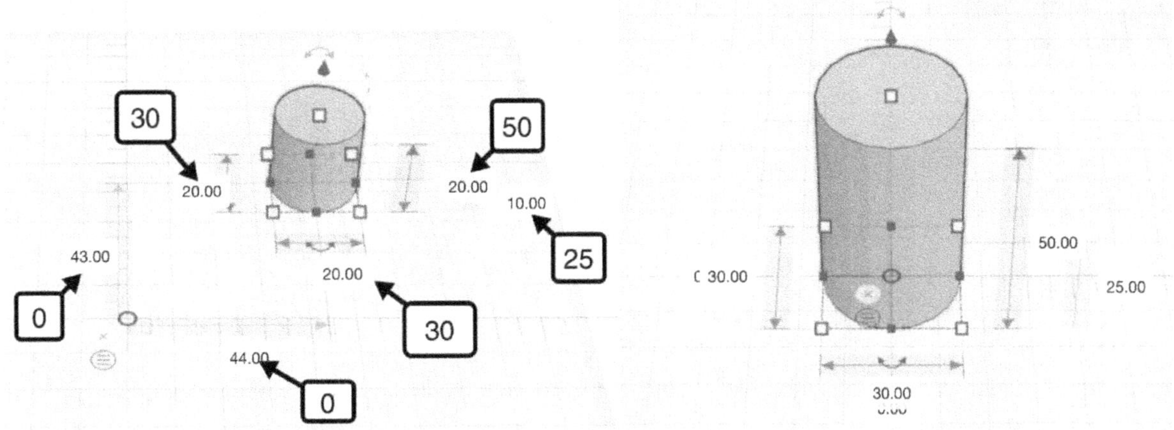

5. Drag the **Cone** shape from the **Shapes** panel and release it on the top face of the cylinder, as shown.
6. Change the measurements, as shown.

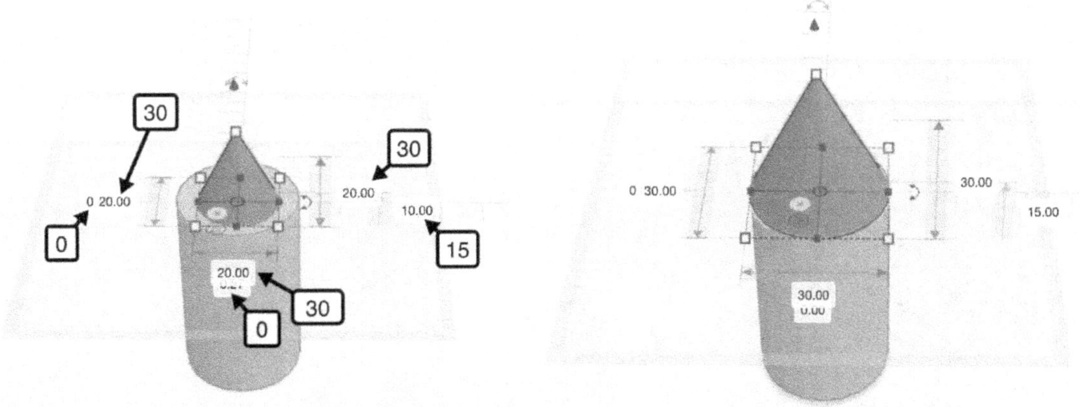

7. Drag and drop the Wedge shape on to the workplane.
8. Click on the Rotate grip displayed on the front side of the wedge. Next, type 90 in the Angle box and press ENTER; the wedge is rotated by 90 degrees.
9. Click on the Width dimension of the wedge and change its value to 5.

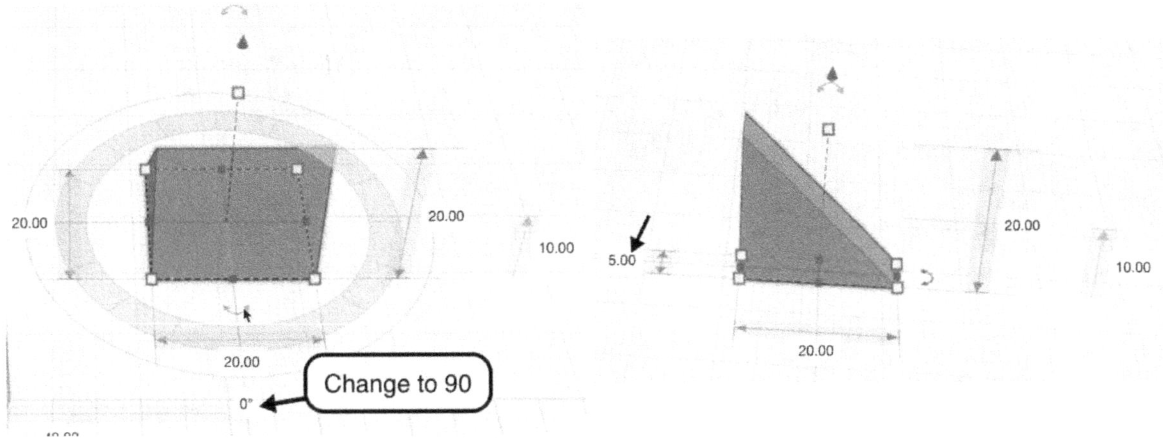

10. Click on the icon with dashes to change it **Use endpoint** mode.

11. Change the measurements between the origin point of the ruler and the corner point of the wedge to **-2.5** and **14**, respectively.

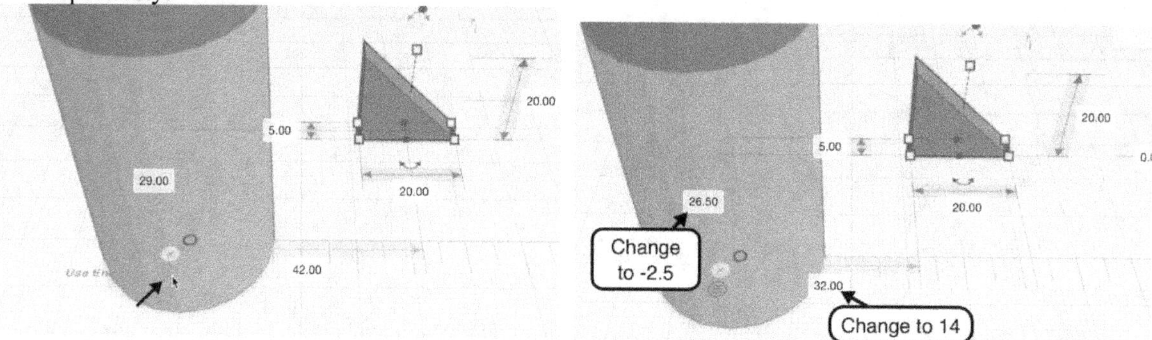

12. Select the Wedge from the workplane and click the **Duplicate** icon on the toolbar; the wedge is duplicated.

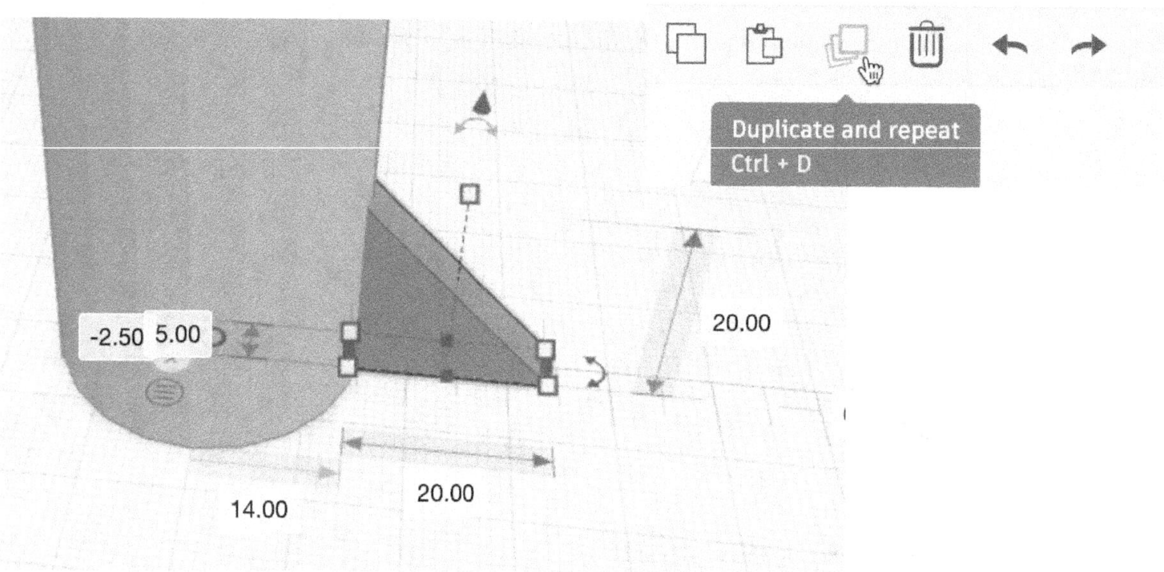

13. Click and drag the highlighted wedge to a new location.

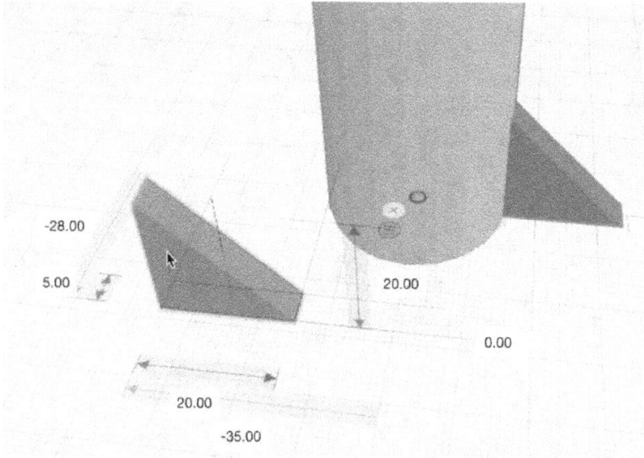

14. Select the duplicated wedge and click the **Mirror** icon on the toolbar. Upon activating the Mirror tool, you will notice three arrows representing the three axes (X, Y, Z) along which you can mirror your object. Hover your mouse over each arrow to preview the mirroring effect.

15. Click on the arrow corresponding to the X axis to mirror the object.

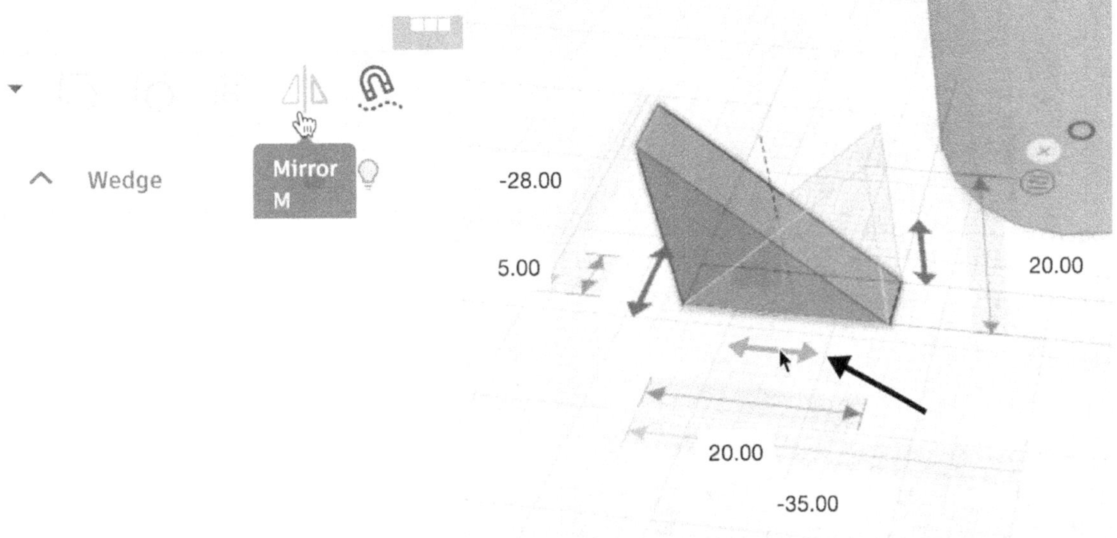

16. Change the measurements between the origin point of the ruler and the corner point of the wedge to **-2.5** and **-34**, respectively.

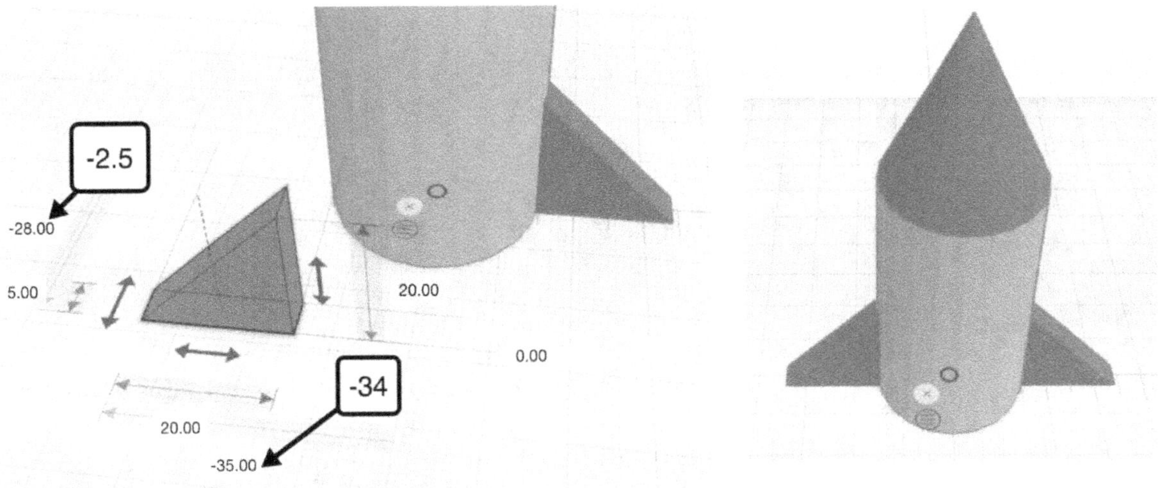

17. Create a selection window across all the objects by pressing and holding the left mouse button and dragging the mouse across all the objects.
18. Click the **Copy** icon on the toolbar; the selected objects are copied.

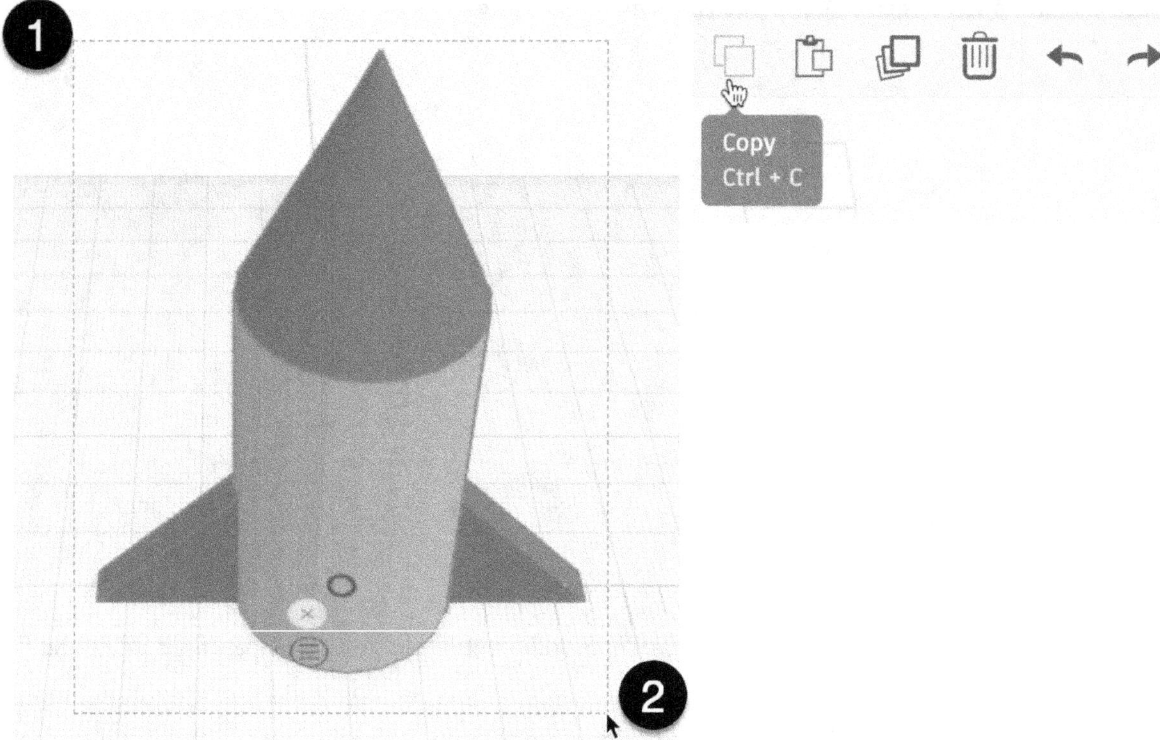

19. Click anywhere on the workplane and click the **Paste** icon on the toolbar; the copied objects are pasted.
20. Click and drag the pasted objects to a new location.

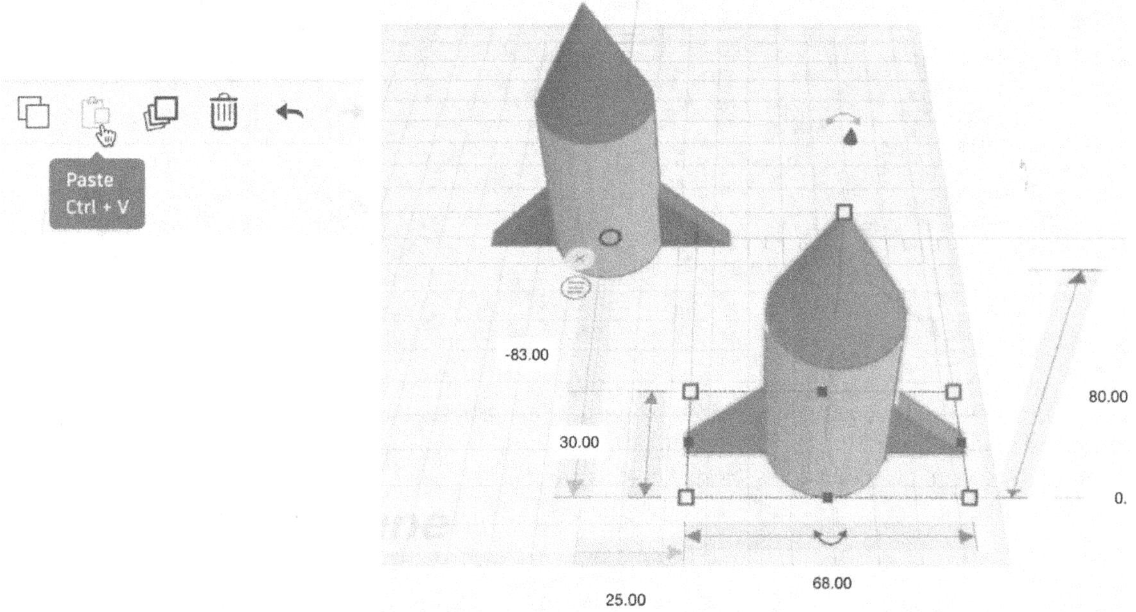

21. Create a selection window across the first set of objects.
22. To group these objects into a single entity, click on the "Group" button located at the top right of the workspace or use the shortcut Command + G (or Control + G on a PC). This will combine the three objects into a single grouped object.

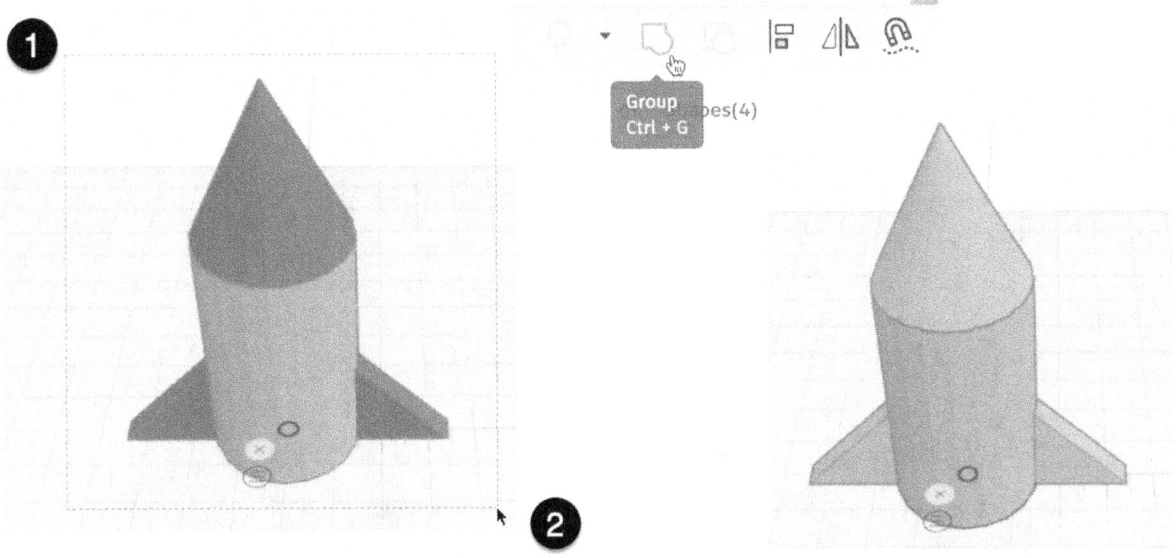

23. For the second set of objects, first click on the cone, then Shift-click on the cylinder and choose "Group." Next, hold down Shift, select the two wedges, and click "Group" again. Note that when grouping objects, the group will take the color of the first object you selected.

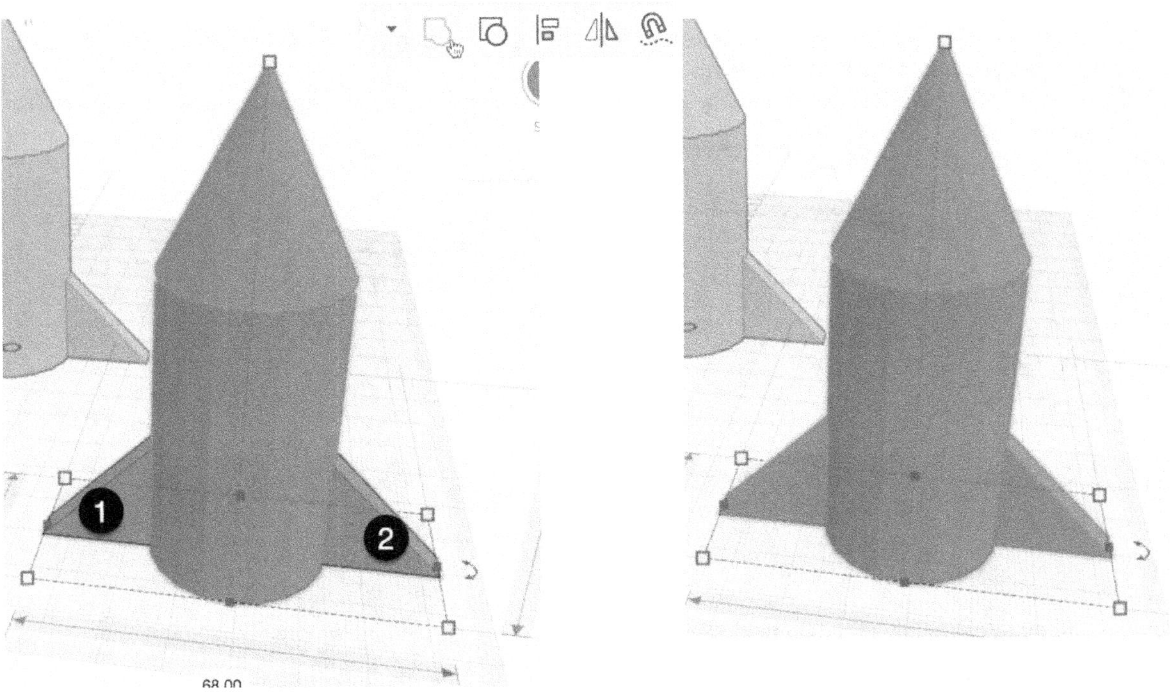

24. Double-click on it on the first group to enter edit mode. You'll notice a transparent red outline on the work plane, indicating that you're in edit mode.

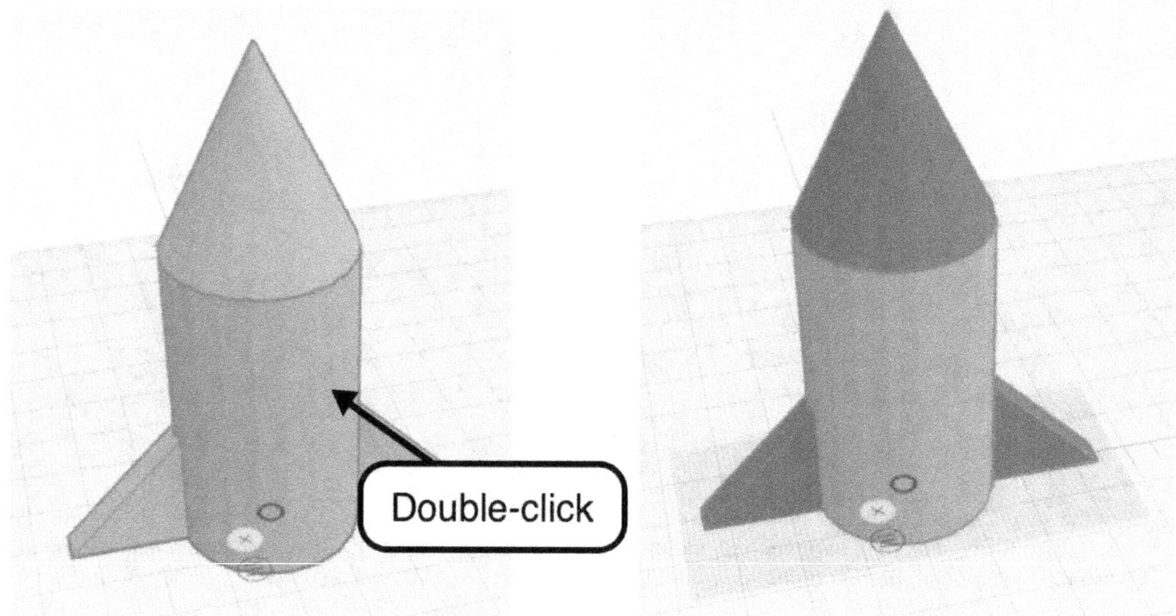

25. Within the Edit mode, you can make adjustments to the design. For example, click on the top vertex of the cone and drag it; the height of the cone is modified.
26. Click anywhere on the work plane outside the grouped object to exit Edit mode. The group will update to reflect your changes.

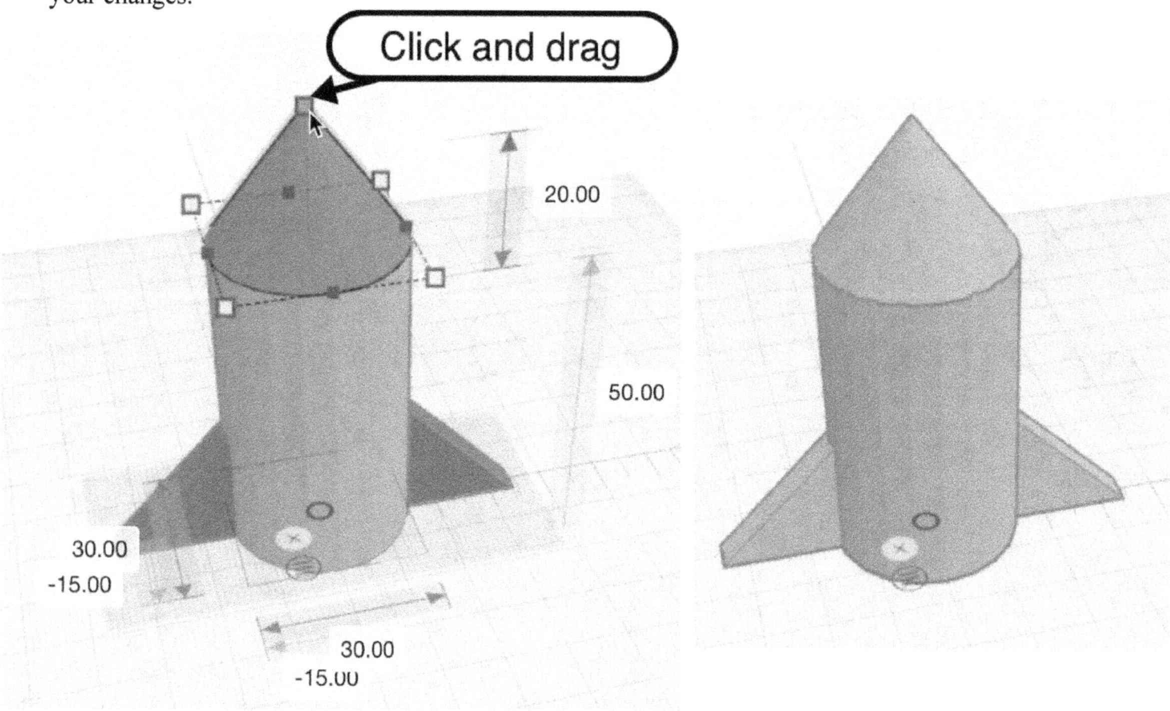

27. Double-click on the second group to enter the Edit mode. Notice that you can edit only the last added objects of the group. So, make sure that you select the objects to be grouped by creating a selection window.
28. Click anywhere in the workplane to deactivate the Edit mode.

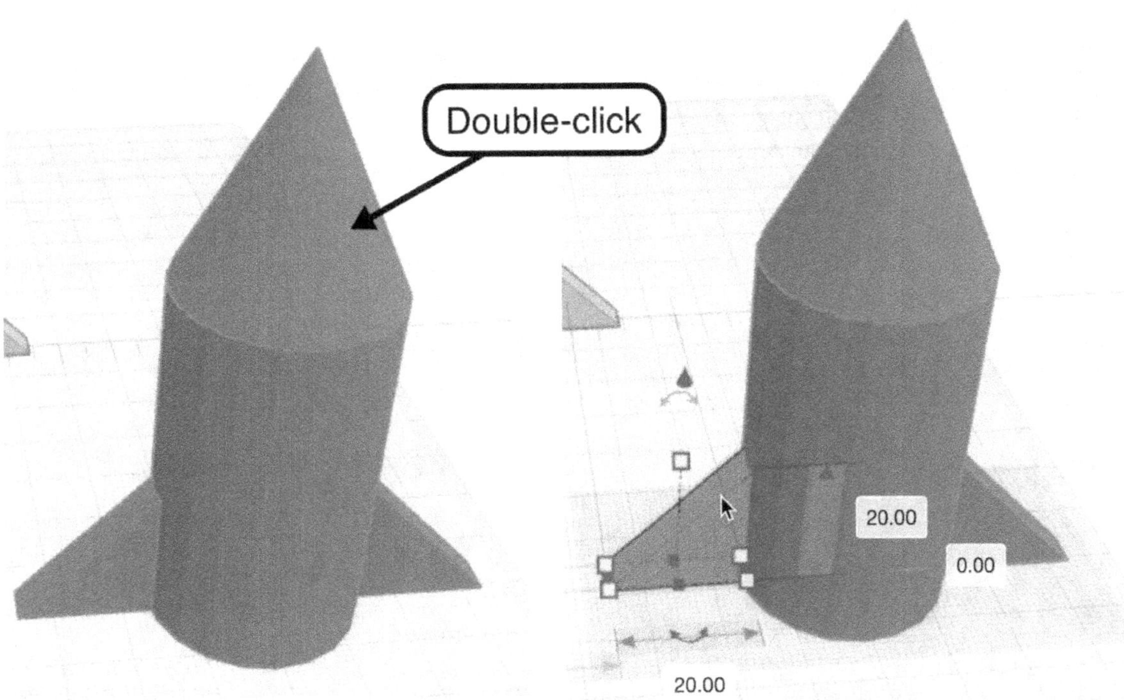

If you need to make changes to individual objects within a group, you can ungroup them.

29. Click "**Ungroup**" on the toolbar or using the shortcut Control + Shift + G. This will break the group down into its individual components, allowing you to modify each one separately.

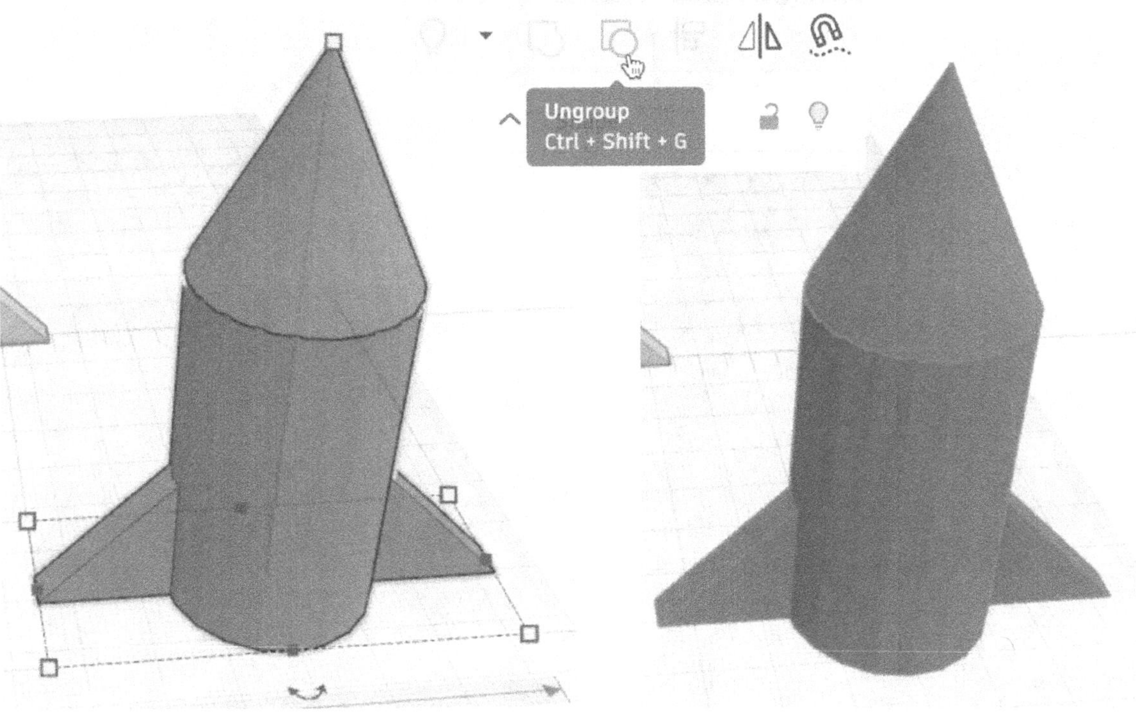

Tutorial 2

In this tutorial, you'll learn how to align shapes, create holes, slice with holes, and create intersection shapes.

1. On the Dashboard, click **Create > 3D Design**.
2. Drag a Sphere, two Boxes, and a Cylinder from the Shapes panel onto the workplane.
3. Press and hold the SHIFT key and click on the two boxes.
4. Navigate to the **Align** tool in the toolbar, or use the shortcut key L to quickly access it. Notice the alignment dots along the X,Y, and Z axes respectively.

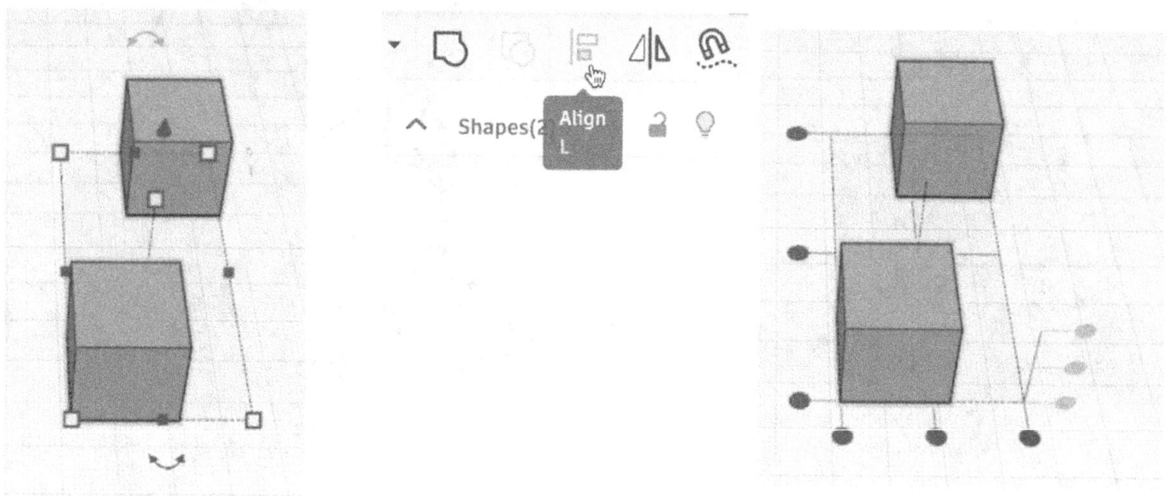

5. Hover the mouse cursor over each alignment option to preview how the boxes will be aligned.

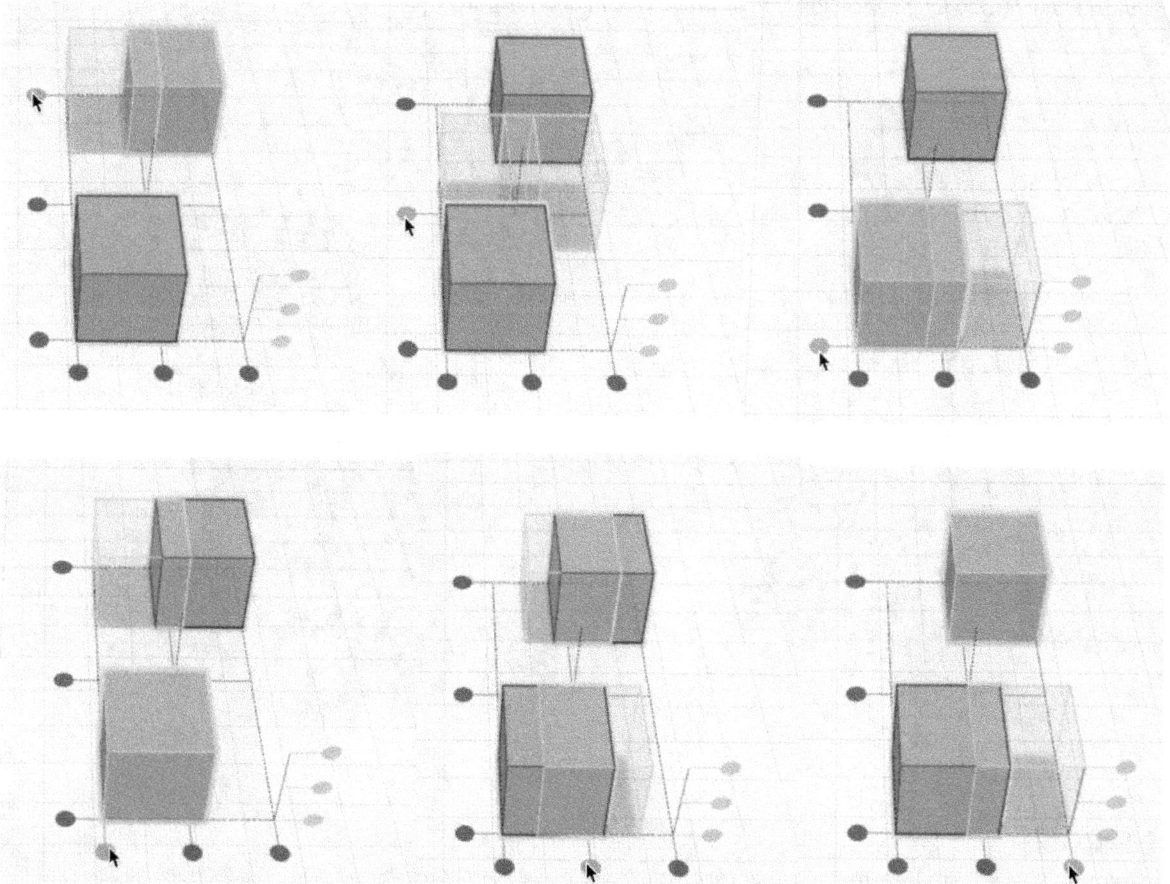

If the alignment dot is grayed out, it indicates that the letters are already aligned.

6. Select the dot is positioned at the center of the X-axis. Once you click on this dot, the boxes will automatically align themselves to the center.

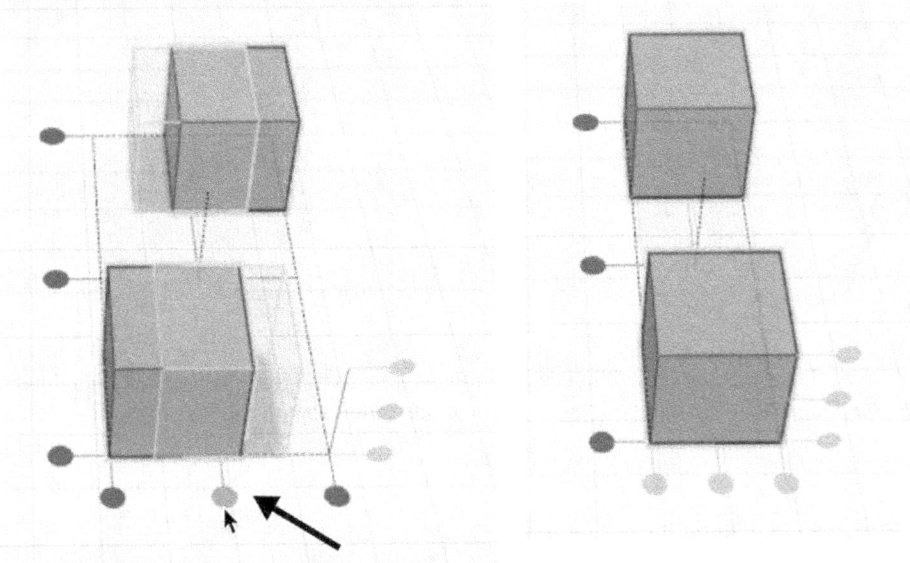

7. Locate the Ruler tool which is typically found above the Shapes panel. Click and drag this tool, positioning its origin (the zero point) on the vertical centerline that is located between the two boxes. This will serve as your reference point for the following steps.
8. Select the box that is positioned lower relative to the Ruler's origin. Once selected, adjust its position so that the distance between the Ruler's origin and the vertex (corner point) of the box is -25 units. The negative value indicates that the box should be placed below the origin.
9. After adjusting the position of the lower box, click anywhere on the workplane. This action will deselect the box and the Ruler tool, allowing you to proceed with the next step without any interference.
10. Select the box that is positioned above the Ruler's origin. Similar to step 8, adjust its position so that the distance between the Ruler's origin and the box's vertex is 5 units. This positive value indicates that the box should be placed above the origin.

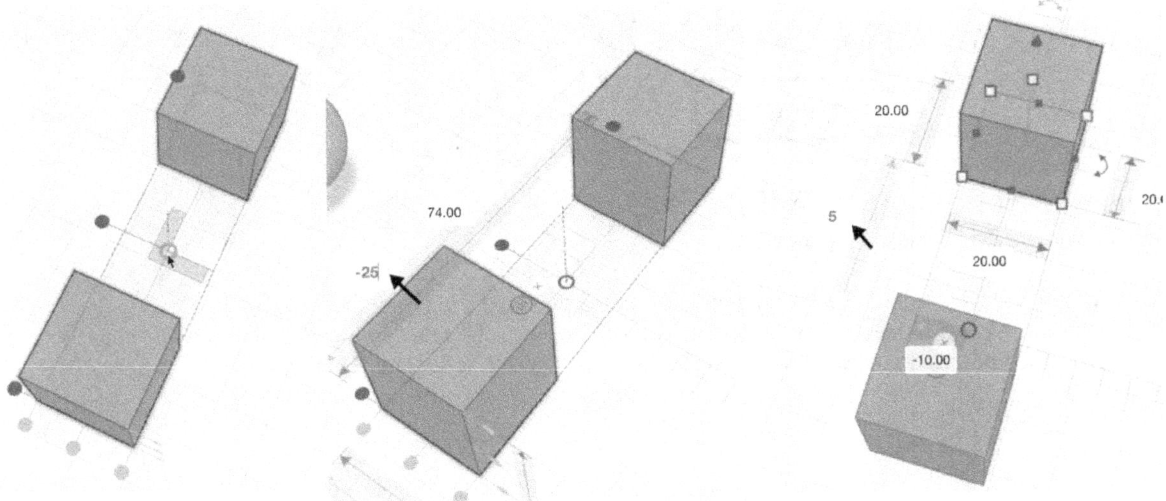

11. Find the icon with three horizontal lines, located next to the Ruler origin.

12. Click on this icon to switch the measurement mode to 'Use Midpoint'. This mode allows us to measure distances from the midpoint of an object.
13. Select the cylinder in your workspace.
14. Change the length and width values of the cylinder to 16. Next, you need to adjust its position relative to the Ruler origin.

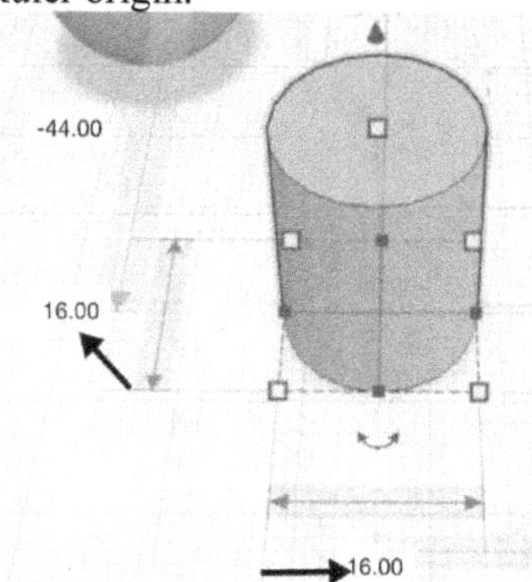

15. Look for the distance values that represent the cylinder's position relative to the Ruler origin. Change these values to '0' along two axes. This action aligns the center point of the cylinder with the Ruler origin.

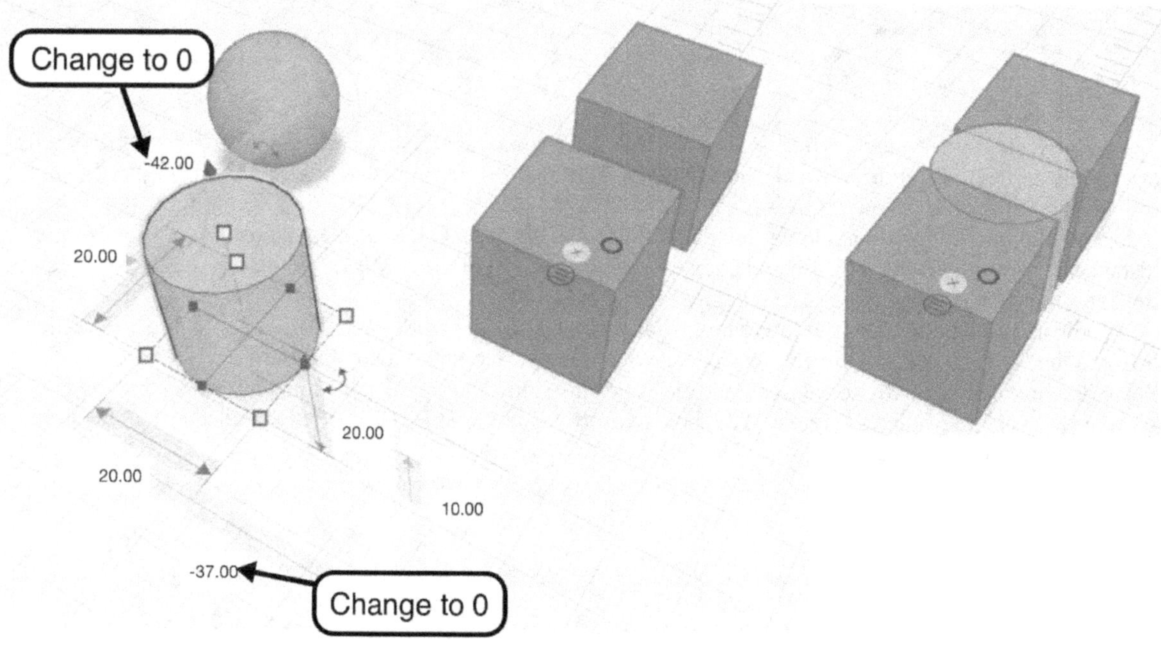

Converting Solid Shapes to Hole Shapes

You can convert any solid shape to a hole shape.

1. To start, press and hold the SHIFT key, then click on the two boxes to select them.
2. In the Inspector panel, select the 'Hole' option. This will change the selected boxes into holes. For quick access, you can use keyboard shortcuts: press 'F' to change an object to a solid, and 'H' to convert it to a hole.

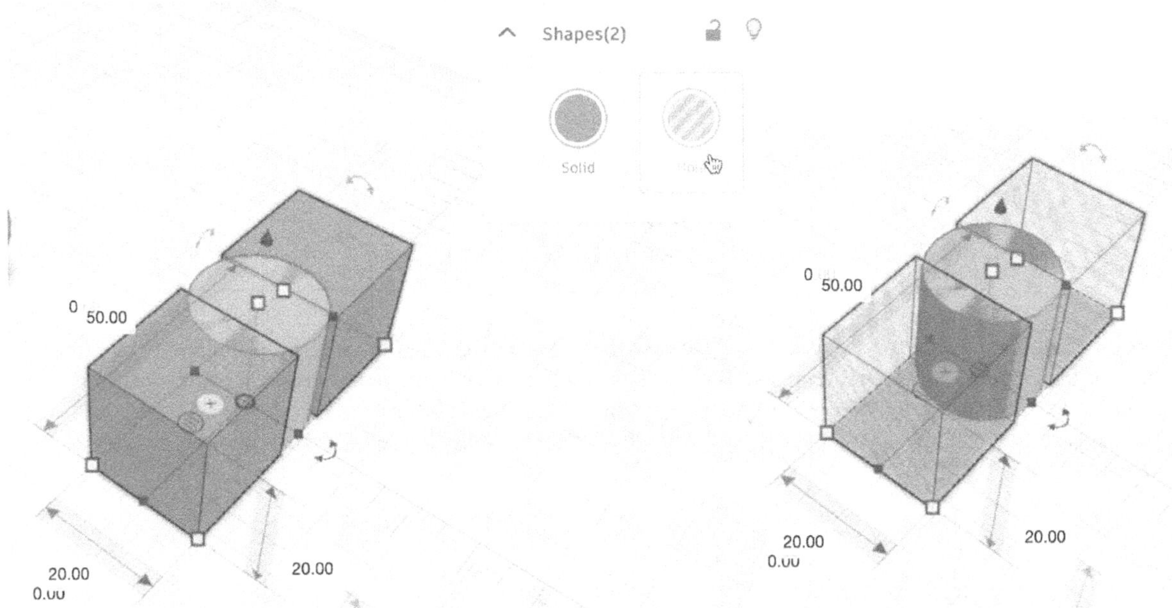

3. Create a selection window across the two boxes and the cylinder. This can be done by clicking and dragging your mouse across these objects.

4. Click on the '**Group**' icon located on the toolbar. This action groups the selected objects together and removes the material from the cylinder, creating a hole in its place.

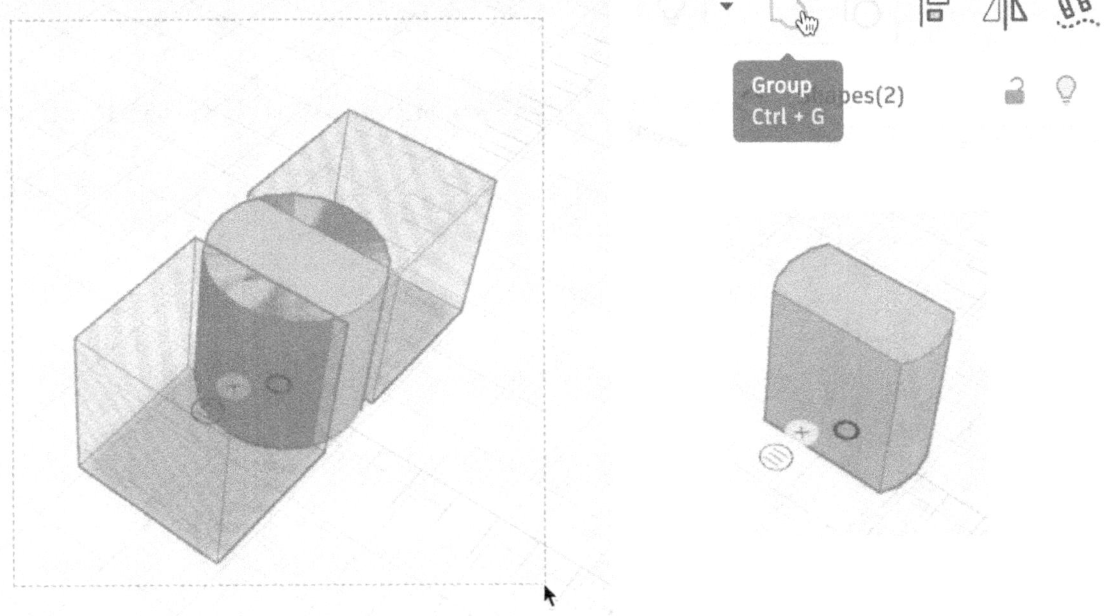

5. Select the resultant solid shape and click the Hole option on the Inspection window; the solid shape is converted into hole shape.

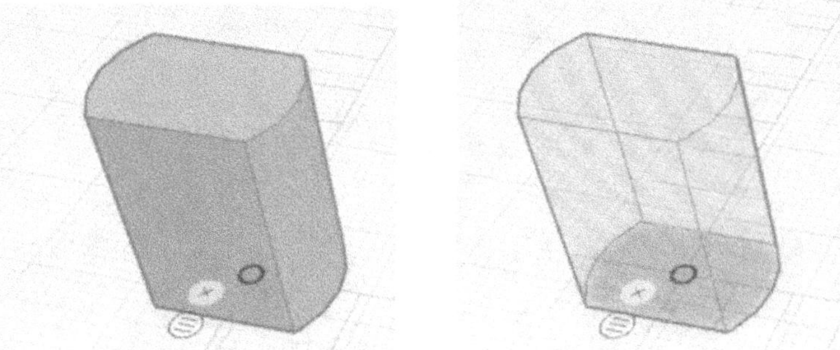

6. Start by dragging the **Box** to the work plane. Release the click to place the box on the work plane.
7. Look for the distance values that represent the box's position relative to the Ruler origin. Change these values to '0' for perfect alignment; the box is now perfectly positioned at the Ruler origin.
8. Create a selection window across the box and click the Group icon on the toolbar; the material is removed from the box.

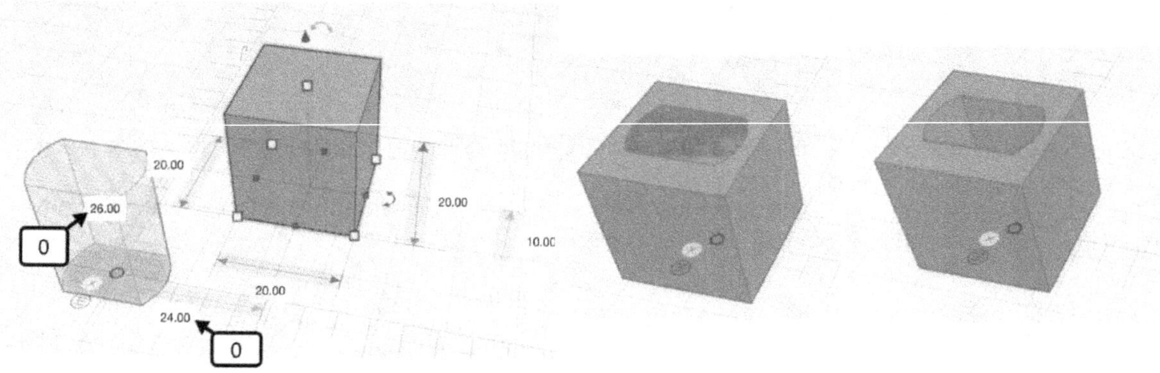

9. Select the newly created solid shape and click the Hole option on the Inspection Window; the solid shape is converted into hole.

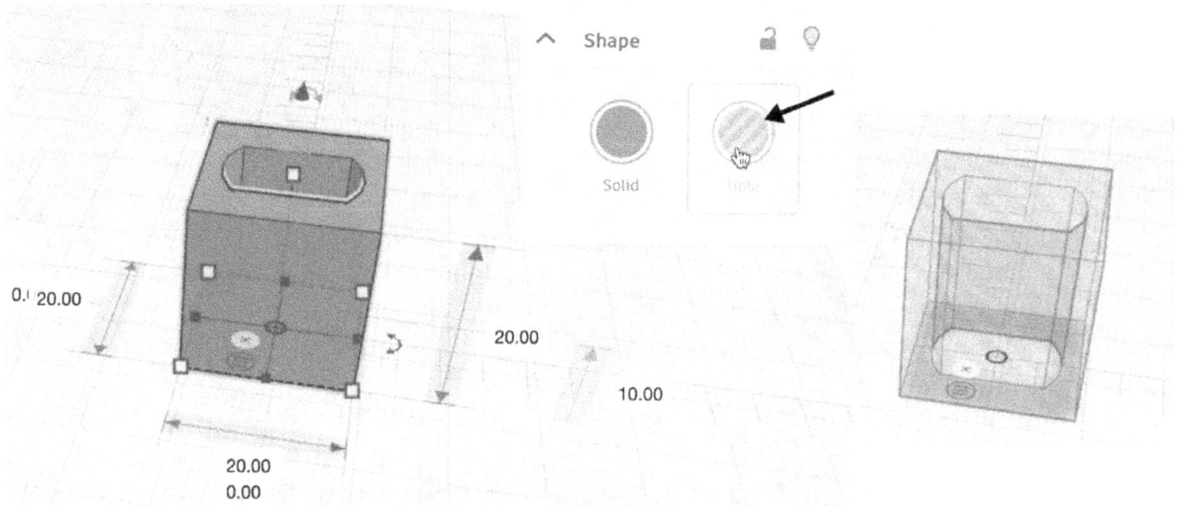

10. Select the sphere within the workspace.
11. Proceed to adjust the sphere's position. This is achieved by modifying the distance values that correspond to the sphere's position relative to the Ruler origin. The objective is to set these values to '0', thereby ensuring perfect alignment. Upon successful adjustment of these values, the sphere will be accurately positioned at the Ruler origin.

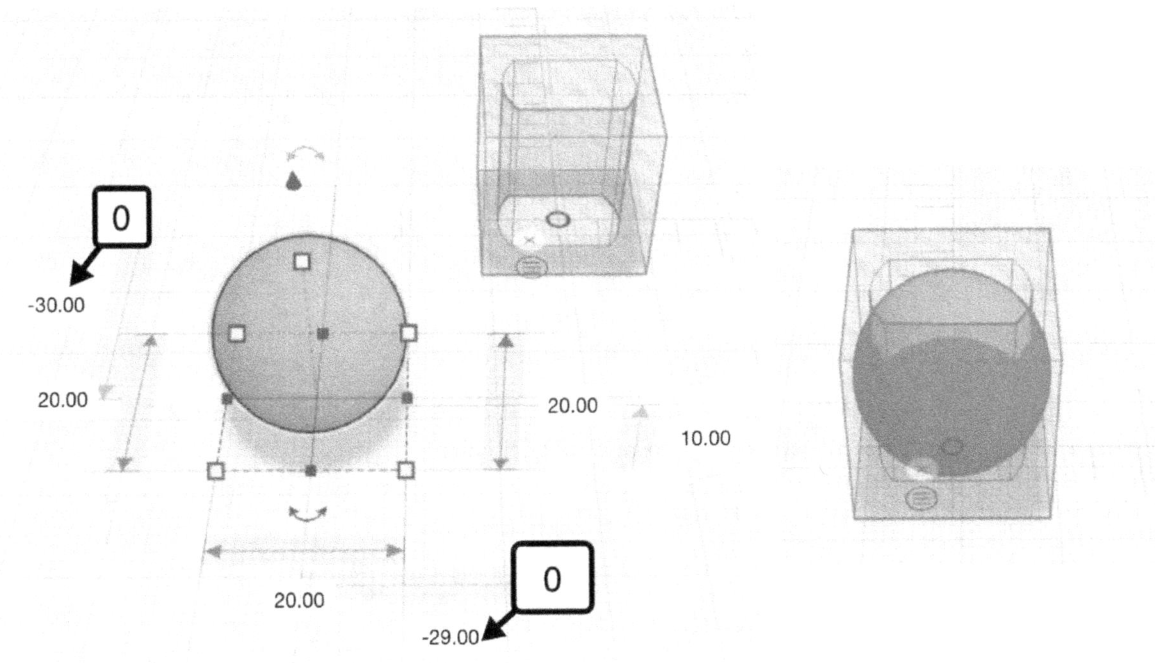

10. Click and drag your cursor across the area of the screen that contains both the sphere and the hole shape. This will create a selection window.
11. Locate the Group icon on the toolbar, which is usually at the top or side of your screen. Click on this icon. Once you've clicked the Group icon, the material will be removed from the sphere using the hole shape.

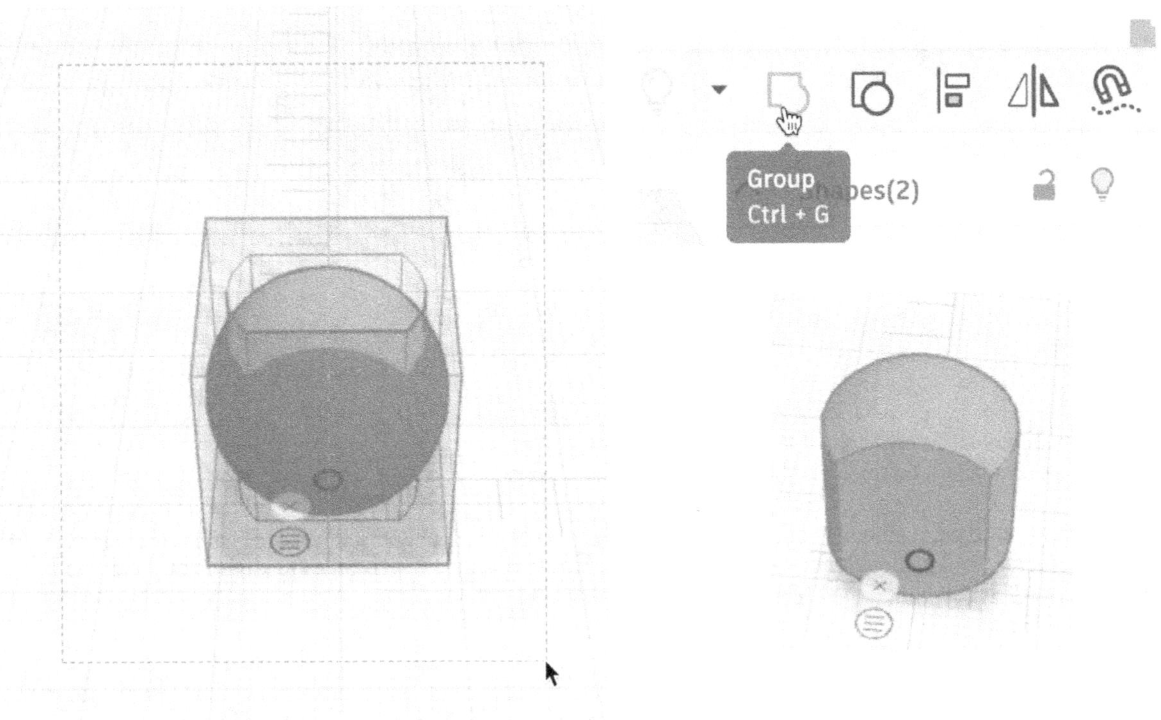

12. Drag a box and a cylinder hole onto the workplane. Then, change the length and width of the cylinder hole to 18, respectively.

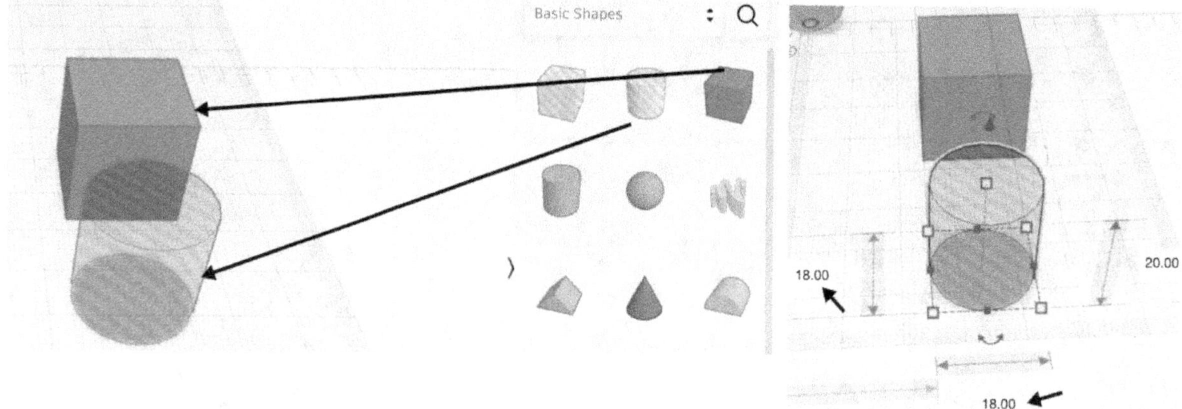

5. Create a selection window encompassing the Box and Cylinder hole.
6. Click the 'Align' icon located on the toolbar.
7. Select the alignment dot at the rear end, along the Y-axis.

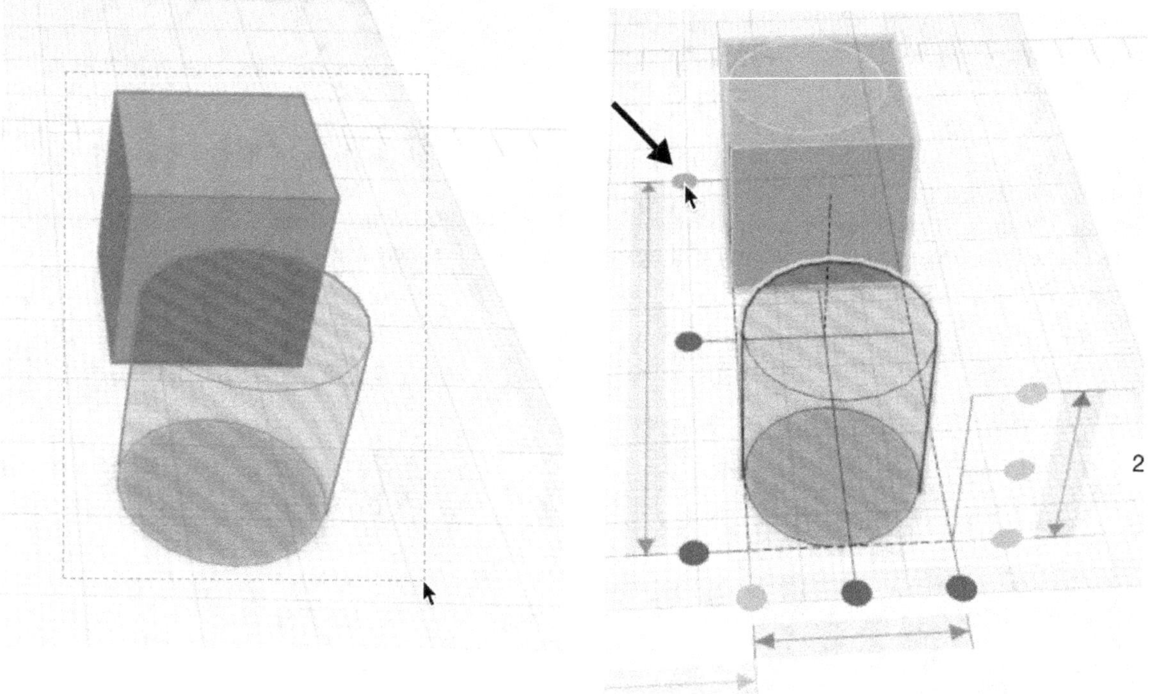

8. Select the alignment dot situated at the center, along the X-axis.
9. Select the alignment dot situated at the center, along the Y-axis.

These steps are used to align an object at the center of a specific axis. By selecting the alignment dot at the center of the X-axis, the object will be positioned horizontally at the center. Similarly, selecting the alignment dot at the center of the Y-axis will position the object vertically at the center.

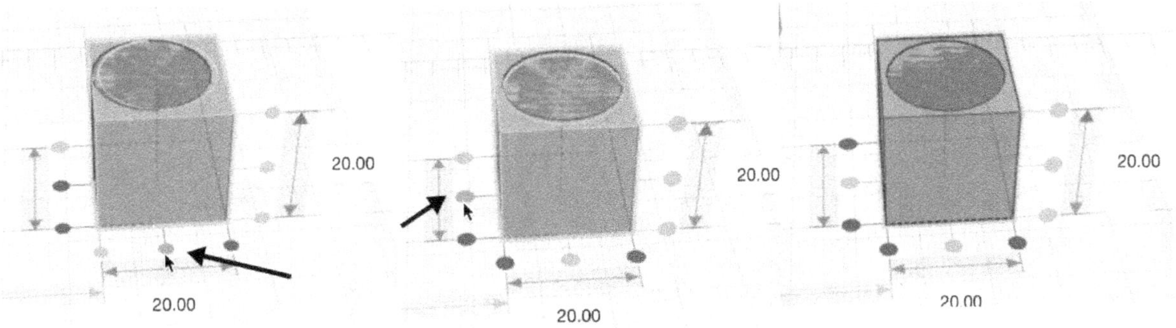

10. Create a selection window across the two aligned objects and click the Group icon on the toolbar. A hole is created on the box.

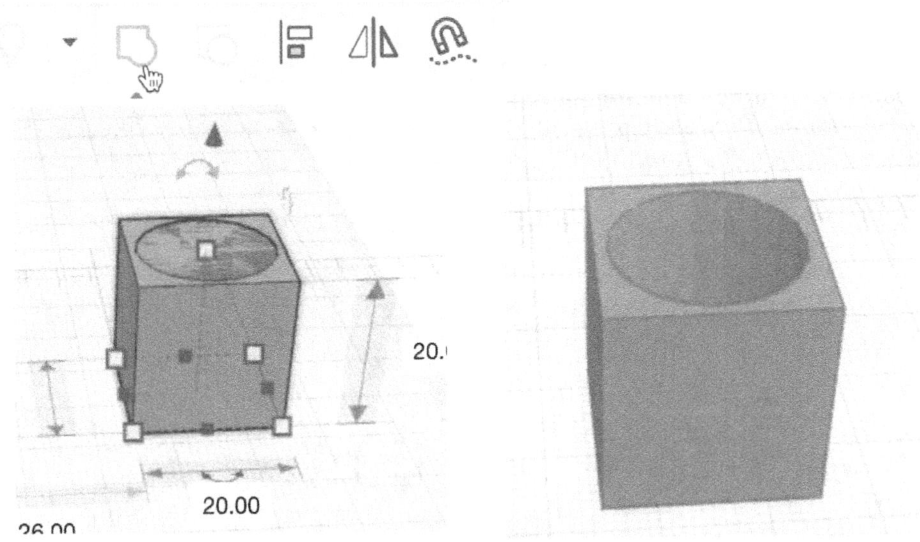

11. Select the box containing the hole and adjust its height to 0.5.
12. Ensure the box remains selected, then click the 'Hole' option in the Inspection window.

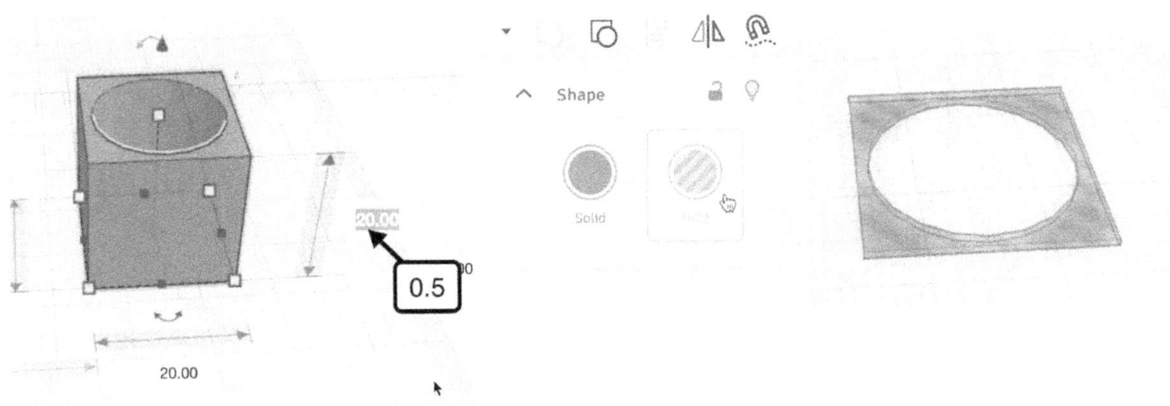

13. Select the hole shape and click on the Rotate grip displayed at the top. Next, change the angle value to 90 degrees; the hole shape is rotated by 90 degrees.
14. Click on the Rotate grip displayed on the front side. Type 90 in the angle box and press ENTER.

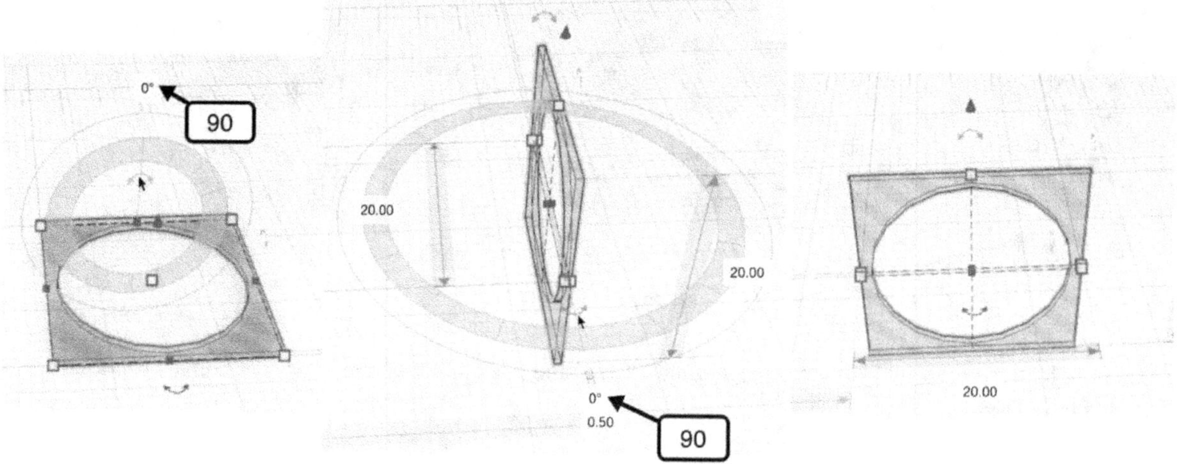

15. Select the hole shape.
16. Click on the icon with three dashes next to the Ruler origin to switch the measurement mode to 'Use Midpoint'. This mode allows us to measure distances from the midpoint of an object.
17. Look for the distance values that represent the hole shape's position relative to the Ruler origin. Change these values to 0 and 2.5 along the X and Y-axis respectively.

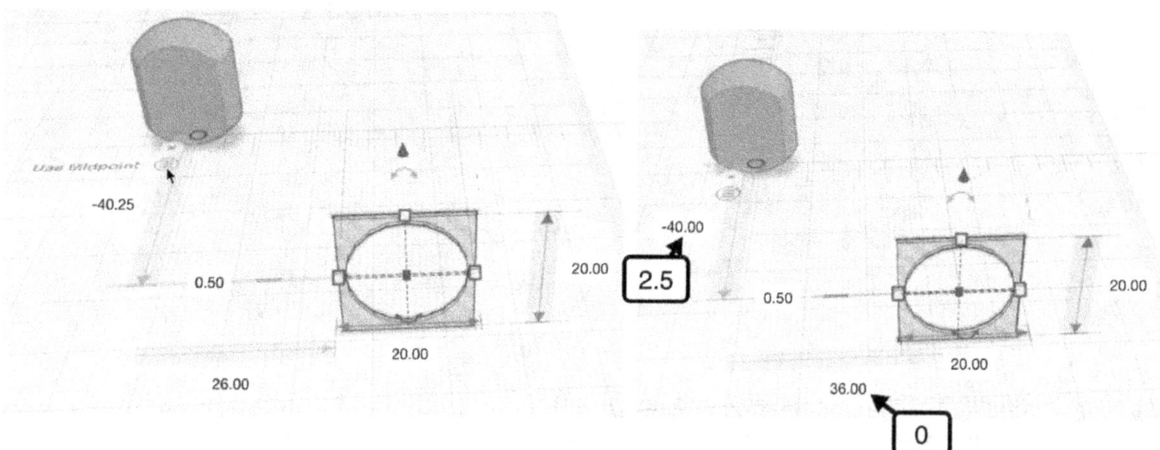

18. Change the distance between the ruler origin and the center point of the hole shape along the Z-axis to 10.

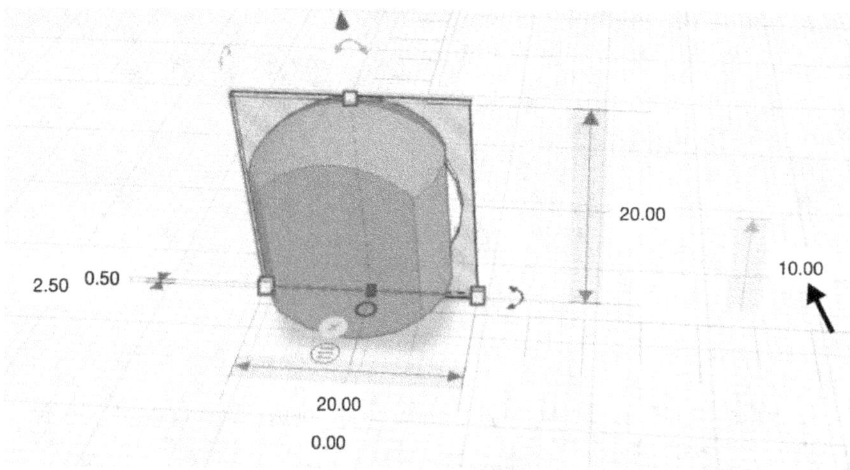

19. Select the hole shape and click the **Duplicate** icon on the toolbar.
20. Drag the duplicated hole shape towards the front.

21. Adjust the Y-axis distance between the ruler origin and the duplicated hole shape to -2.5.

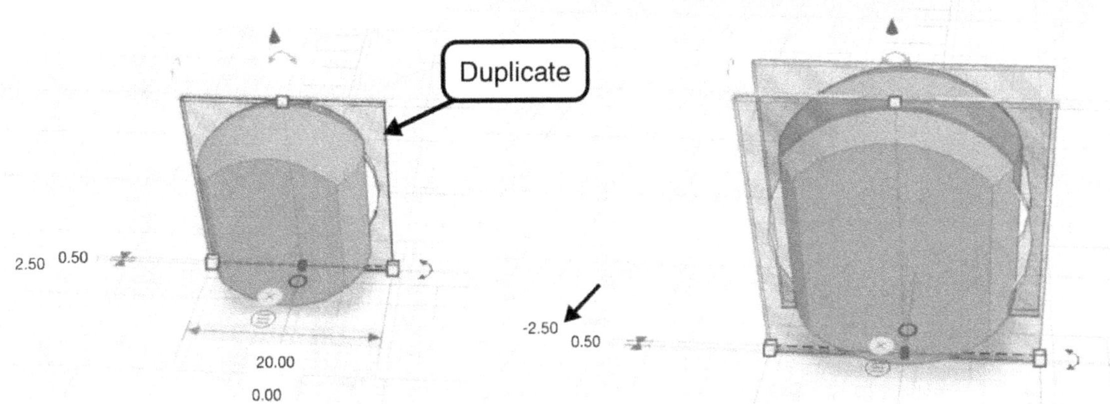

22. Create a selection window across all the objects and click the **Group** icon on the toolbar; the material is removed from the solid shape using the two hole shapes.

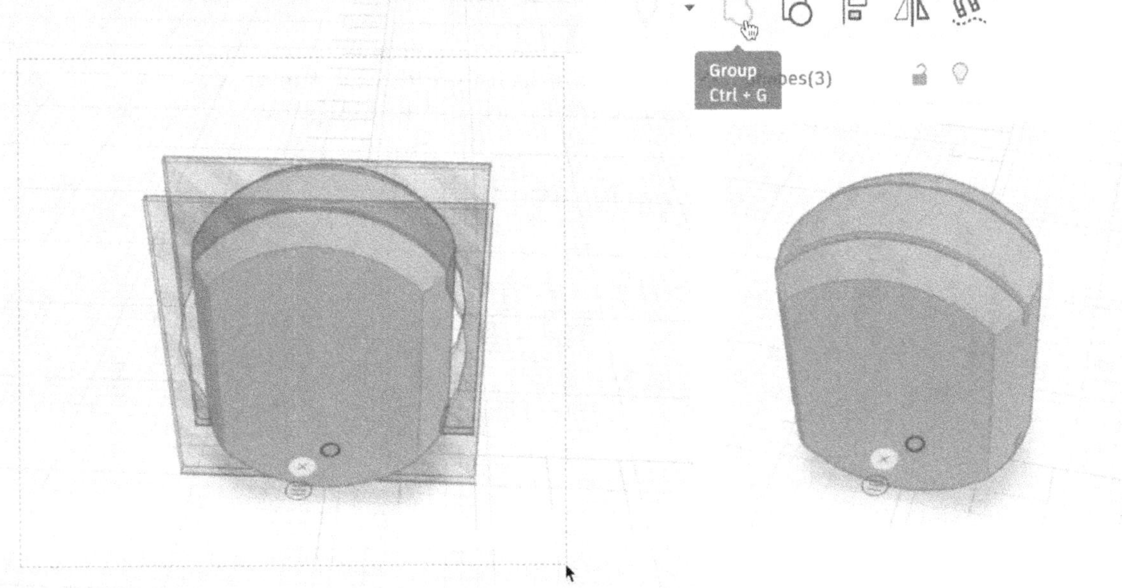

23. Select the solid object from the workplane and click the **Duplicate** icon on the toolbar.
24. Click the Rotate grip located at the bottom right side, and then type 90 in the **Angle** box.
25. Click the Rotate grip located at the top left side, and then type 90 in the **Angle** box.

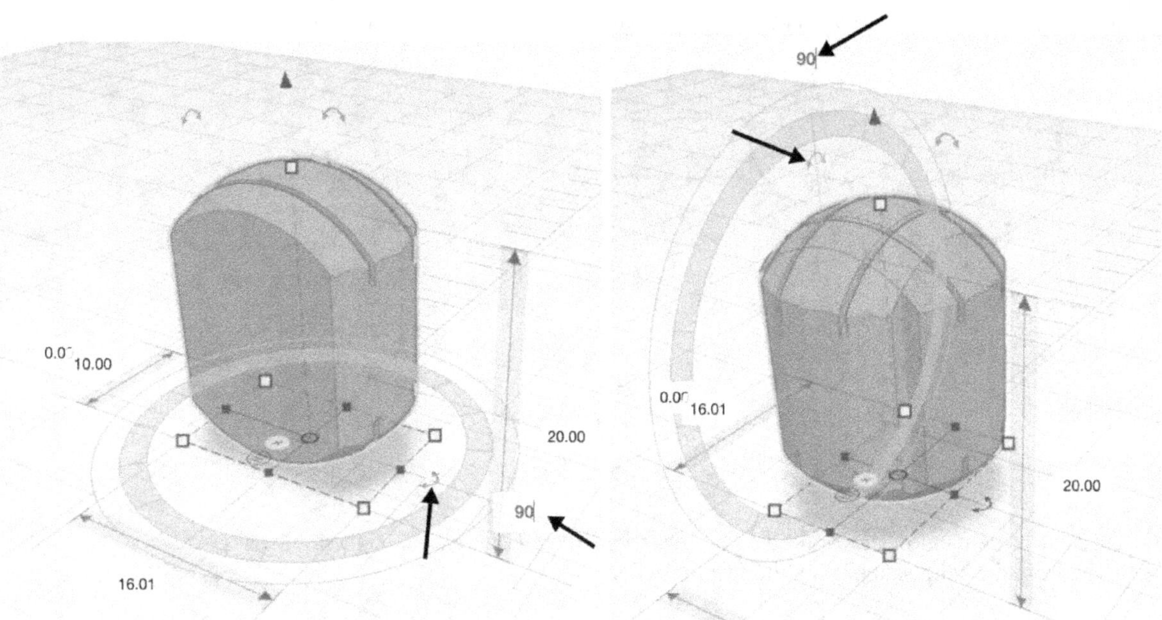

26. Select the rotated solid object from the workplane and click the **Duplicate** icon on the toolbar.
27. Click the Rotate grip located at the bottom front side, and then type 90 in the **Angle** box.
28. Click the Rotate grip located at the upper left side, and then type 90 in the **Angle** box.

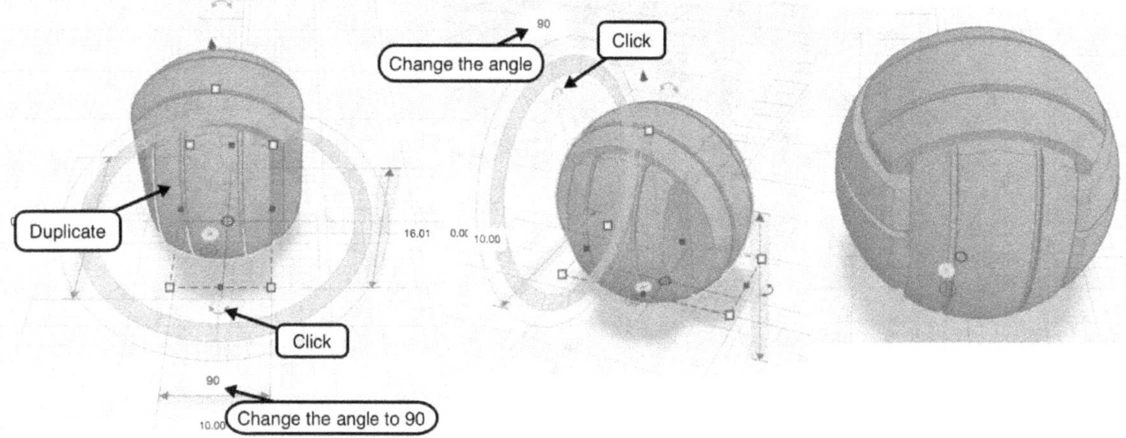

Chapter 4: Patterns and Generators

Creating Patterns Using the Duplicate tool

This section aims to guide you through the process of creating evenly spaced patterns or arrays in Tinkercad using the Duplicate tool.

1.   Select the Shape

Begin by selecting the shape that you wish to duplicate to create your pattern. This shape will serve as the base for your pattern.

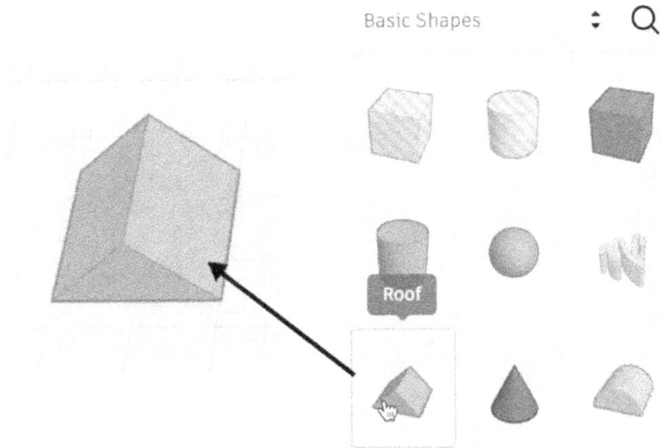

2.   Duplicate the Shape

Select the shape and use Ctrl + D (or Command + D on a Mac) to duplicate it. The duplicate will appear directly over the original shape.

3.   Move the Duplicated Shape

Move the duplicated shape to the desired location. Hold the Shift key while moving to ensure precise alignment.

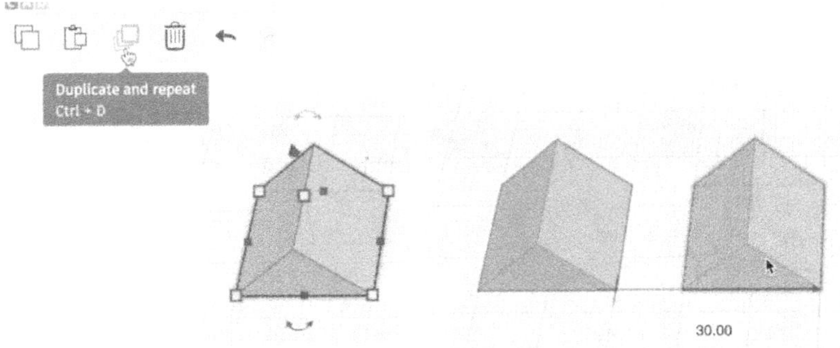

4.   Duplicate and Offset the Shape

After positioning the duplicated shape, duplicate it again with Ctrl + D (or Command + D). The new duplicate will offset from the previous shape by the same distance and direction.

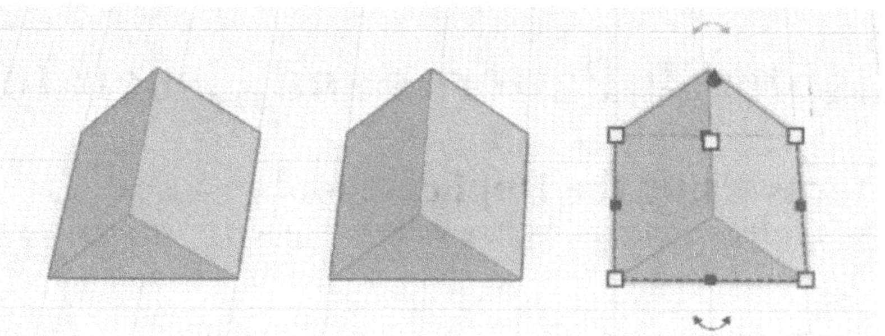

5. Create a Pattern

Continue to press CTRL+D to create a pattern. Each new duplicate will maintain the same offset, resulting in an evenly spaced pattern.

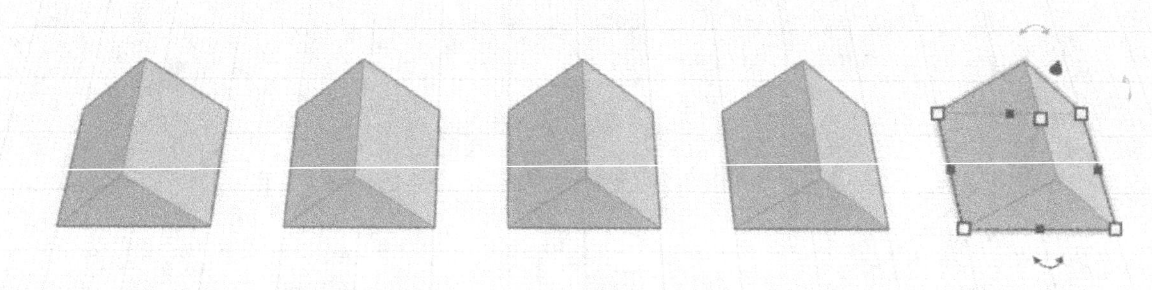

6. Duplicate Multiple Shapes (Optional)

To duplicate multiple shapes simultaneously, select all desired shapes, press Ctrl + D (or Command + D on a Mac), and move them to the desired location. This maintains their relative positions.

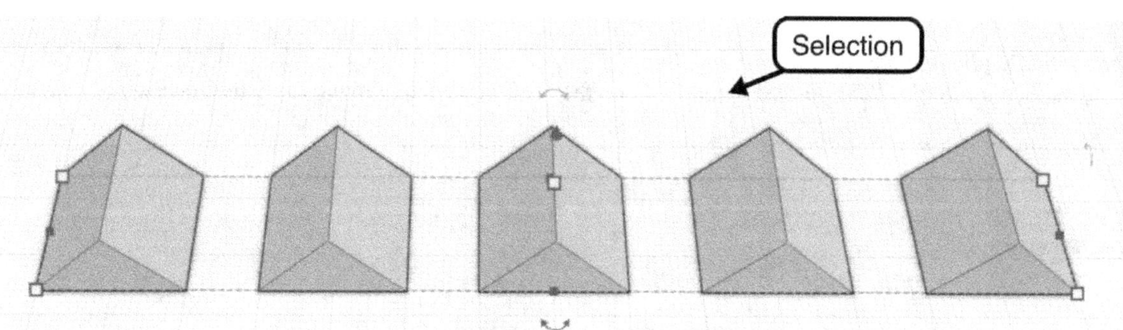

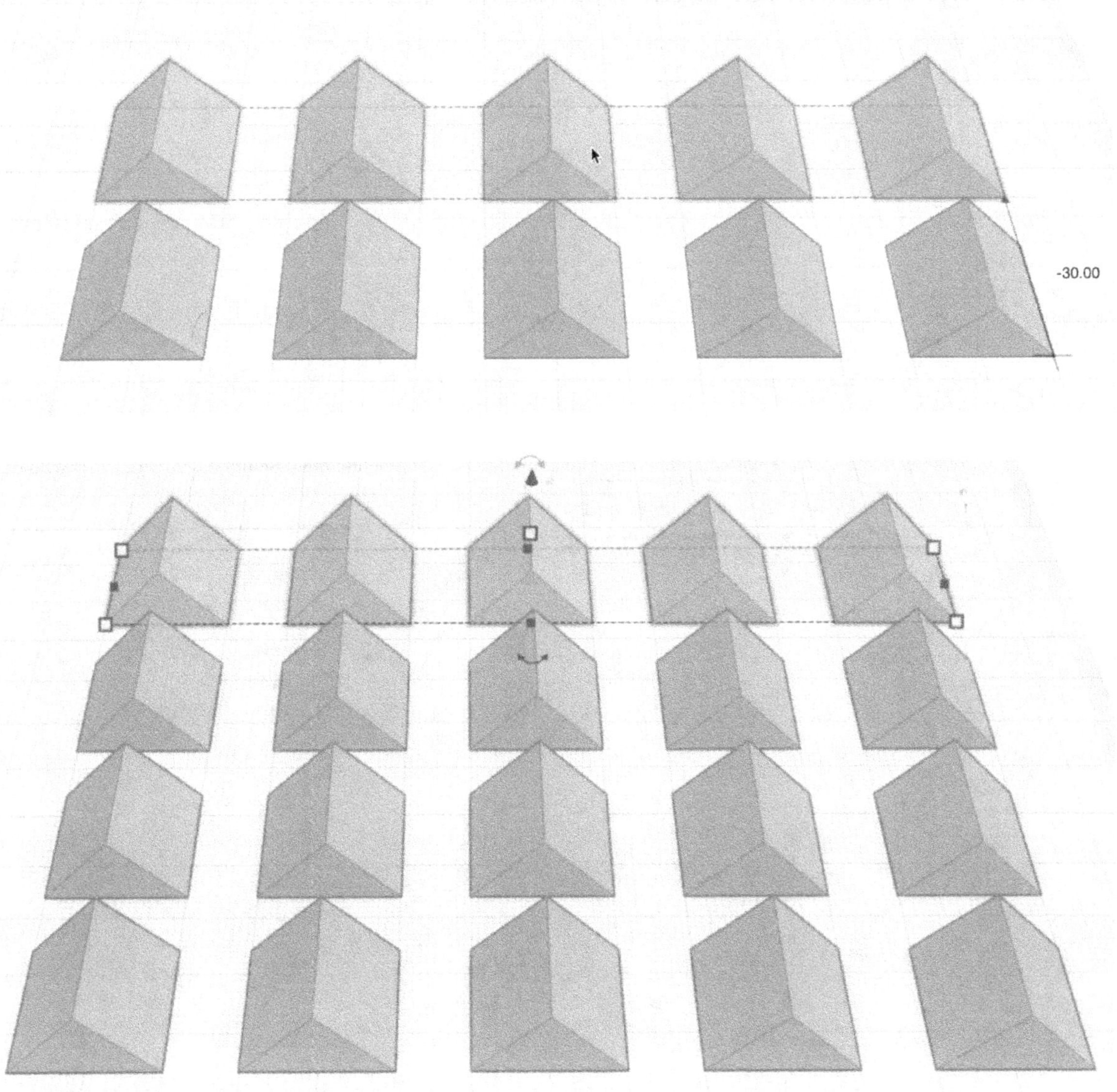

7. Use the Mirror Tool (Optional)

For a mirrored pattern, use the Mirror tool to flip the shape along a chosen axis, creating a reflection of the original shape.

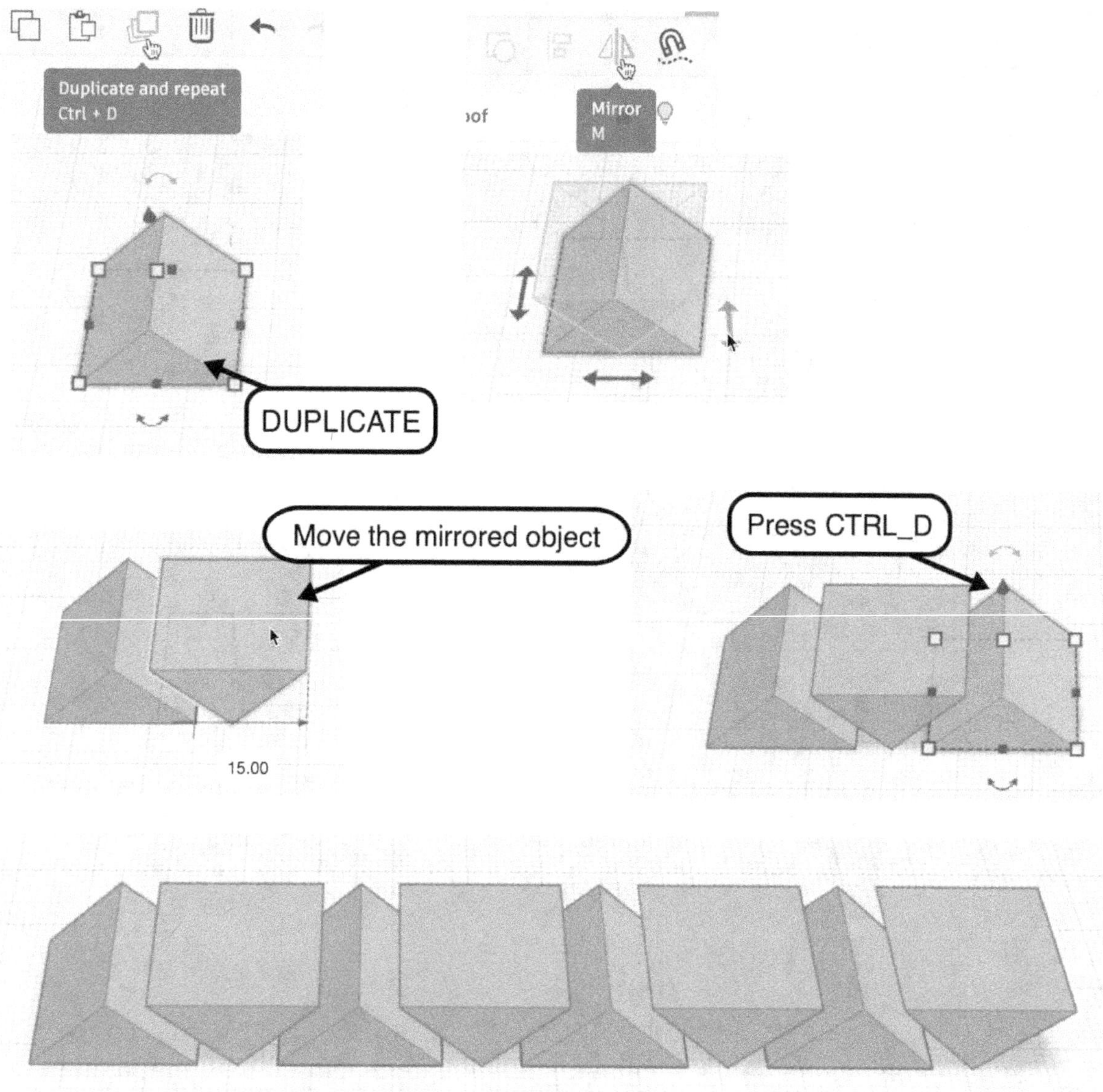

Experiment with combining these methods to create more intricate patterns. Utilize other Tinkercad tools, such as the Rotate tool, in conjunction with the Duplicate tool for advanced design possibilities.

Create a circular pattern

1. Placing the Initial Shape:

Click and drag the Tube shape from the Shapes panel and release on the workplane. This will be the base of our pattern. Next, change the dimensions of the tube using the Inspection window, as shown.

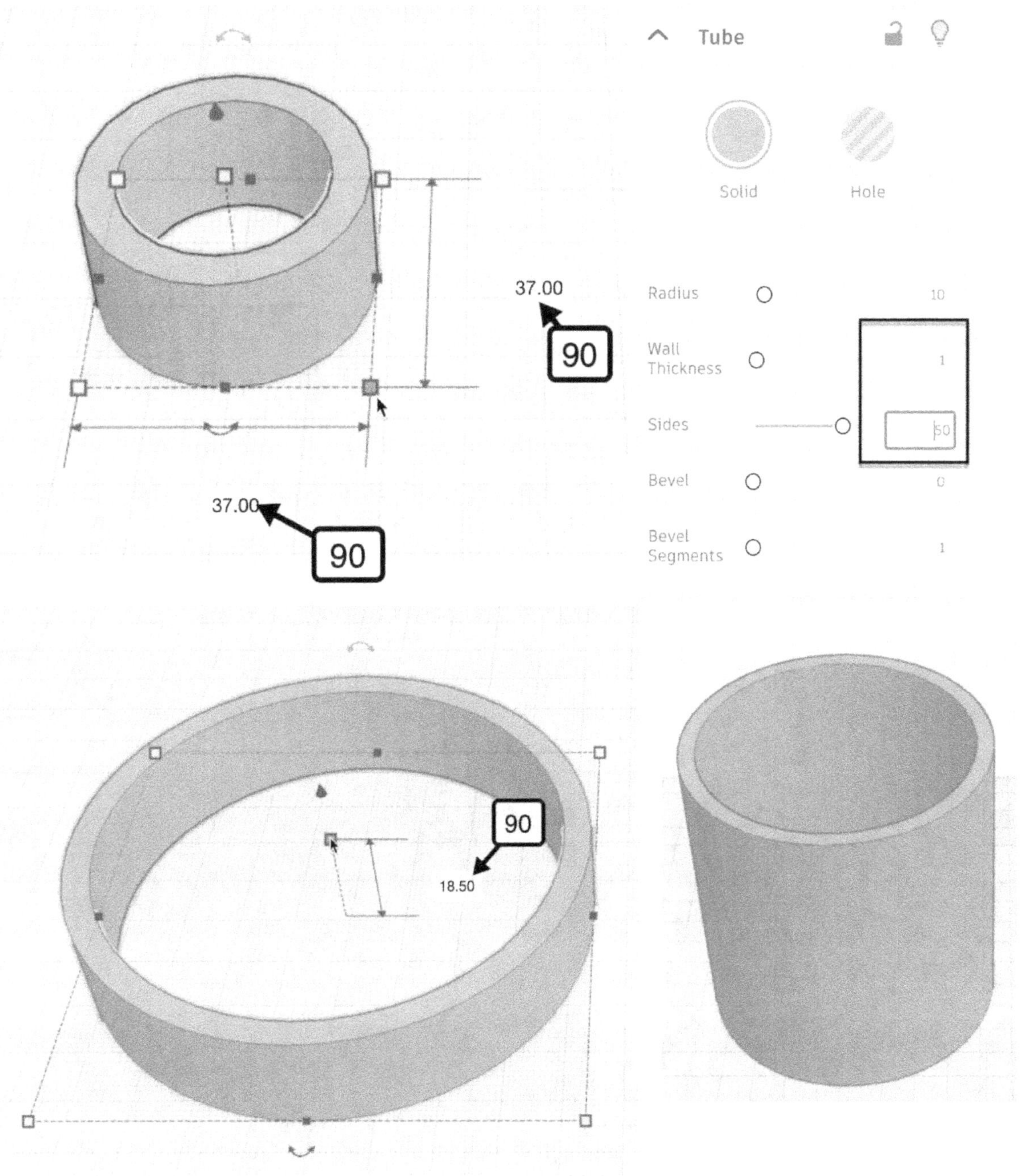

2. **Place the Cylinder Hole Shape:** Drag and drop the "Cylinder Hole" shape from the Shapes panel onto the workplane.
3. **Adjust the Sides:** In the Inspection Window, slide the "Sides" control to its maximum value.

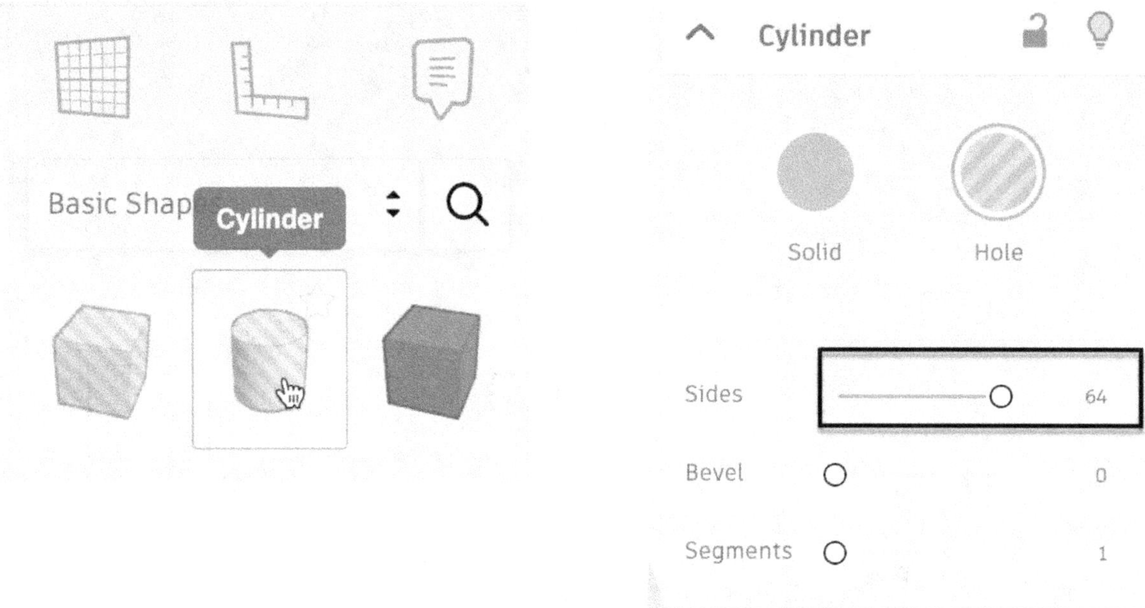

4. **Set the Dimensions:** To change the diameter and height of the cylinder hole, click on the respective dimension values displayed next to it. Enter 15 for the diameter and 100 for the height.

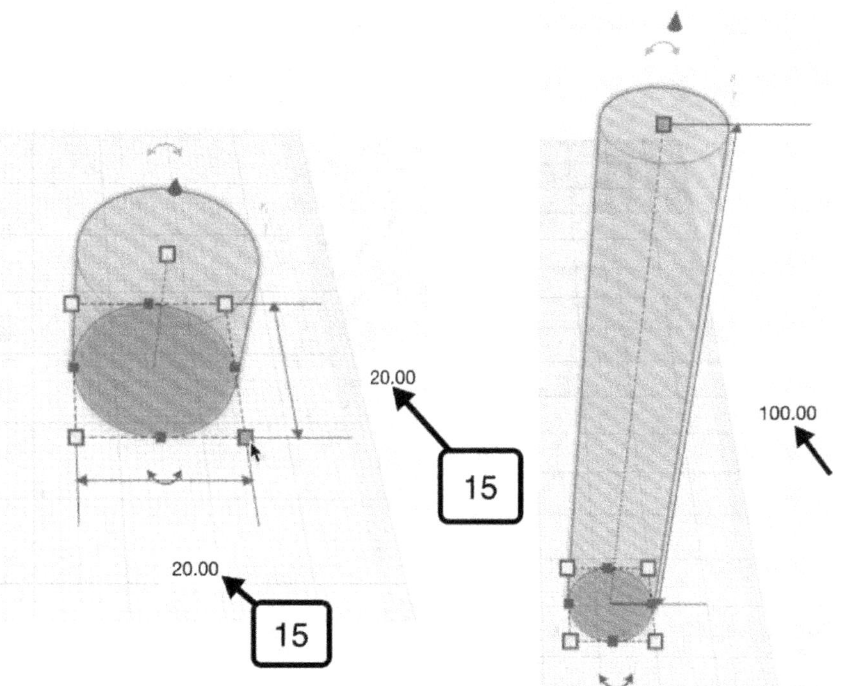

5. Hold down the right mouse button, then drag it to the left to orbit the model view.
6. Select the rotate handle located at the bottom, and enter "90" in the Angle field. This will rotate the cylinder hole by 90 degrees.

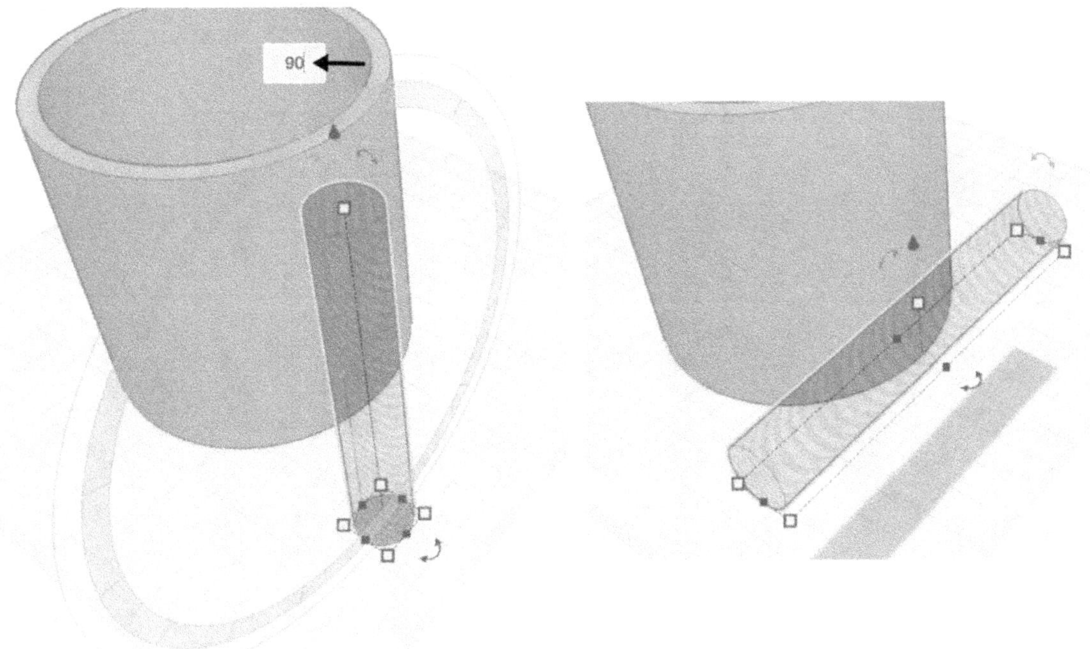

7. Press and hold the SHIFT key and click on the tube and the cylinder hole.

8. Navigate to the **Align** tool in the toolbar, or use the shortcut key L to quickly access it. Notice the alignment dots along the X,Y, and Z axes respectively.

9. Select the dot positioned at the bottom of the Z-axis; the cylinder hole is aligned to the bottom plane of the tube.

10. Select the dot positioned at the center of the X-axis. Once you click on this dot, the tube and cylinder hole will automatically align themselves to the center.

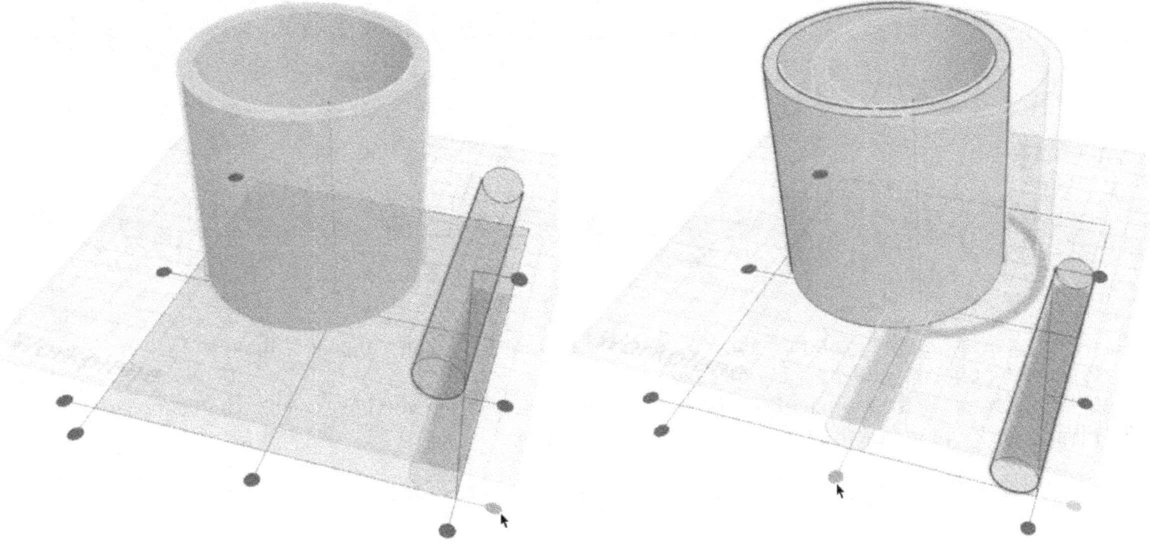

11. Select the dot positioned at the center of the Y-axis; the tube and cylinder hole are aligned at the center along the Y-axis.

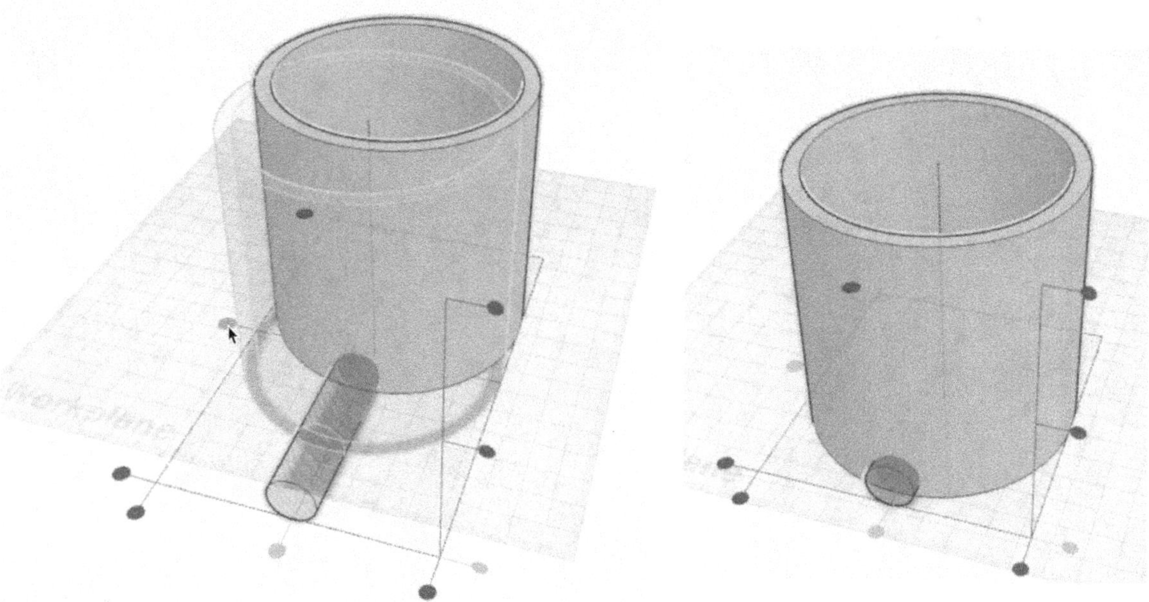

12. Select Front from the View Cube (usually found in a corner of the screen) to get a front perspective.
13. Choose Orthographic for a flat, undistorted view.

14. Begin by selecting the cylinder hole. You will see a cone-shaped grip appear at the top.
15. Proceed by clicking and dragging this grip.
16. Continue to move the cylinder hole upwards, stopping only when you have reached a distance of 4 units.
17. Finally, let go of the mouse button to complete the action.

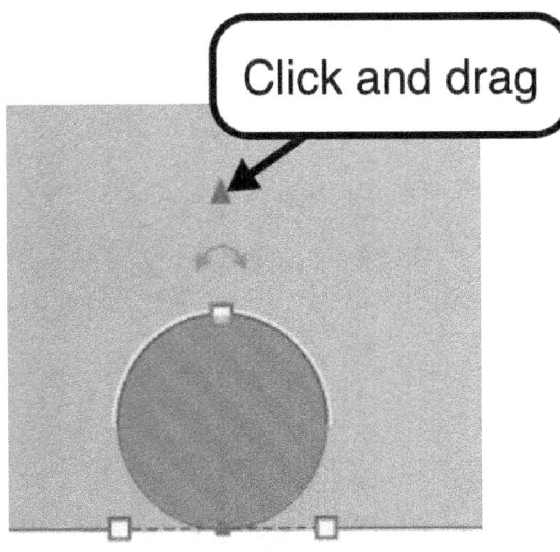

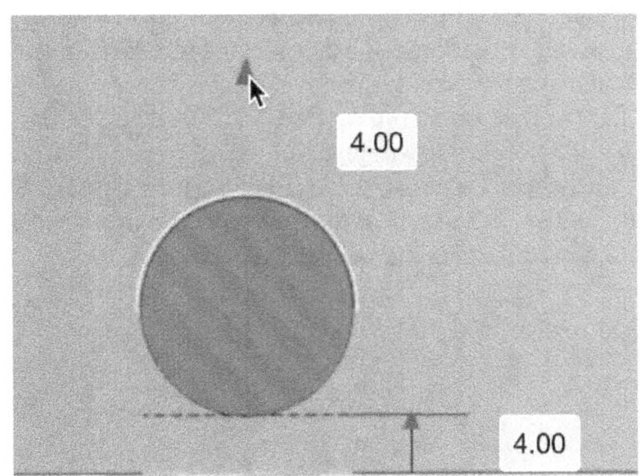

18. **Orient to Top View:** Click the rotation arrow at the top of View Cube to switch the active view to the Top orientation.

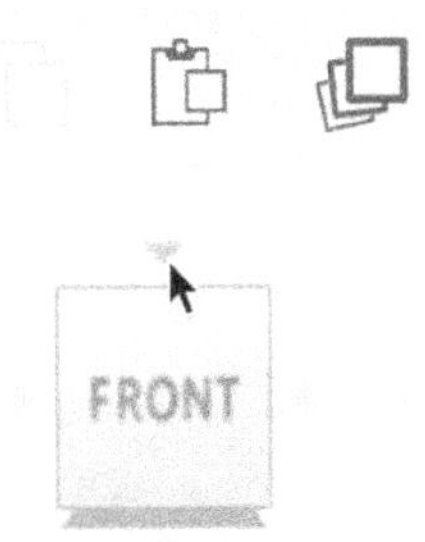

19. **Duplicate the Cylinder Hole:** Select the existing cylinder hole you want to duplicate. Locate the **Duplicate** tool on the toolbar and click it.
20. **Prepare for Rotation:** Select the newly duplicated cylinder hole. Click on the **Rotate** grip, which appears when the object is selected.
21. **Rotate the Duplicate:** In the **Angle** input box, type **30** and press **Enter**. This rotates the duplicated cylinder hole by 30 degrees.
22. **Create the Circular Pattern:** Press the **Ctrl+D** key combination on your keyboard **four** times. This repeats the duplication and rotation action, resulting in a circular pattern of cylinder holes.

23. **Orient to Front View**: To change the active view to the Front orientation, click the rotation arrow at the bottom of the View Cube.
24. **Select All Objects**: To select all objects, use the keyboard shortcut CTRL+A.
25. **Deselect the Tube**: To deselect the tube from the selected objects, press and hold the SHIFT key, then click on the tube.
26. **Duplicate the Circular Pattern**: With the circular pattern selected, use the Duplicate tool available on the toolbar to create a duplicate.
27. **Move the Duplicated Circular Pattern Up**: To move the duplicated circular pattern upward, click on the conical-shaped grip at the bottom or top of the pattern. Then, drag the pointer up by a distance of 20 units before releasing the pointer.

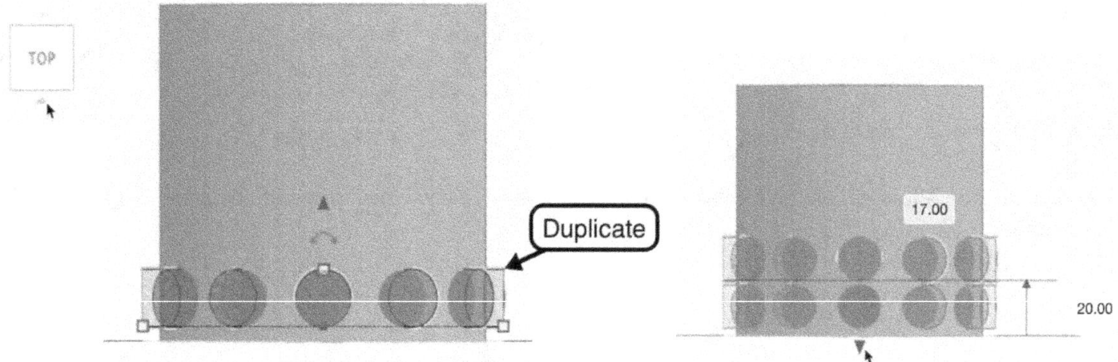

28. **Orient to Top View:** To switch the active view to top orientation, click the rotation arrow located at the top of the View Cube.
29. **Rotate the Duplicated Circular Pattern:** Select the rotate handle, enter 15 in the Angle box, and then press ENTER.
30. **Create a Staggered Linear Pattern:** Utilize the Duplicate tool from the toolbar. Click on it three times to generate the desired staggered linear pattern.

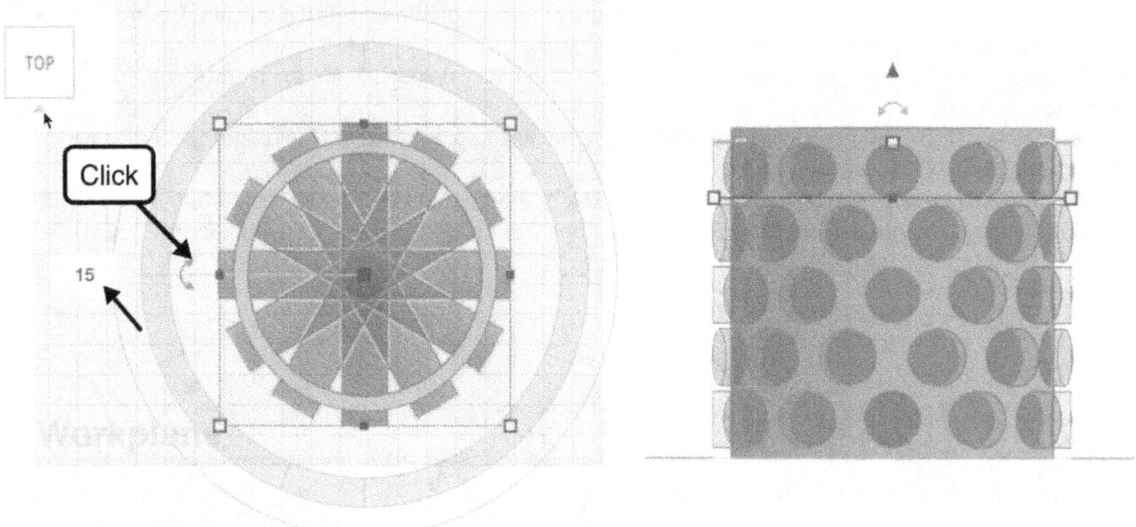

31. Press the CTRL+A to select all the objects.
32. Click on the '**Group**' icon located on the toolbar. This action groups the selected objects together and removes the material.

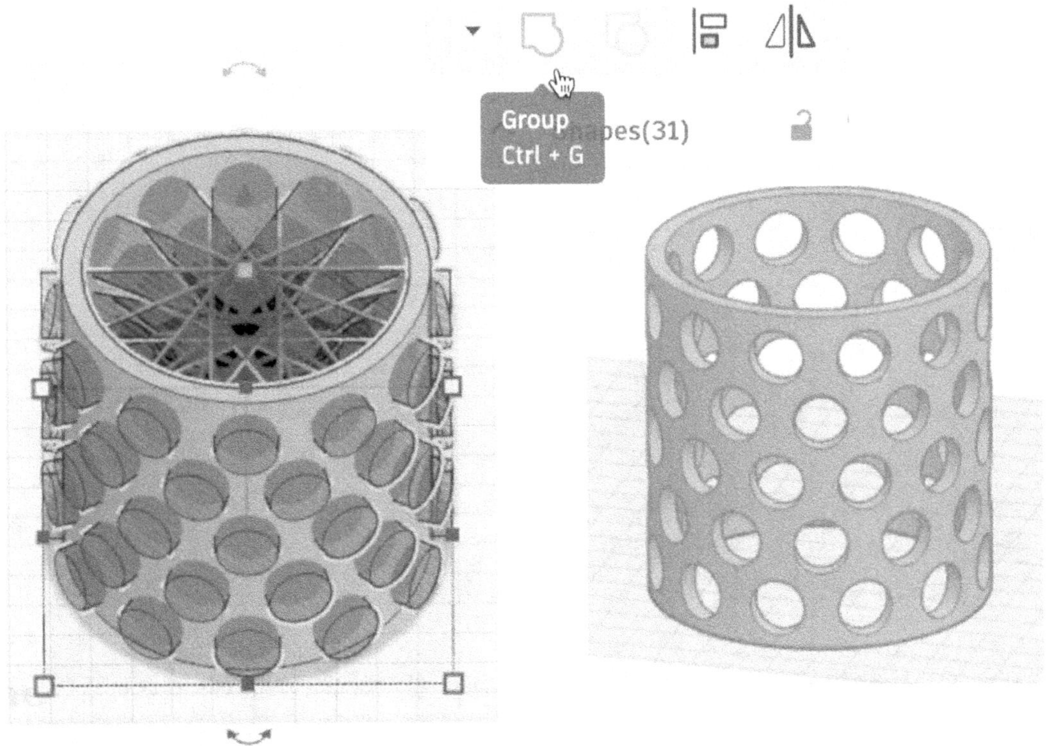

Creating a Linear Scaled Pattern

1. Select the 'Star' shape from the geometric shapes in Tinkercad.

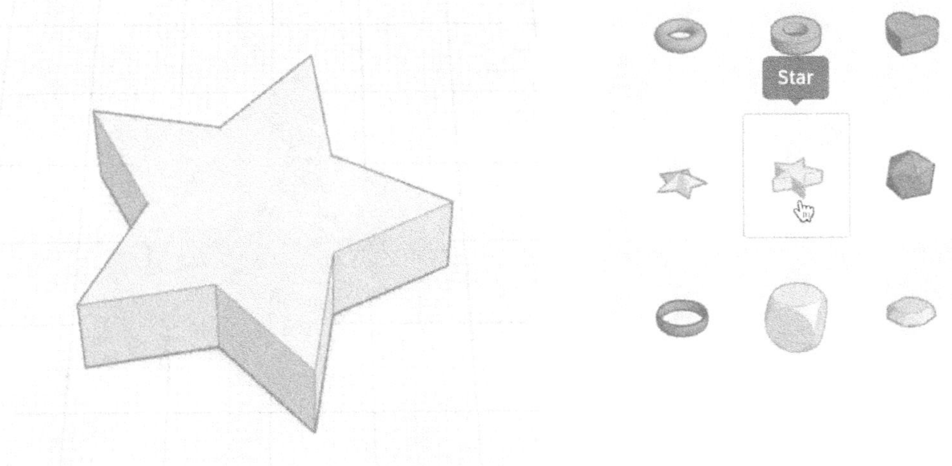

2. Duplicate the star by selecting it and using 'Duplicate' or pressing 'Ctrl+D'.
3. Move the duplicated star to the side by clicking and dragging it.
4. Scale down the duplicated star using the corner grips. Hold 'Shift' to maintain proportions.

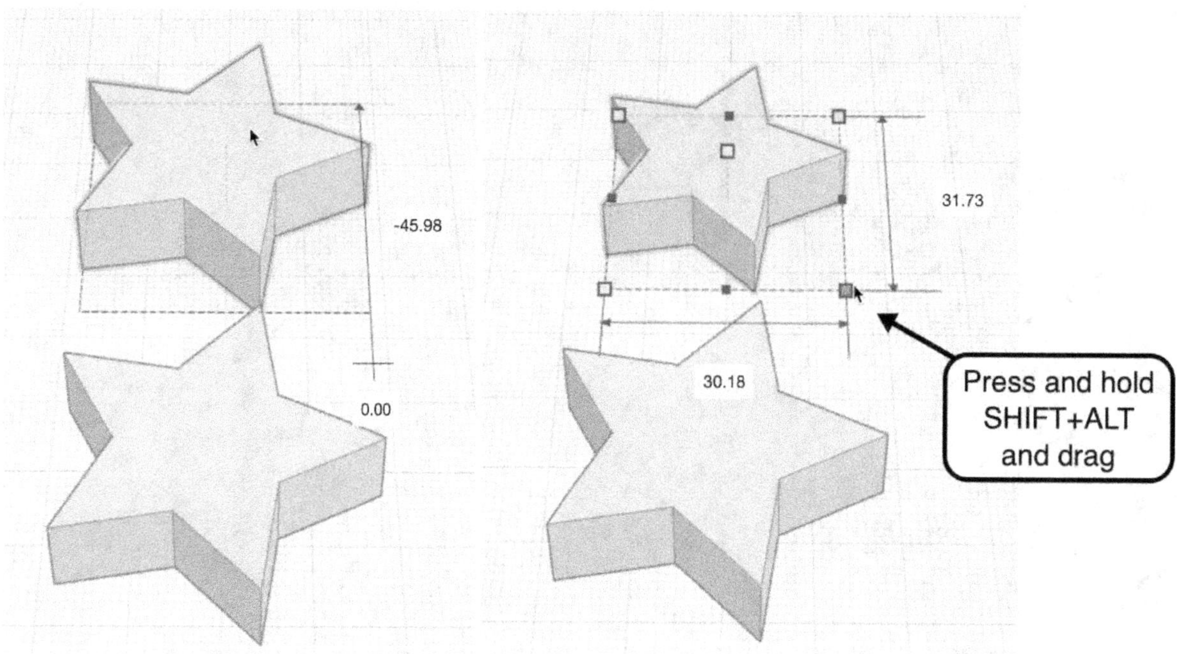

5. Repeat steps 2 times to create a linear scaling pattern. Each new star should be smaller than the previous one.

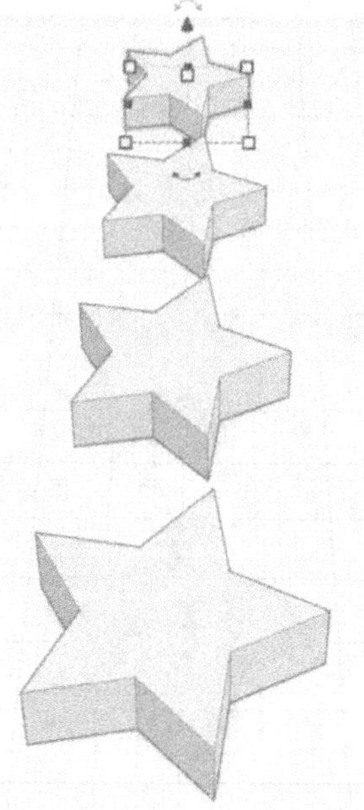

Using shape generators

Tinkercad provides you with shape generators to simplify the creation of intricate 3D models. These generators you to generate complex shapes and forms using basic geometric primitives as building blocks.

Key Advantages:
- **Efficiency:** Shape generators eliminate the need to manually construct complex shapes, saving time and effort.
- **User-Friendly:** The intuitive interface and adjustable parameters make them accessible to users of all skill levels.
- **Design Versatility:** A wide range of generators are available, enabling you to create gears, springs, text, numbers, and much more.

Step 1: Accessing Shape Generators

1. Locate the dropdown menu in Tinkercad's interface. This is typically found in the top left corner of the screen.
2. Click on the dropdown menu and select "Shape Generators" from the list of options. This will display a variety of generators that you can use to create custom shapes for your 3D designs.

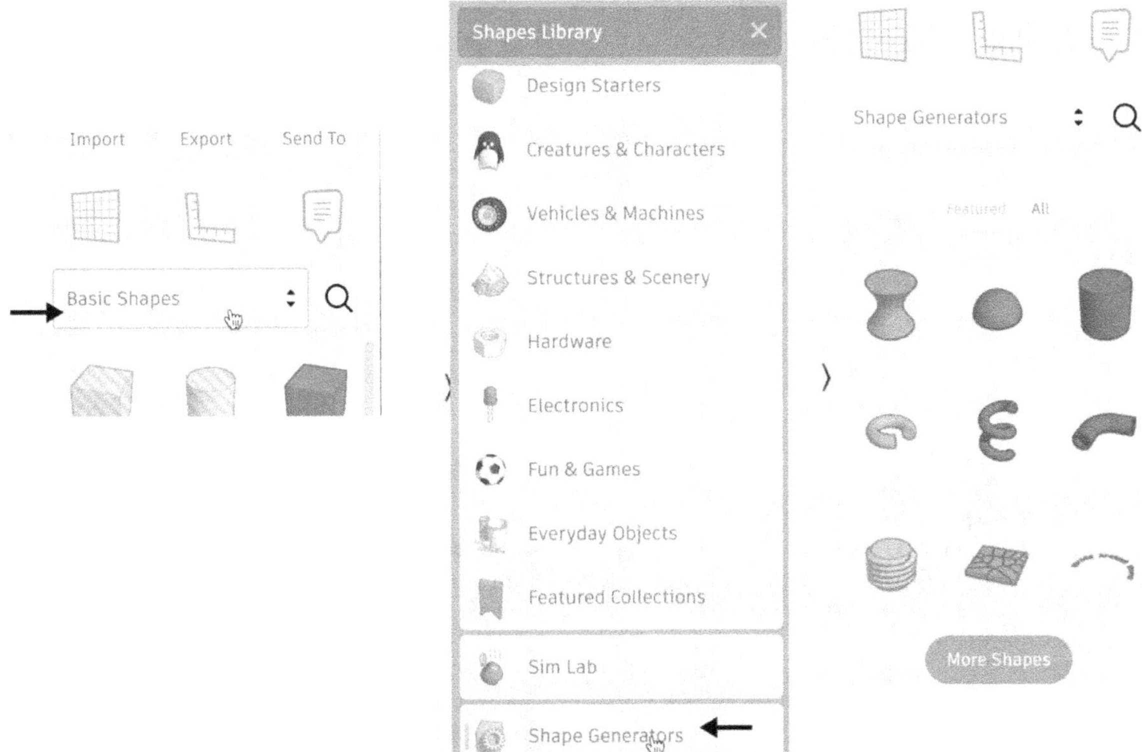

Step 2: Using the Extrusion Generator

1. Select the "Extrusion" generator from the list of shape generators. This tool allows you to create organic, extruded shapes by manipulating points on a 2D profile.
2. Click and drag this generator onto the workplane. The Inspection window displays a 2D profile.

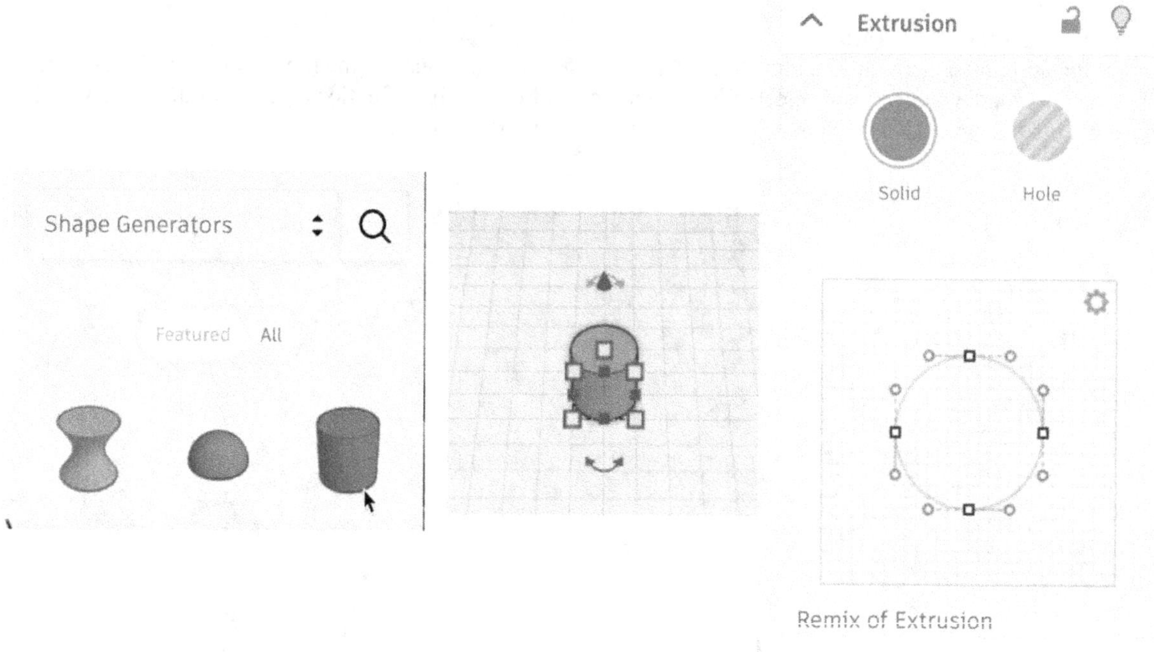

Step 3: Adjusting Shapes

1. Click and drag the points on the 2D profile to adjust the shape.
2. Pull points outwards or inwards to achieve your desired form.
3. For sharp corners, hold down the Alt or Option key and drag the handles. This allows you to create precise, angular shapes.

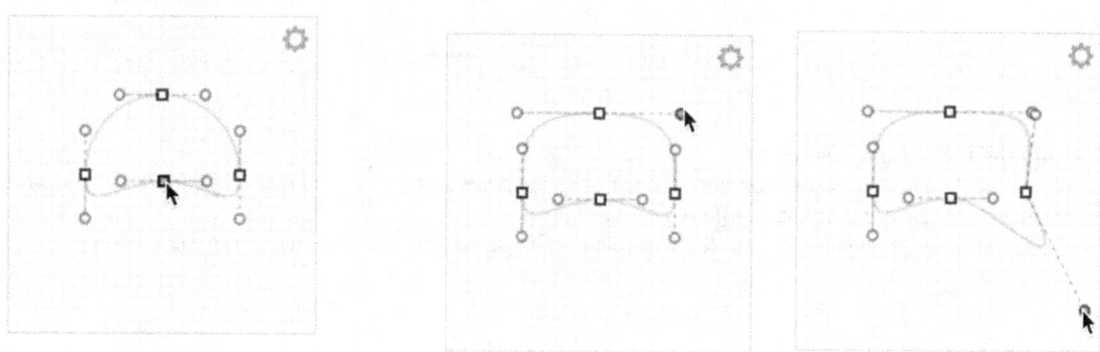

Step 4: Utilizing the Snap option

Click the **Edit Sketch Settings** icon and check the Snap option. The **Snap** option automatically aligns points in one-millimeter increments. This option is particularly helpful for ensuring precise measurements in your designs.

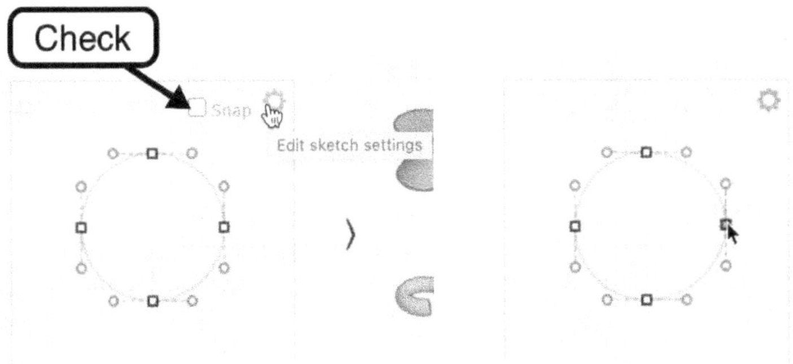

Using the SVG Revolver

The "SVG Revolver" is another valuable tool for creating unique shapes. This generator revolves a circle or a closed profile from the uploaded SVG file around a circle to generate a three-dimensional form.

1. Click and drag the SVG Revolver onto the workplane.
2. Change the parameters of the shape such as **Sketch Height**, **Inside Diameter**, **Number of Sides**, **Sketch Rotation**, and **Revolve Angle** on the Inspection window. You can also use custom shape as the cross-section. To do this, click the **Or choose one** button on the Inspection window and select a .svg file containing the shape.

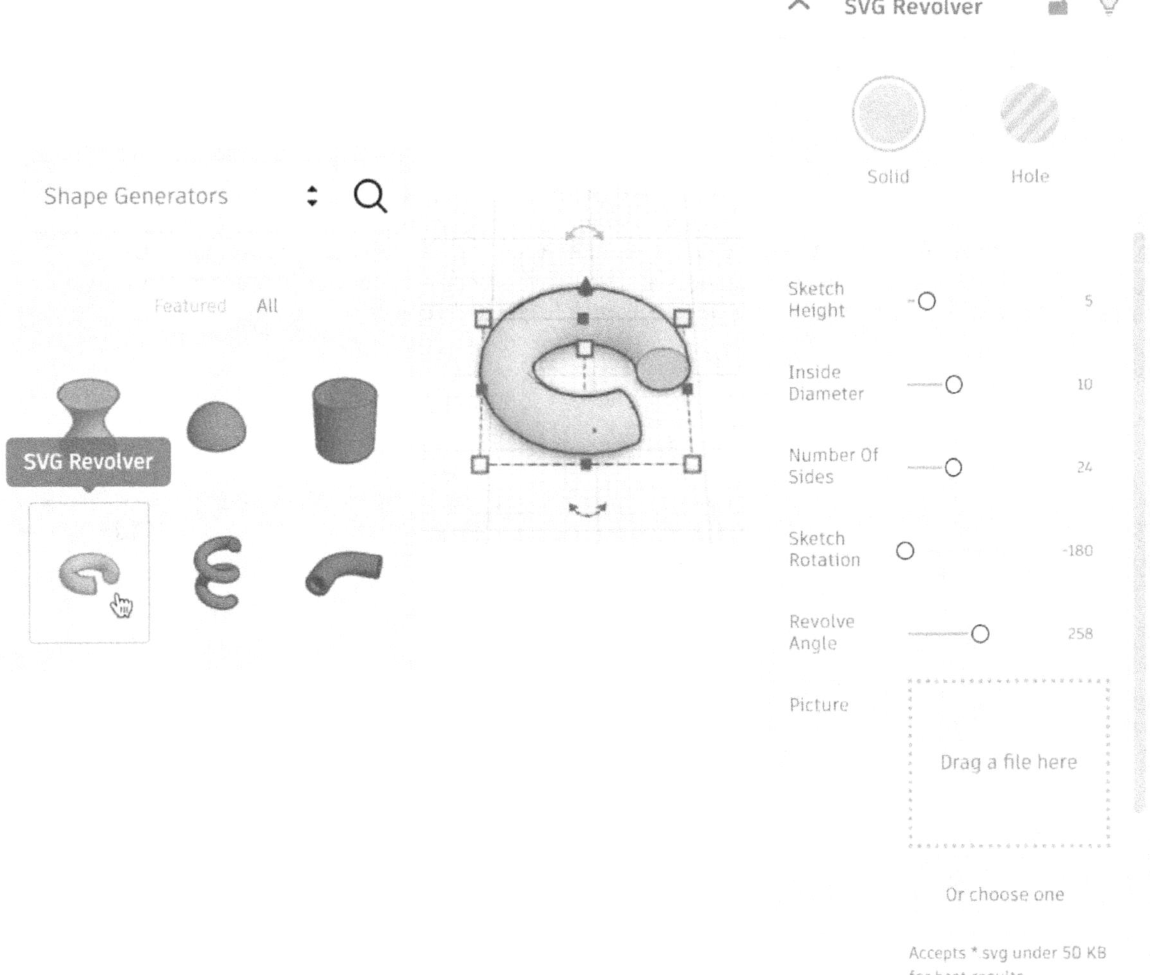

Using the Scribble Tool

This tool allows you to create freeform shapes and lines, adding a personal touch to your designs. Whether you're sketching out a rough idea or refining the details of a complex design, the Scribble tool provides the versatility you need.

1. Accessing the Scribble Tool:
- Select the **Basic Shapes** option from the drop-down available on **Shapes** panel.
- Click on the **Scribble** tool. Next, place the scribble shape onto the workplane.

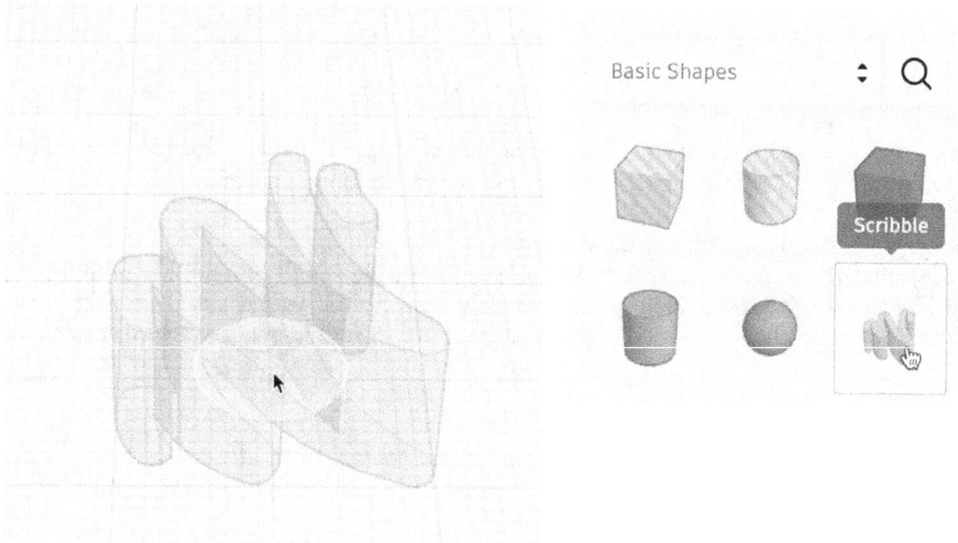

2. Drawing Your Shape:
- Imagine drawing on paper. Click and drag your mouse cursor on the Workplane to create a 2D outline. Once satisfied with your outline, simply release the mouse button. Tinkercad automatically extrudes your 2D scribble into a 3D object, giving it height and volume.

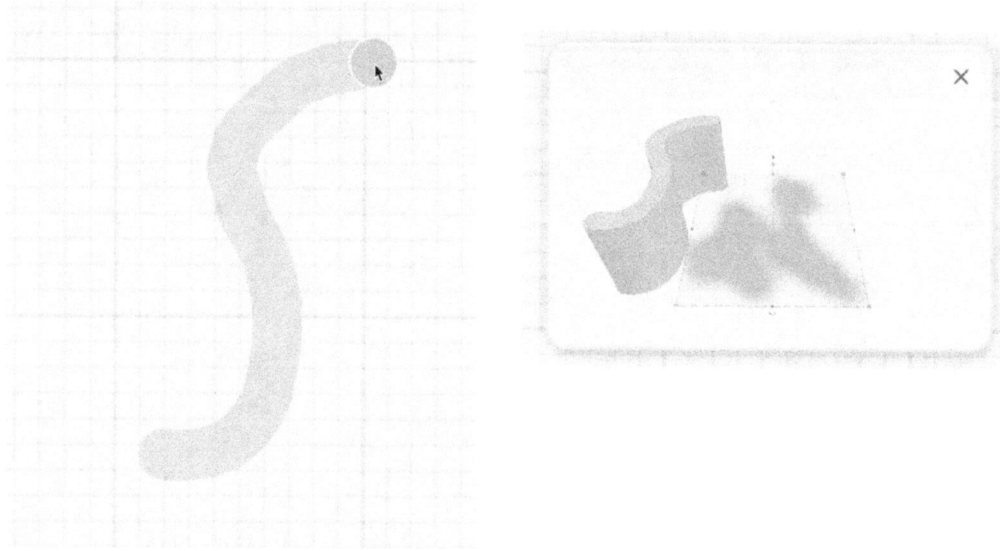

3. Erasing Mistakes:
- Click the **Erase** icon.
- Click and drag over the parts of your shape you want to remove.

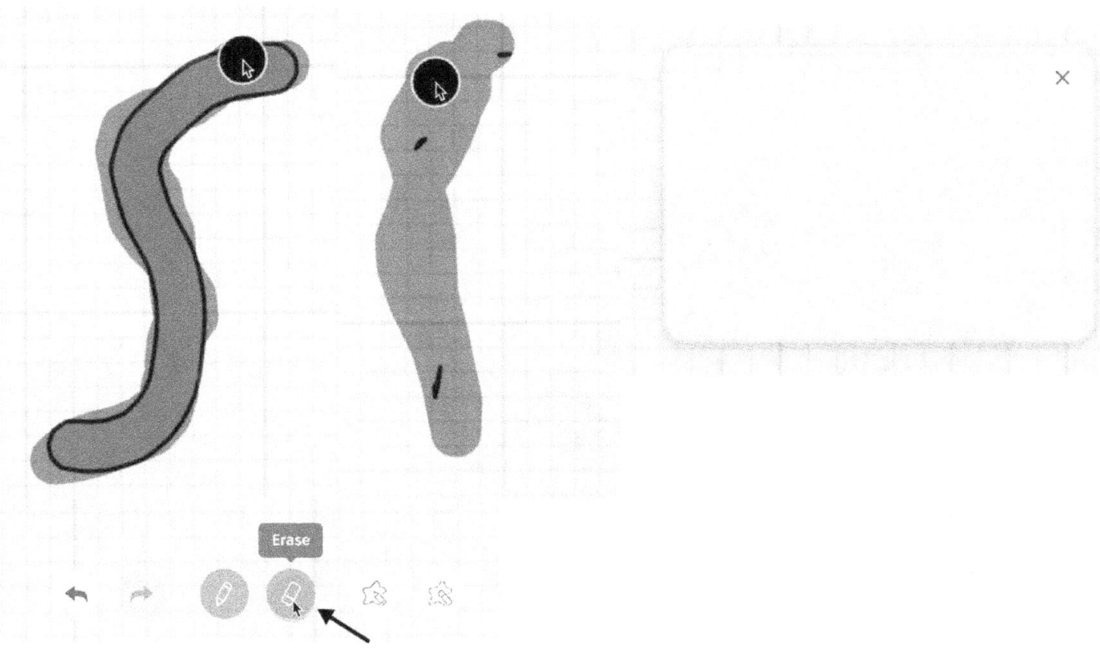

4. Using the Draw Shape Mode:
- Click on the **Draw Shape** icon.
- Press and hold the left mouse button and drag the pointer to create a bounding shape.

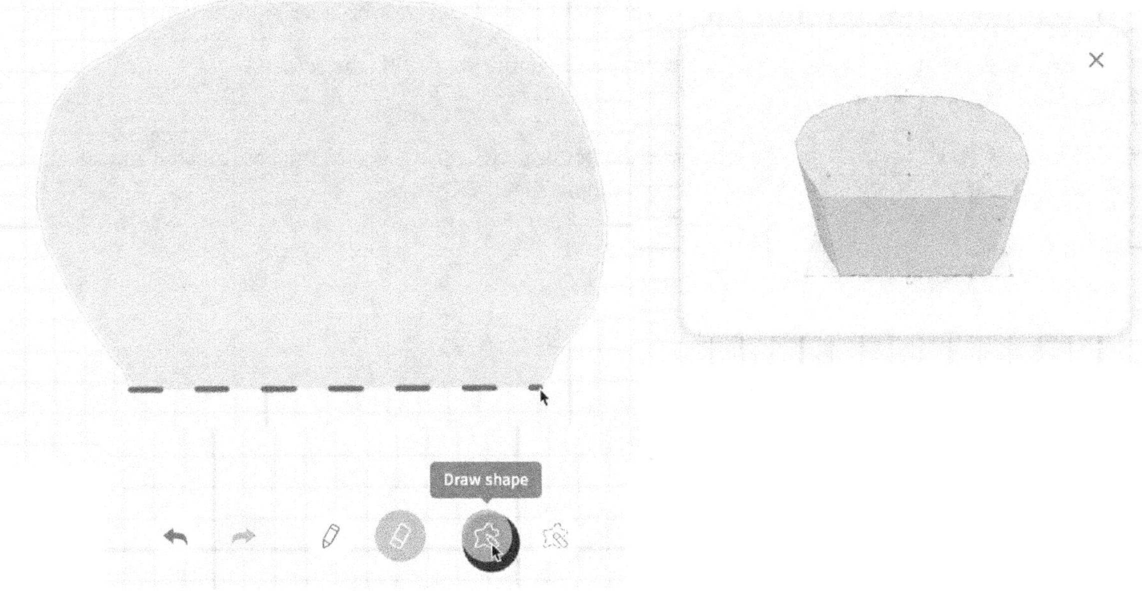

- Click the **Erase with shape** icon.
- Create a bounding shape enclosing the scribbled solid to erase it.

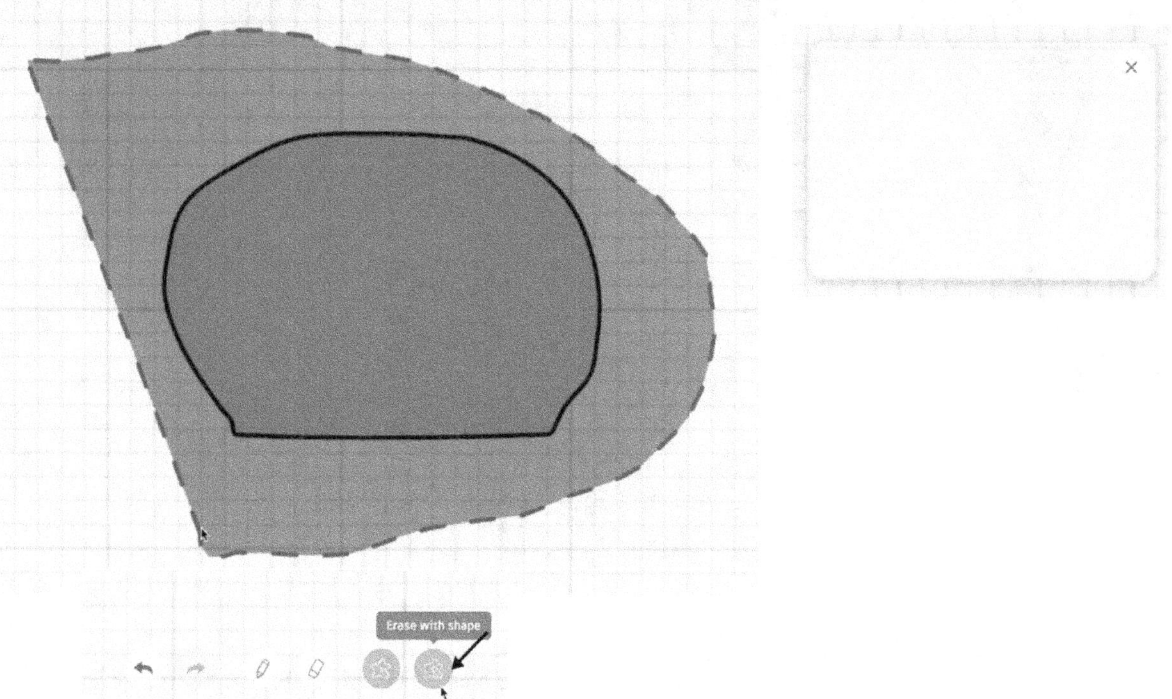

5. Zooming and Adjusting the View:

- Use the middle mouse button to zoom in or zoom out to get a closer or broader view of your shape.
- Click **"Fit to View"** to adjust the view so that the entire shape fills the screen.

6. Clearing, Undoing, and Redoing:

- Click the **"Clear"** button located at the bottom left corner to erase the entire shape and start over.
- Use the **Undo** and **Redo** buttons to reverse or reapply specific changes.

7. Hiding the Preview:

- Click **"Hide Preview"** if the preview is distracting.

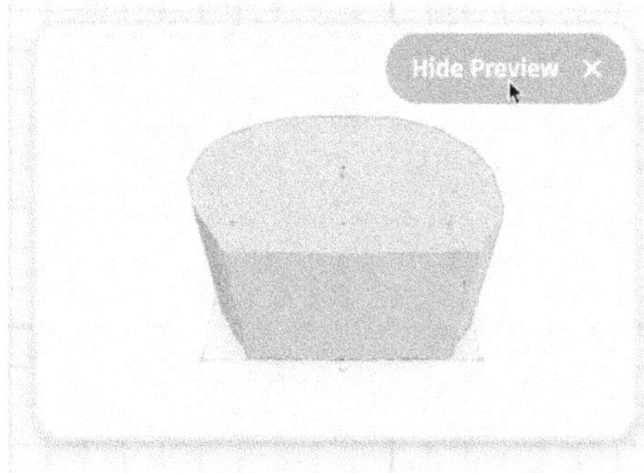

8. Finishing Your Shape:

- Click **"Done"** located at the bottom right corner of the window when you're happy with your shape.
- You can now adjust the shape using the grips and change its height as needed.

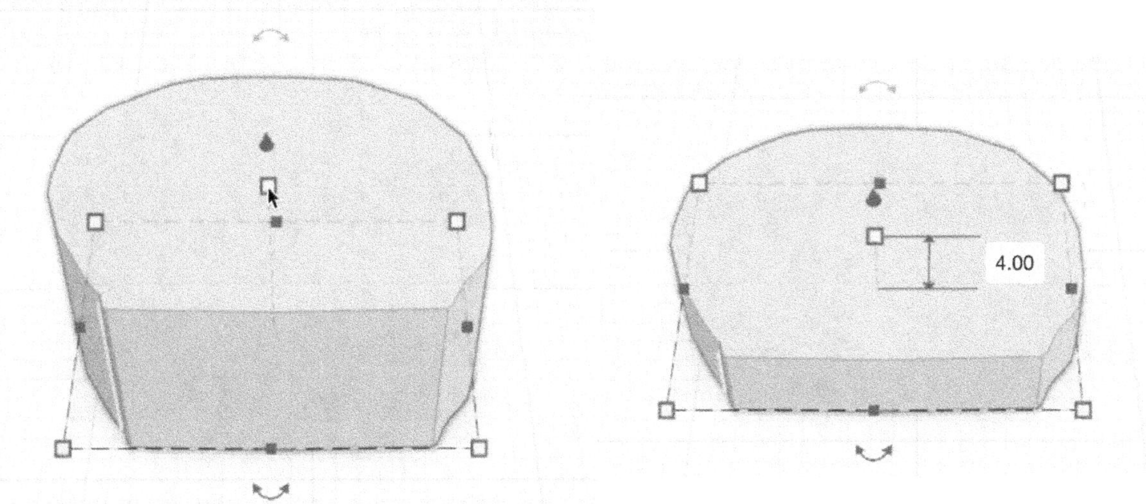

- Click the **Edit Scribble** button on the Inspection window to go back to scribble mode and edit the shape. Next, make changes to the shape and click **Done**.

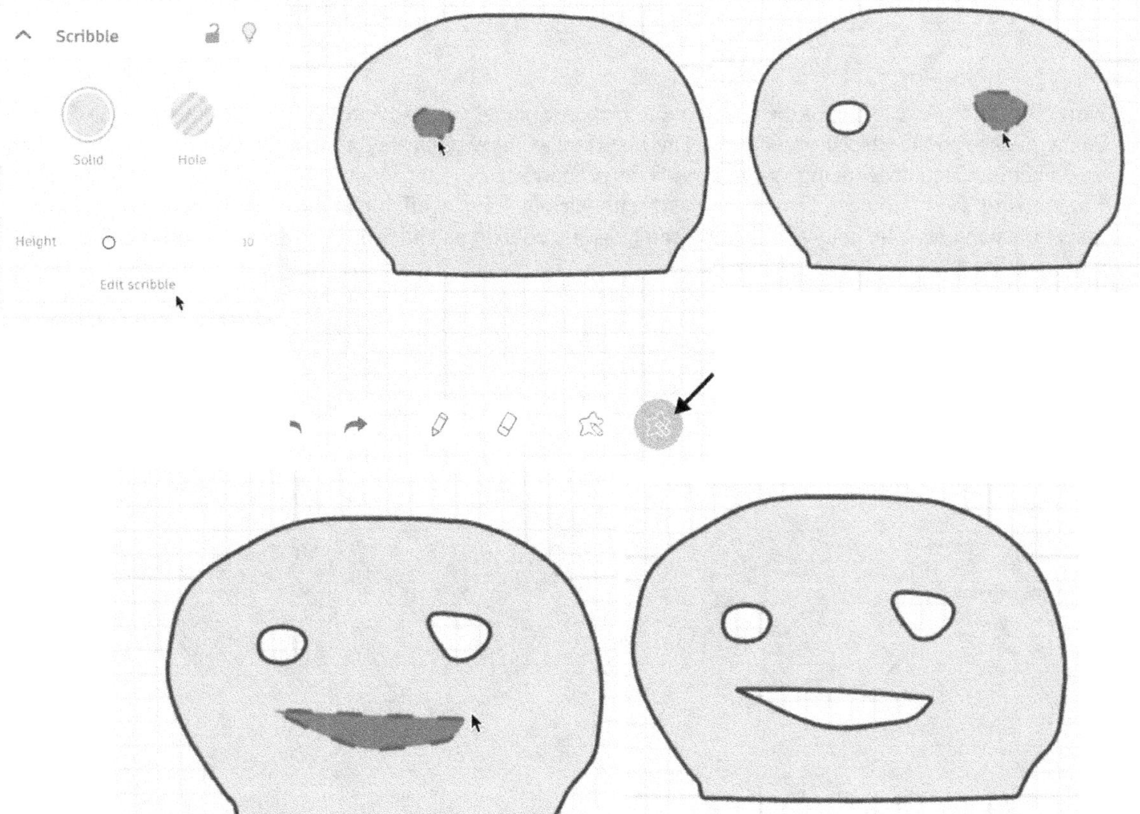

Using the Text Tool

The **Text** tool allows you to create 3D text that can be easily edited, positioned, and styled. This tool is perfect for adding labels, titles, or any other text-based elements to your designs. With the Text tool, you can create text in various fonts, sizes, and orientations, giving you complete control over the appearance of your design.

1. **Accessing the Text Tool**: To use the text tool in Tinkercad, navigate to the **"Basic Shapes"** section in the Shapes panel on the right side of the interface. Click on the **"Text"** option to select it.
2. **Placing the Text Tool**: Once selected, click and drag the text tool onto the work plane. The work plane is the area where you design and create your 3D models.

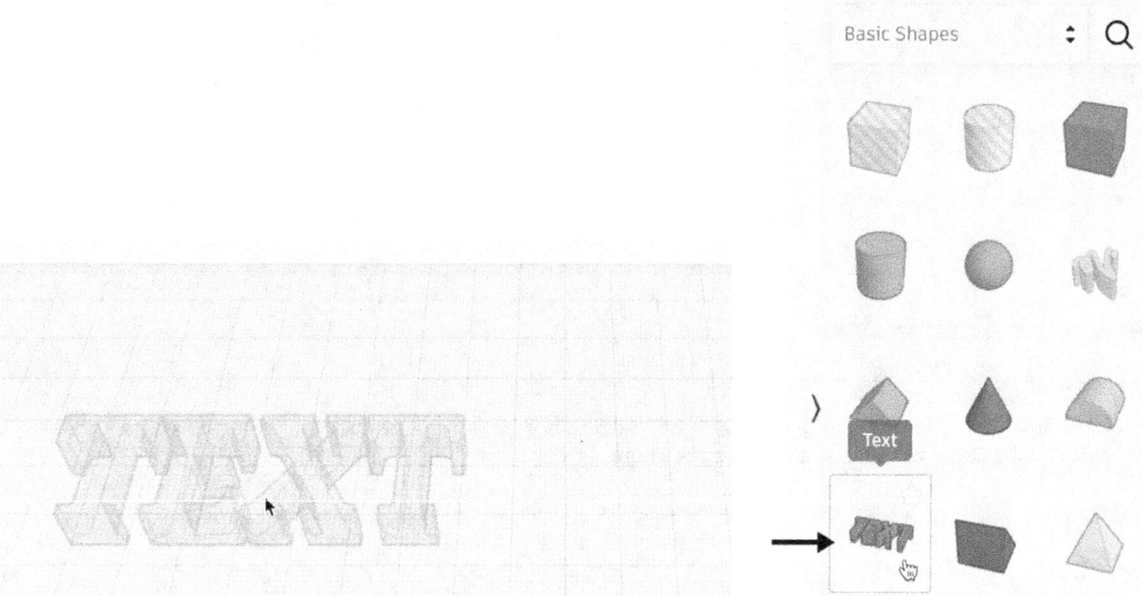

3. **Entering Text**: After placing the text tool on the work plane, you can enter your desired text in the **Text** box available on the Inspector window. The Inspector window appears on the right side of the screen when an object is selected, allowing you to modify its properties.
4. **Formatting Text**: You can format your text with various fonts available in the dropdown menu in the Inspector window. The height of the text can be adjusted using a slider or by typing a specific value in the provided field.

5. **Adjusting Bevel**: To make your text bold, increase the bevel value.

6. **Adjusting the Segments**: Drag the **Segments** slider. This will also allow you to add segments to the top and bottom edges of your text for a more stylized look.

Chapter 5: Saving and Exporting Designs

Save a shape as a component in PartMaker for future reuse

1. **Creating a Bolt**:
    - Drag a cylinder onto the workplane and change its height and number of sides.

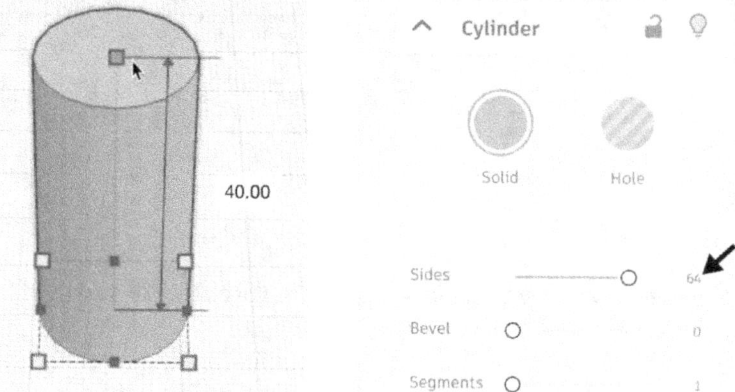

    - Drag a Polygon shape, and then release it on the top face of the cylinder.
    - Change the dimensions of the polygon, as shown.

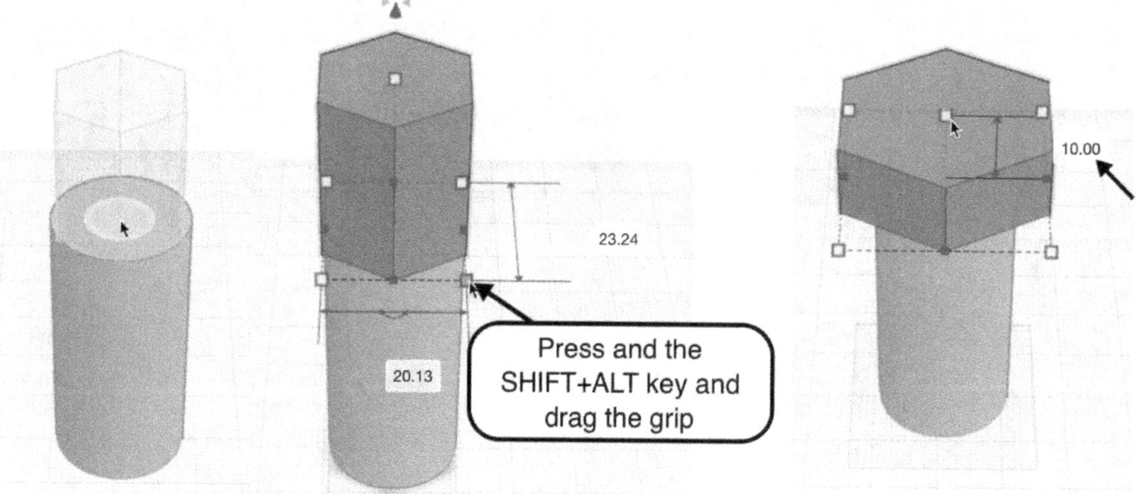

    - Press CTRL+A to select all the shapes.
    - Click the **Group** icon on the toolbar.

2. **Shape Selection**: Click on the group of shapes created in the last step.
3. **Accessing the Your Creations Menu**: Click the dropdown menu located at the top of the Shapes panel. Under the **"Your Creations"** section, select the **"Create Shape"** option. This will open a new dialog box where you can input the details of your new part.

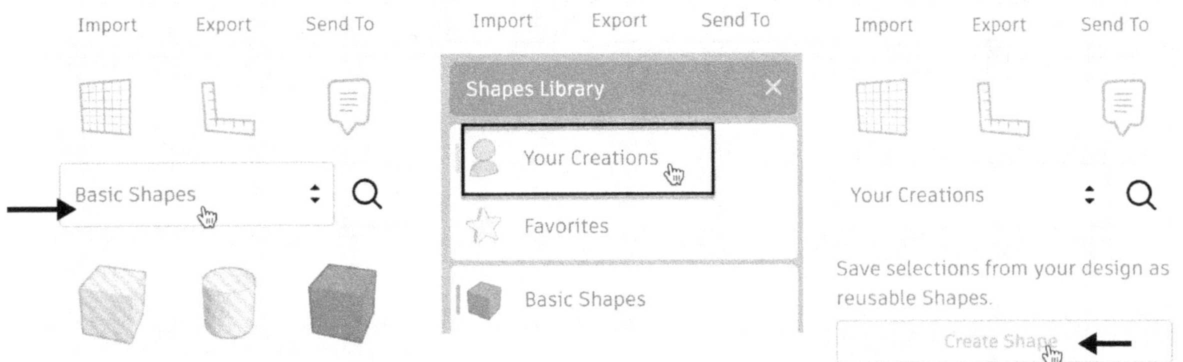

4. **Shape Details Input**: In the "**Create Shape**" dialog, enter a distinctive **Name** for easy identification, add a **Description** detailing its application or features, and optionally include **Tags** for efficient organization and search.

5. **Part Type and Size Configuration:** Specify whether the part is a solid or a hole. This choice depends on the nature of the shape you are saving. Decide if you want to lock the part size to prevent scaling. If you select the **Lock part size** option, the part will keep its original dimensions whenever it is used.

6. **Saving the Shape**: After filling in all necessary details and configuring the part type and size, click the "**Save Shape**" button. This will save the shape as a reusable component in your Shapes library, ready for future use.

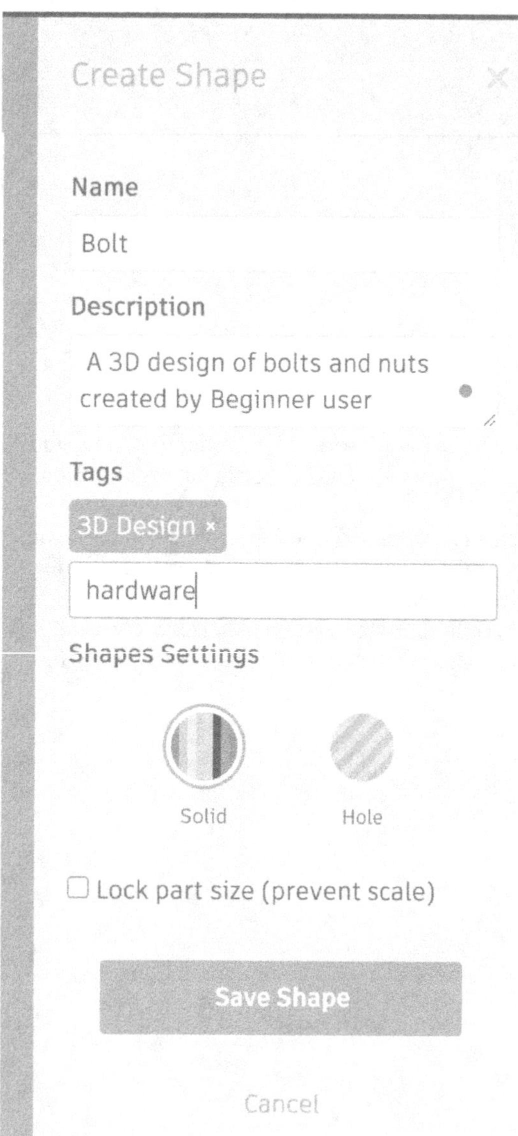

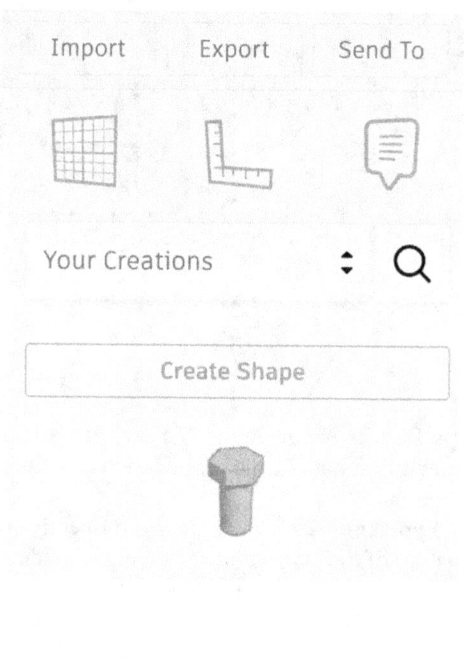

Importing Files

Importing files into Tinkercad is a useful feature that allows you to incorporate external 3D models or designs into your Tinkercad projects. Follow these steps to import files into Tinkercad.

1. **Supported File Formats:** Tinkercad accepts three file formats for import, such as STL, OBJ, and SVG.
2. **Importing from Local Files:** To import a file from your computer, click the **"Import"** button in Tinkercad's top-right interface corner. Choose **"Choose File"** and select the desired file from your local storage.

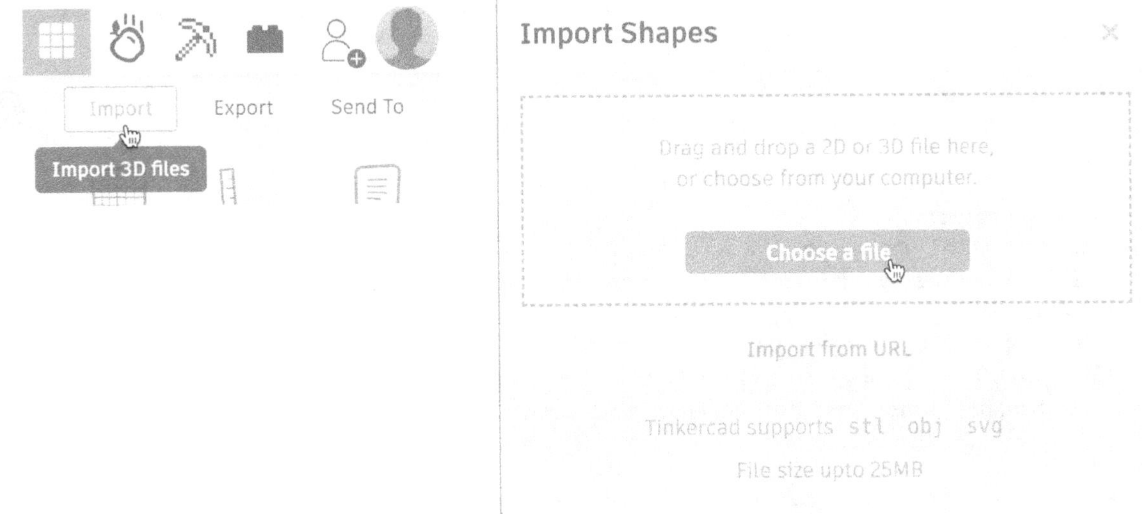

3. **Importing from Online Sources:** Tinkercad also lets you import files from online sources like Thingiverse or GrabCAD. Click the **"Import"** button, select **"Import from URL,"** and input the URL of the file you wish to import.

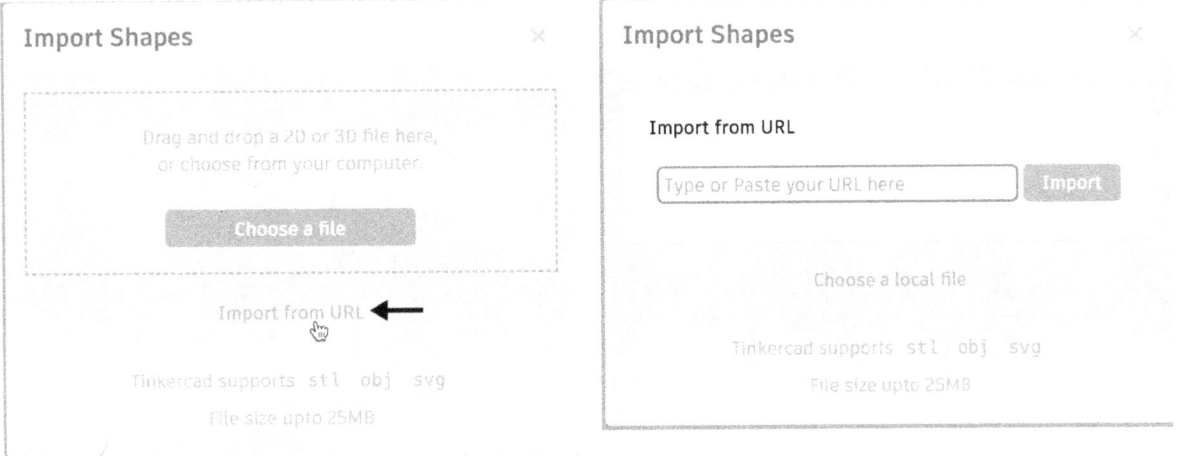

4. **Positioning and Scaling:** Once imported, use Tinkercad's standard translation and scaling tools to position and scale the file within the workspace. You can rotate the imported model as needed.
5. **Editing Imported Models:** Although Tinkercad's editing capabilities for imported models are limited, you can still perform basic operations like cutting, grouping, and ungrouping components of the imported model.
6. **Combining with Native Designs:** Importing files into Tinkercad allows you to merge imported models with native Tinkercad designs, creating complex assemblies or enhancing existing designs with imported components.

Exporting a 3D Design

Exporting your designs in Tinkercad is a simple process that prepares them for 3D printing, rendering, or sharing. Follow these steps to export your models efficiently:

1. Prepare Your Design

Ensure your design is complete and error-free. Check for any floating or misaligned parts that might cause issues during printing or further processing.

2. Select the Object

Click on the object or group of objects you want to export. To export the entire design, do not select anything from the workplane (You need to select the **Include > Everything** in the design option from the **Export** dialog).

3. Access the Export Menu
In the upper-right corner of the Tinkercad interface, click the **"Export"** button. This will open the Export dialog box with several options.

4. Choose the Export Format
Select the appropriate file format for your needs:
- **.STL (Stereolithography):** Common for 3D printing; compatible with most 3D printers and slicing software.
- **.OBJ (Object):** Supports color and material properties; useful for detailed models.
- **.GLTF/.GLB (GL Transmission Format):** Ideal for web applications and virtual reality (VR).
- **.SVG (Scalable Vector Graphics):** Suitable for 2D designs like laser cutting.

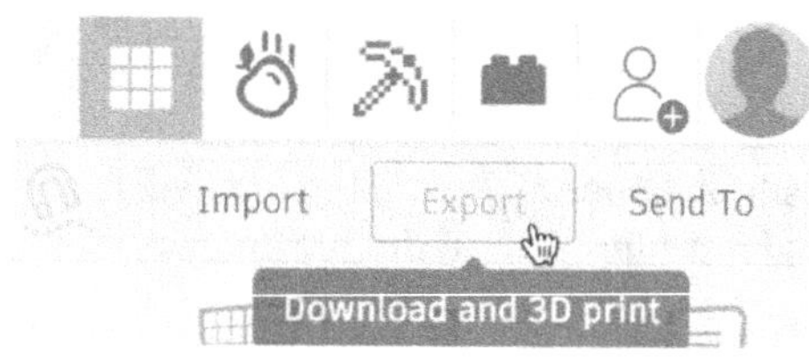

5. Download the File
After selecting the format, Tinkercad will generate the file and prompt you to download it. Save the file to your computer.

6. Post-Processing (if needed)
Depending on the export format and intended use, you may need to take additional steps:
- **For 3D printing:** Import the file into your slicing software (e.g., Cura, PrusaSlicer) to set up the print job.
- **For rendering or further editing:** Open the file in software like Blender, Maya, or other CAD tools.
- **For laser cutting:** Load the SVG file into your laser cutter's software to adjust settings and start the cut.

Collections

This section provides a step-by-step guide on how to utilize the Collections feature. The Collections feature allows users to organize multiple designs under a single category for quick access and efficient management.

1. Creating a Collection:

- To create a new collection, navigate to the Tinkercad dashboard and click on the **Collections** option.
- Click **Create a Collection** to create a new collection.
- Click on the **Edit** button located next to **Add a description**.
- Type the **Name** and **Description** in the **Properties** dialog.
- Click **Save Changes**.

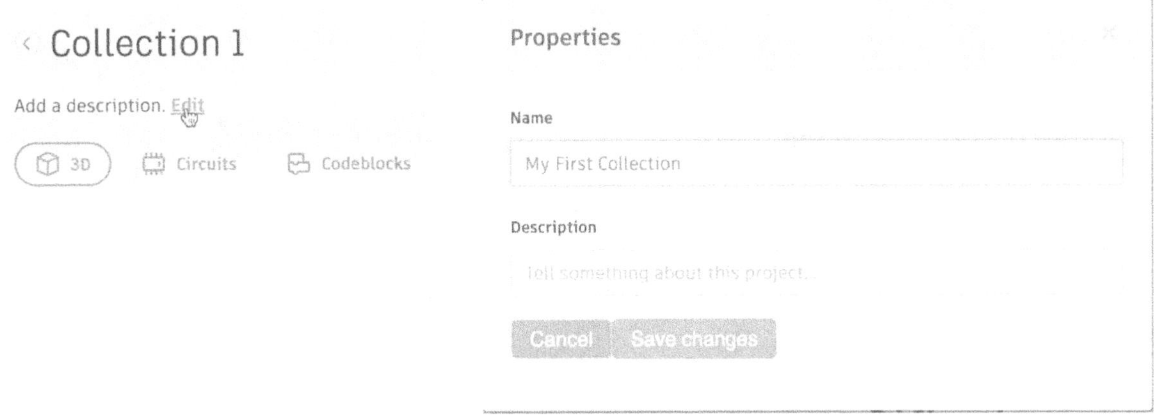

2. Adding Designs to a Collection:

- To add designs to your collection, return to the '**Designs**' section.
- Check the '**Select**' option.
- Choose the designs you would like to add to your collection by selecting the respective checkboxes.

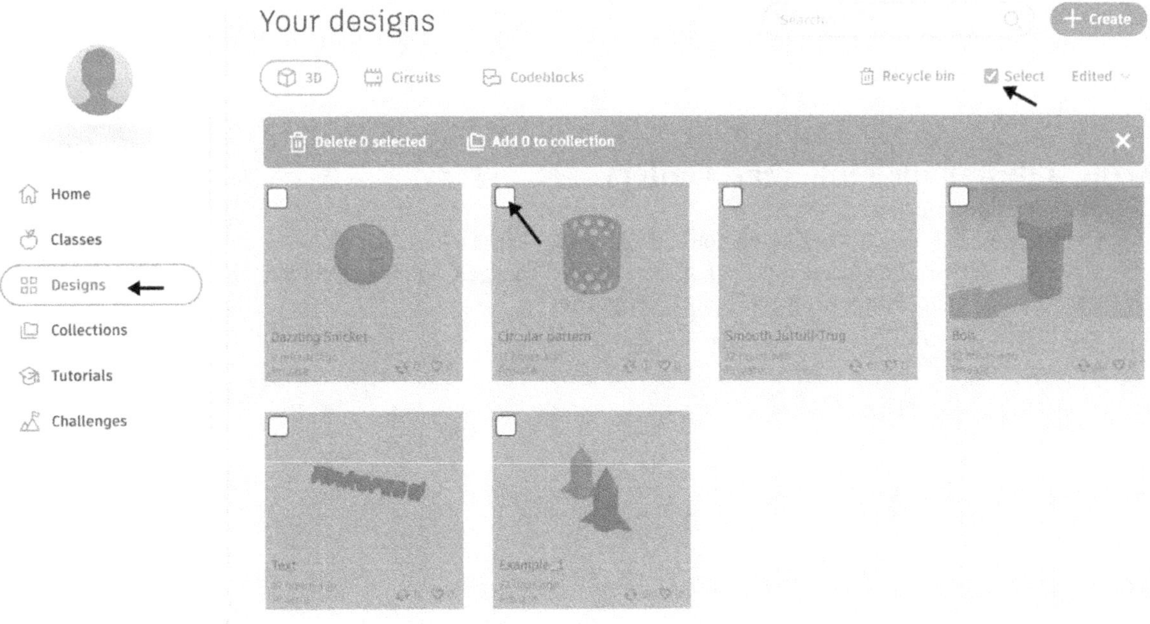

- Click on **Add to collection**.
- Select the collection to which you would like to move the chosen designs. Next, click **Move**.

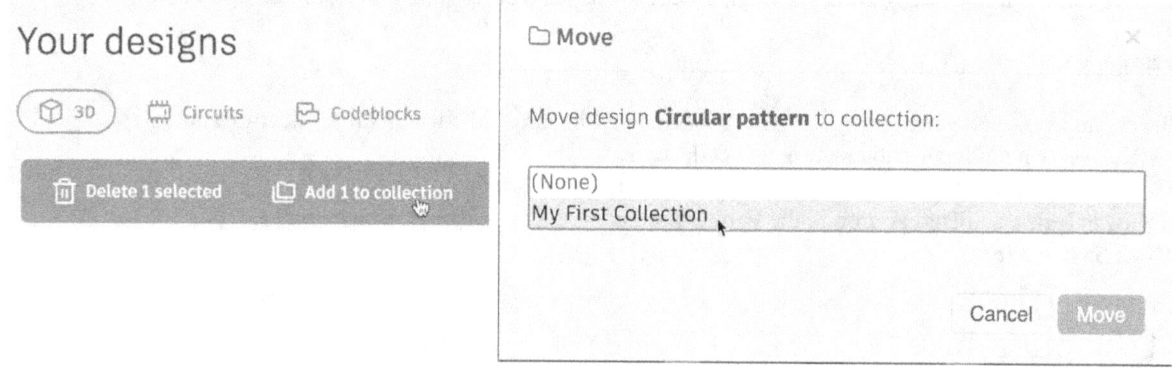

3. Viewing and Deleting a Collection:

- To view the designs within a collection, click on the collection name under the **Collection** section.
- To delete an entire collection, click on the icon with three dots associated with the collection and select **'Delete collection'** from the dropdown menu.
- Confirm the deletion by following the prompts. Deleted collections cannot be recovered.

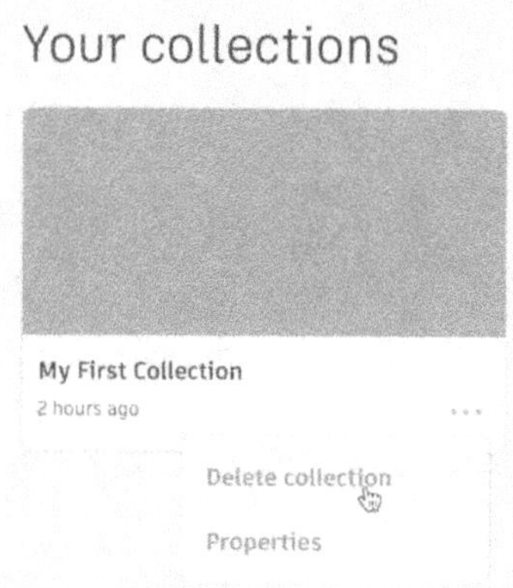

Sharing a design on Tinkercad Gallery

1. **Sharing Your Design:**
   Once you have finished working on your design, go to your Tinkercad dashboard. Your designs are set to private by default. To change this setting, click on the **'Designs'** option and then on the gear icon that appears. From the dropdown menu, select **'Properties'**.

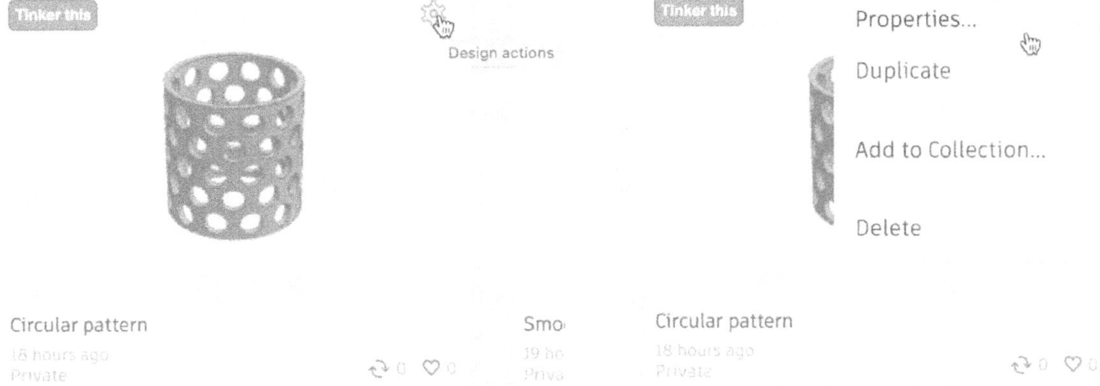

2. **Adding Details:**
    In the 'Design Properties' dialog, include a concise description of your design and relevant tags to make it easier for others to find. If you want to share your design publicly, change the privacy setting from 'Private' to 'Public'. Remember, when your design is public, anyone can download it as an STL, OBJ, or SVG file. You can also choose whether to allow others to copy and modify your design by adjusting the license settings.

⚙ **Design properties**

Design name

Circular pattern

Design description

Give your users something to talk about. Add a short

Tags (10 maximum)

Enter tag(s) here separated by commas. Press Enter to add a tag

Privacy

Please read our Be Nice Policy before sharing your design with our community.

Public

Viewable and discoverable by everyone

✓ I'm not a robot   reCAPTCHA
Privacy - Terms

License

Attribution-ShareAlike 3.0(CC-BY-SA 3.0)

This license lets others remix, tweak, and build upon your work even for commercial purposes, as long as they credit you and license their new creations under the identical terms. More info on Creative Commons licenses

Cancel   Save changes

3. **Saving Your Work:**
   After making these changes, don't forget to save them by clicking on the 'Save changes' button at the bottom of the page. This step ensures that your preferences are applied to your design.

Utilizing Brick Mode

The Brick Mode allows you to transform your 3D designs into brick-based models, similar to LEGO constructions. This mode is particularly useful for those who enjoy building with bricks and want to create physical models of their digital designs using standard brick elements.

1. **Accessing the Brick Mode:** To enter Brick Mode, locate and click on the **Bricks** icon situated in the upper right-hand corner of the interface. This mode will represent your Tinkercad model using bricks.

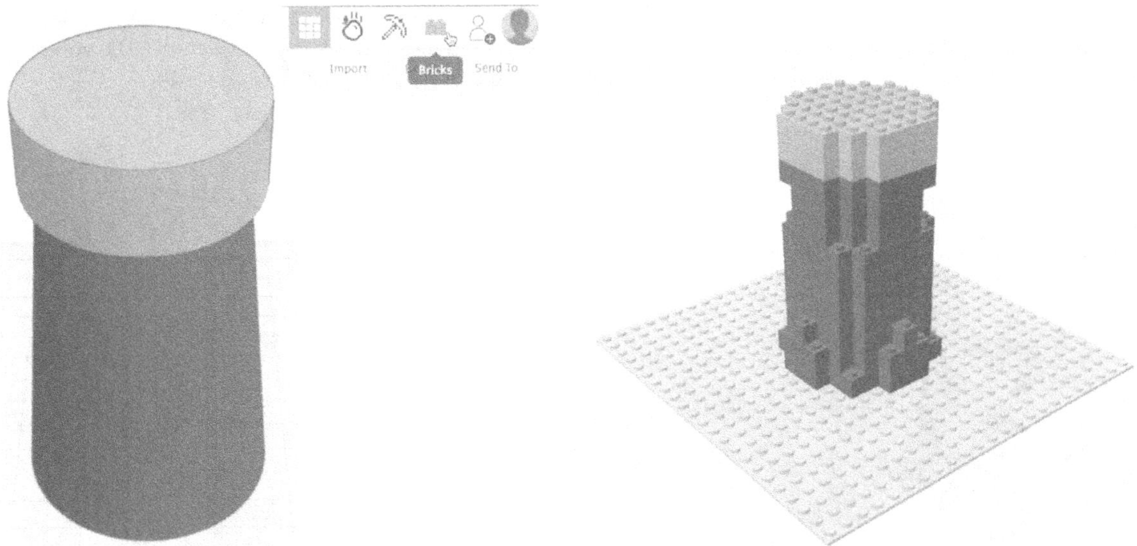

2. **Adjusting Scale:** The first option in the newly appeared toolbar at the top of the screen allows you to adjust the scale of your design. The **"1x"** scale utilizes the least number of bricks, while scaling to **"2x"** provides a more detailed representation.
3. **Ground Toggle:** To toggle the base plate on and off, click on the **"Ground"** option.

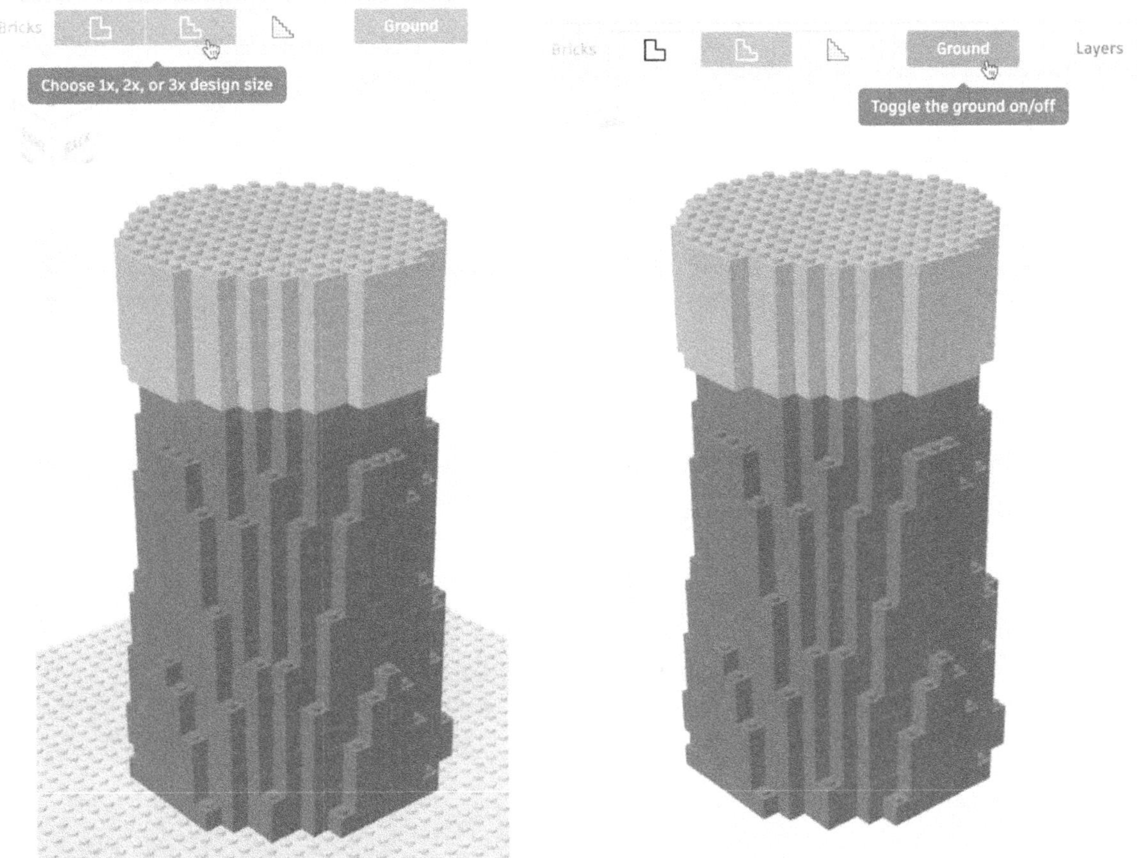

4. **Making Model Changes:** To modify your model, you must return to the 3D workspace, as Brick Mode functions solely as a viewing mode. The translation to brick mode is more effective when the shapes are grouped together first.

Small adjustments can significantly impact how Tinkercad interprets brick placement. By modifying feature size and placement on the grid in small increments, and then alternating between the 3D workspace and Brick Mode, you can achieve a model that aligns more closely with your desired results.

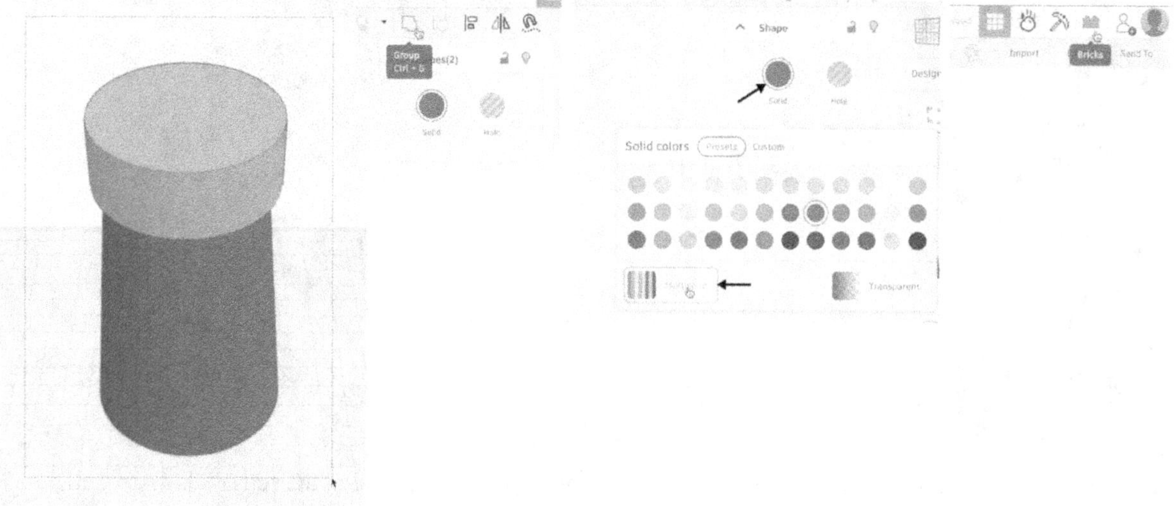

5. **Viewing Layers**: To view the layers, click on the **"Layers"** option. Use the arrow keys to navigate through them one by one. The top layer will be subtly highlighted.

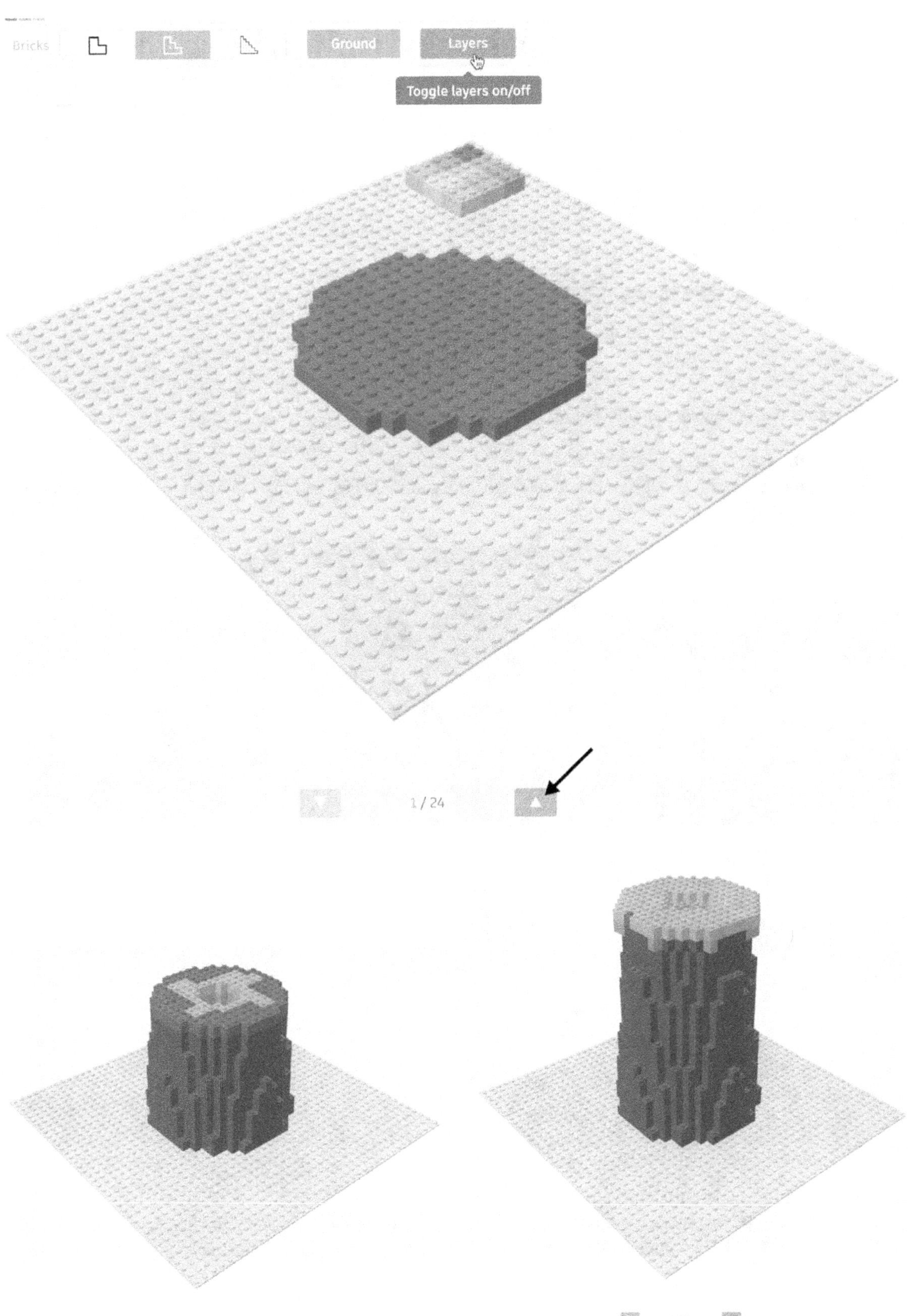

Bricks
Ground
Layers
Toggle layers on/off
1 / 24

Chapter 6: Coding with Tinkercad

Codeblocks is a block-based programming environment integrated with Tinkercad. Through Codeblocks, you can leverage Scratch-like coding to control and animate their 3D designs, merging the worlds of coding and creative design seamlessly. This section will introduce you to the Codeblocks workspace and guide you through creating pattern using variables

1.   Accessing the Codeblocks Workspace

On the Tinkercad dashboard, click Create > Codeblock. Next, click on the file name located at the top-right corner. Type "Bracelet" and click anywhere in window.

2.   Familiarizing with the Workspace Layout

Code Blocks on the Left

On the left side of your screen, you'll find the codeblocks of various shapes, actions, variables, and so on. You can click on individual categories to view the codeblocks.

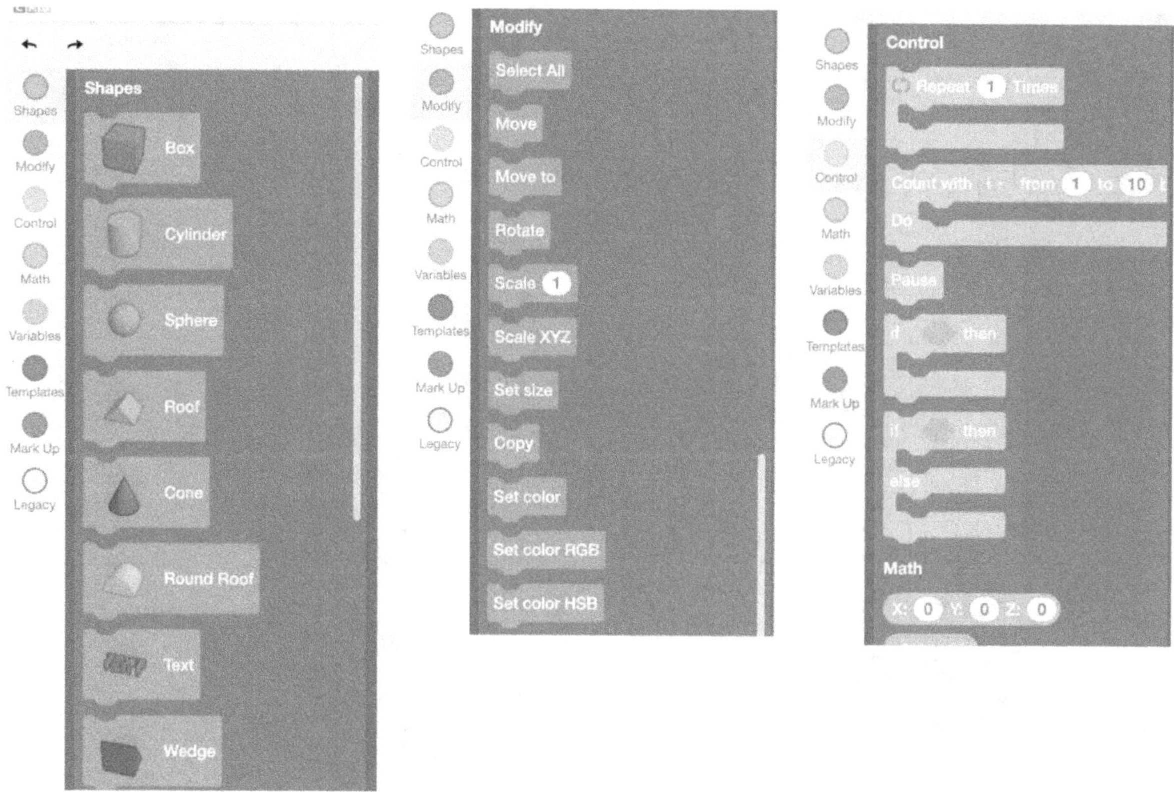

Programming Area in the Middle

In the central part of your workspace, you have the "Programming Area." This is where you'll arrange and connect the codeblocks to create the 3D model. You can drag and drop codeblocks onto the "Programming Area" and add logic and parameters to them.

Display or Renderer on the Right

On the right side of your workspace, you have the workplane. This is where you can visualize the output of your design. You can view your design from different angles and apply various rendering options to see how it will look in the real world.

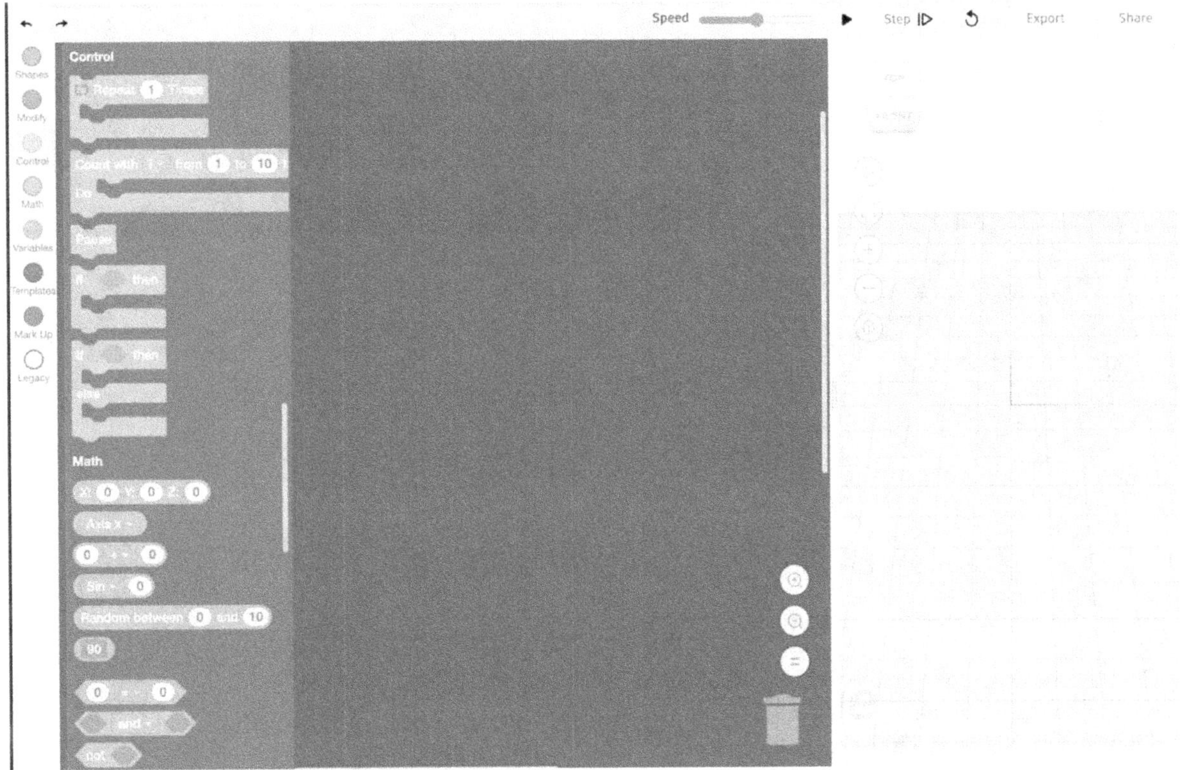

3. Defining Variables Using Math Blocks

- Click the Math codeblock category.
- Click '**Create number Variable**' button.
- Type **Tube size** in the **New variable name** box and click **OK**.

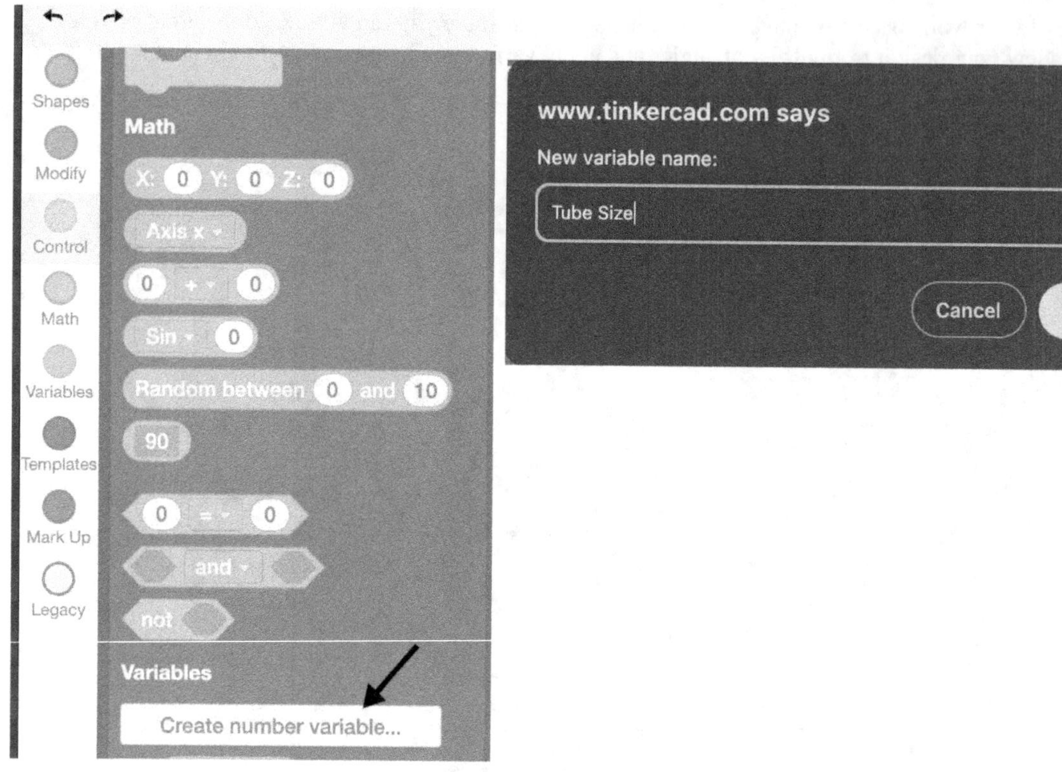

- Click on the drop-down in the Set my variable to 0 codeblock and select Tube Size.
- Set the Tube Size to **40**.
- Click and drag the **Set Tube size to 40** codeblock into the Programming area.

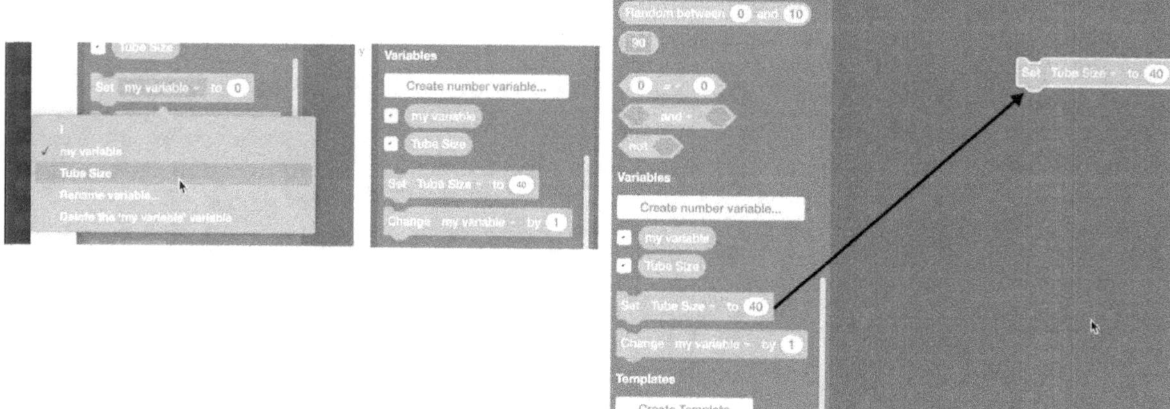

- Likewise, create the **Hole Depth**, **Hole Orientation**, **Hole Quantity**, **Hole Rotation**, and **Hole Size** variables.
- Click on the drop-down in the **Set my variable to 0** codeblock and select **Hole Orientation**.
- Set the **Hole Orientation** to **90**.
- Drag and drop the **Hole Orientation to 90** codeblock into the Programming area.
- Likewise, set the **Hole Quantity**, **Hole Rotation**, **Hole Size**, and **Hole Depth** to **12, 0, 5,** and **0**.
- Drag and drop all the set variable values onto the Programming area.

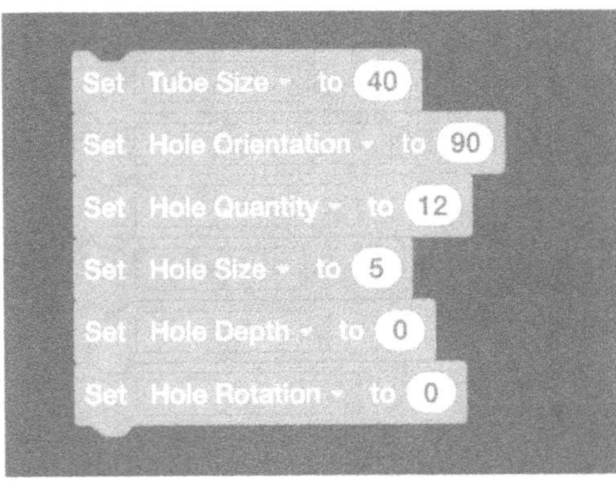

- Drag and drop the **Arithmetic** block from the **Math** section into the Programming area.

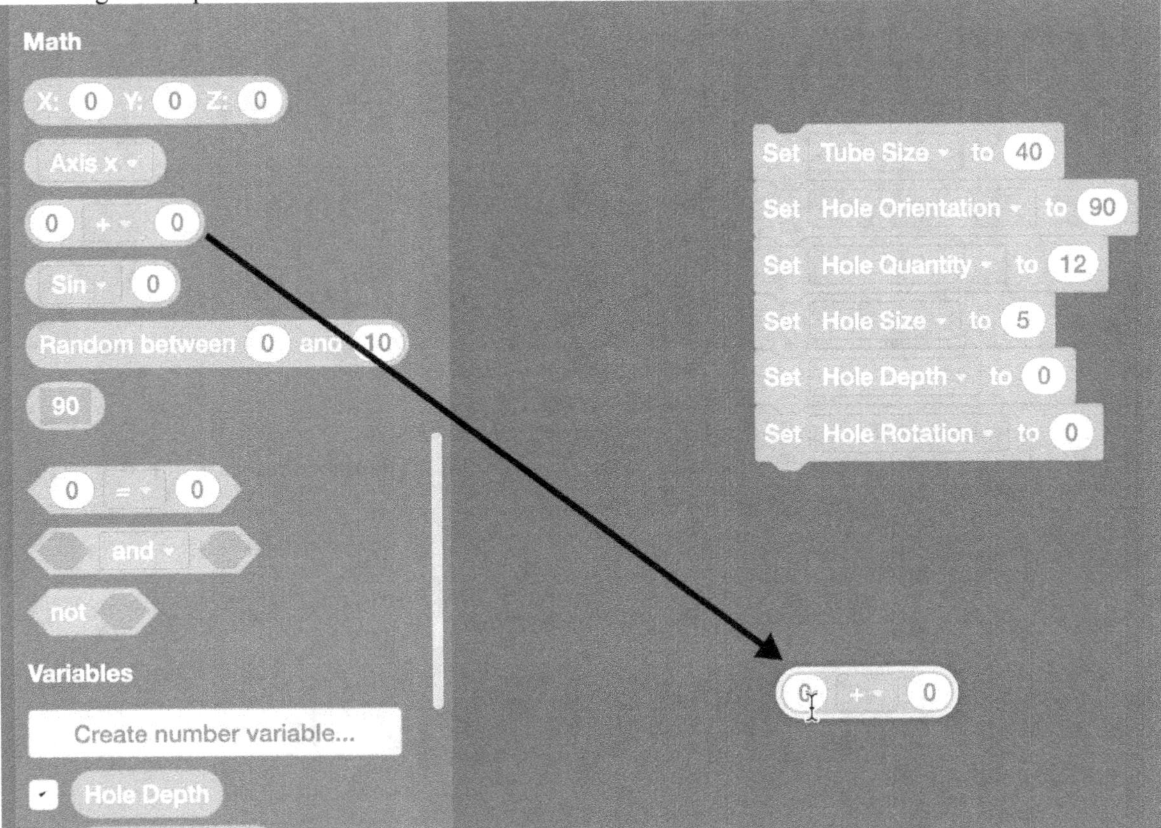

- Drag the drop the **Tube Size** block into the second value box of the **Arithmetic** block.
- Click the drop-down on the Arithmetic block and select
- Type **2** in the first value box of the **Arithmetic** block.

- Drag and drop the whole **Arithmetic** block into the value box of the **Hole Depth** variable block.

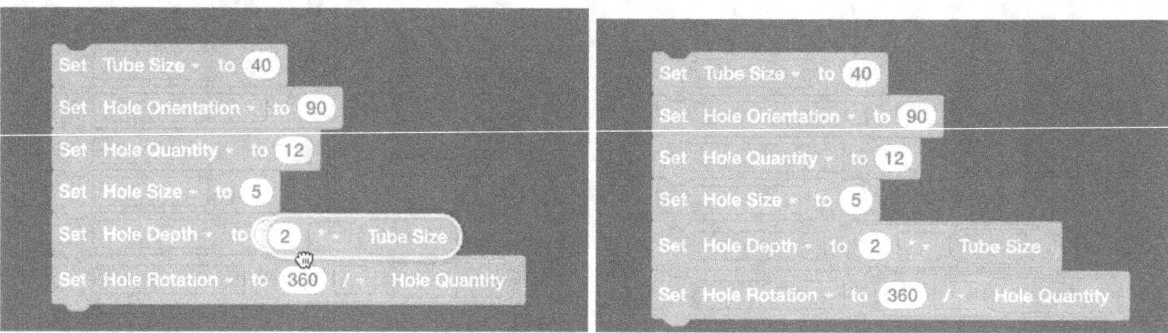

- Drag and drop another Arithmetic block into the Programming area.
- Click the drop-down available on the Arithmetic block and select /.
- Drag and drop the Hole Quantity block into the second value box of the Arithmetic block.
- Type **360** in the first value box of the Arithmetic block.

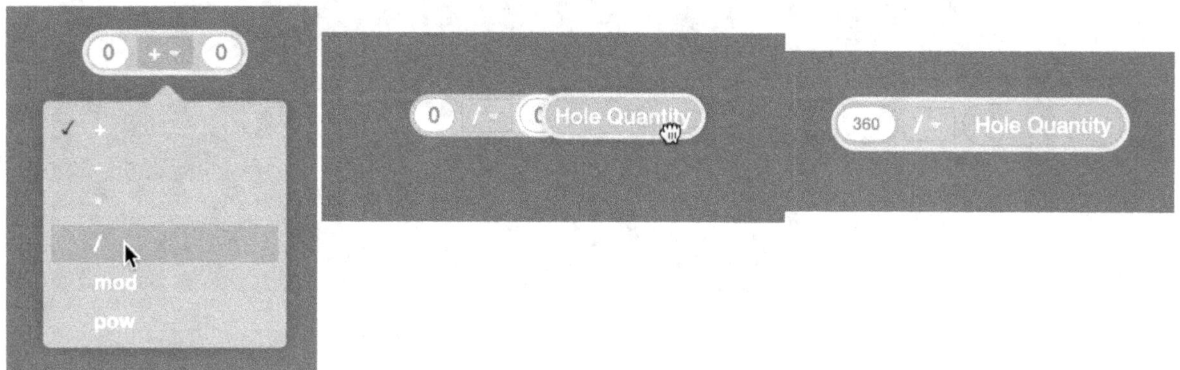

- Drag and drop the whole **Arithmetic** block into the value box of the **Hole Rotation** variable block.

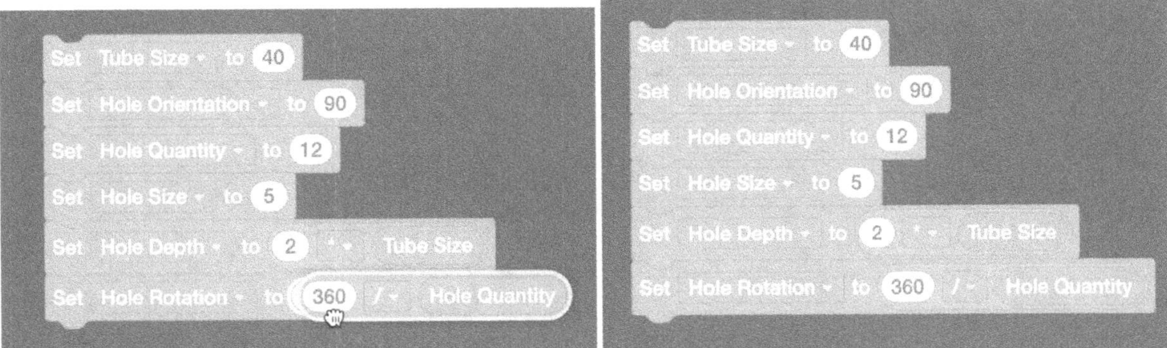

4. Working with Geometry

- In the shapes blocks, look for a 'Tube' and drag it onto the Programming area.
- Position it below the lowest variable block.
- Click on the arrow on the Tube block to expand it.

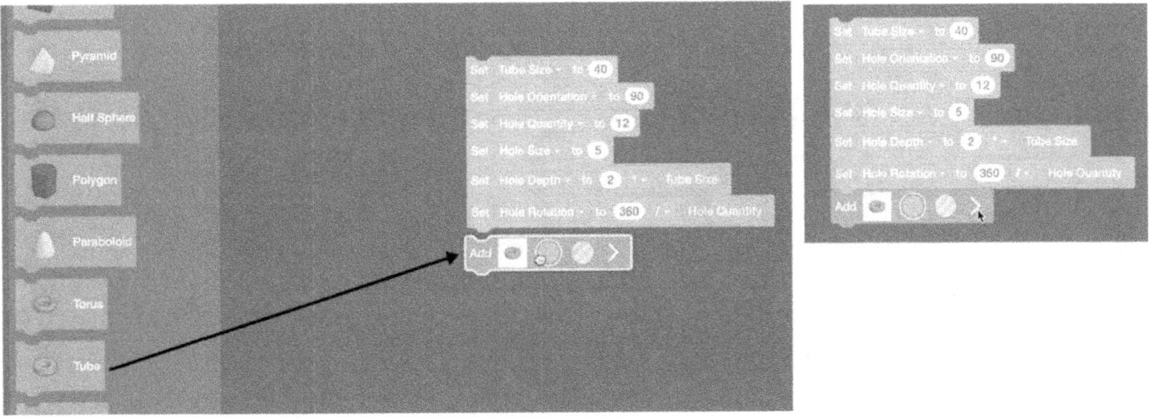

- Go to the **Variable** section of codeblock. Next, drag and drop the **Tube Size** block into the **Radius** box of the Tube block.

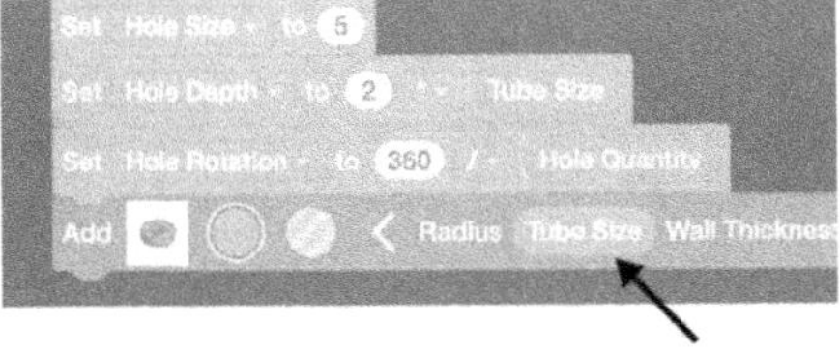

- Change the **Sides** value to **64**.
- Click the **Play** button on the toolbar; the design generated from the code is displayed on the workplane.

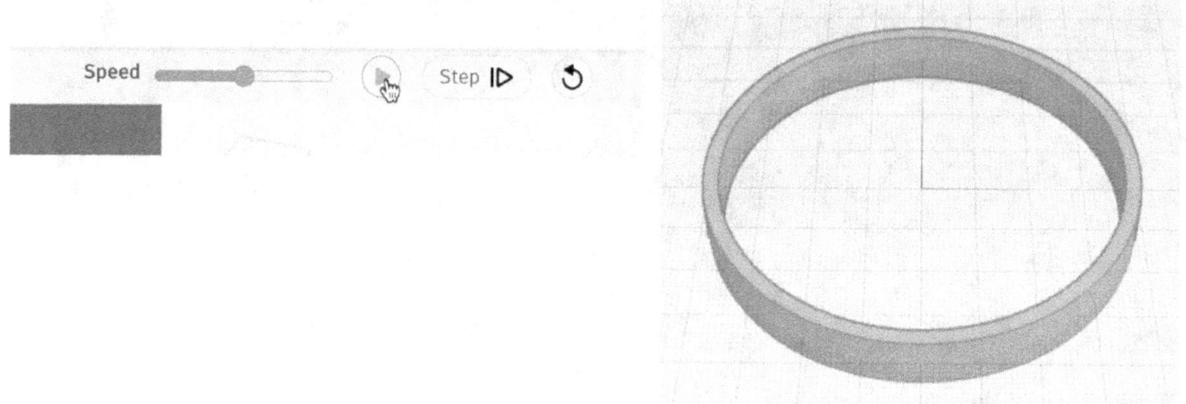

5. Establishing the Circular Pattern of Hole

- Go to **Control** section and drag and drop the **'Count with'** block into the programming area.

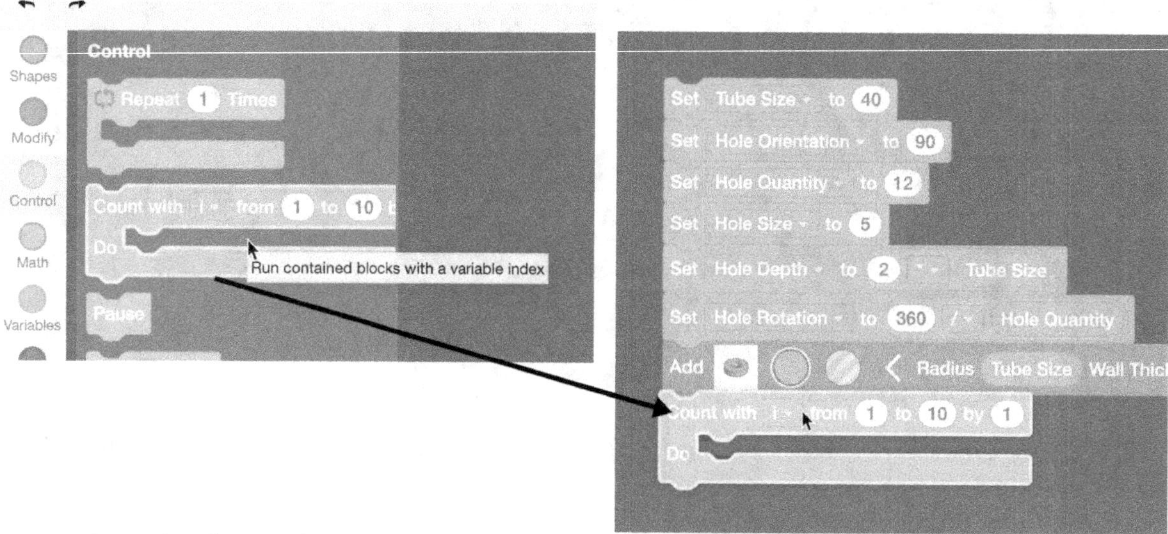

- Leave **i** as the counting variable.
- Type **1** in the from box to count from zero up to the number of holes.
- From the **Variable** section, drag the **'Hole quantity'** and drop it into the second value box.

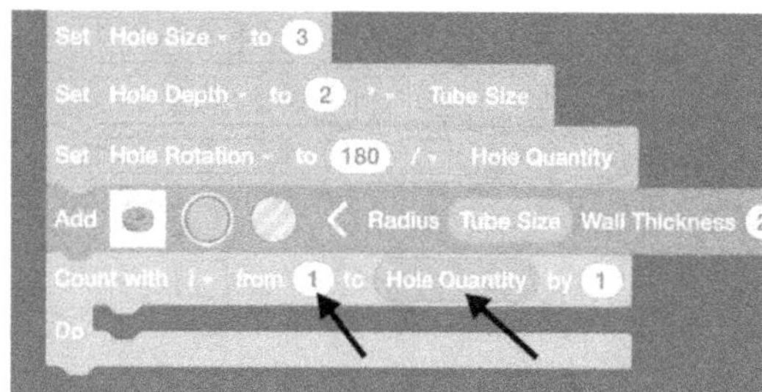

- From Shapes, select the **'Cylinder'** block and drag it in the middle of the **Count with** block.

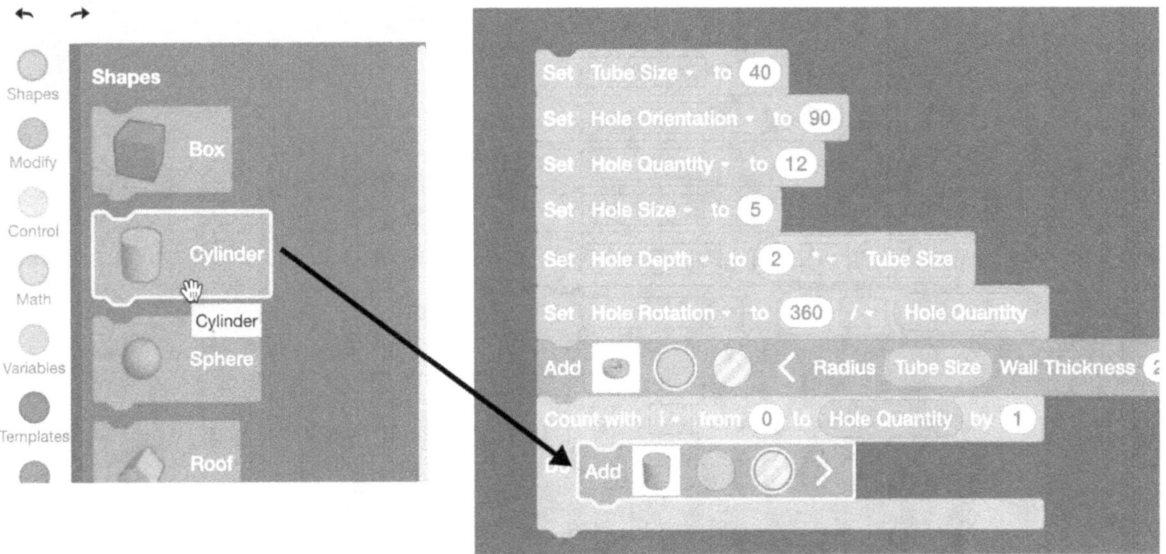

- Select the **Hole** swatch from the Cylinder block and click on the arrow for more options.
- From Variable blocks, choose **Hole size** and place in the **Radius** box.
- Type **64** in the **Sides** box of the **Cylinder** block.
- From Variable blocks, choose **Hole Depth** and place in the **H** box.

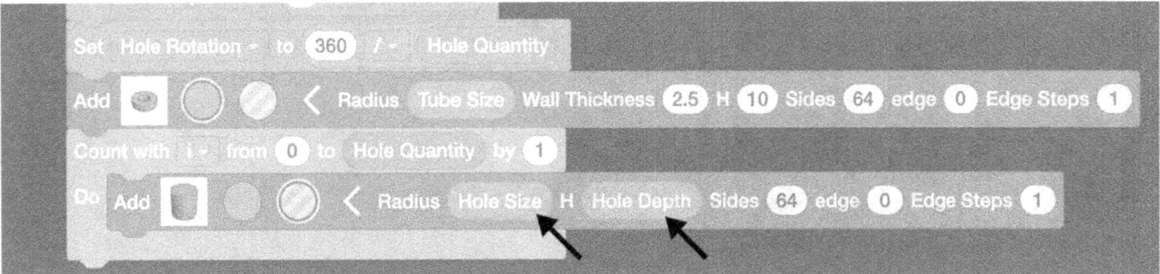

- From the **Modify** section, drag and drop the Rotate block below the Cylinder block.
- Select Axis x from the axis drop-down available on the Rotate block.
- Drag the Hole Orientation block from the Variable section and drop in the Angle box.

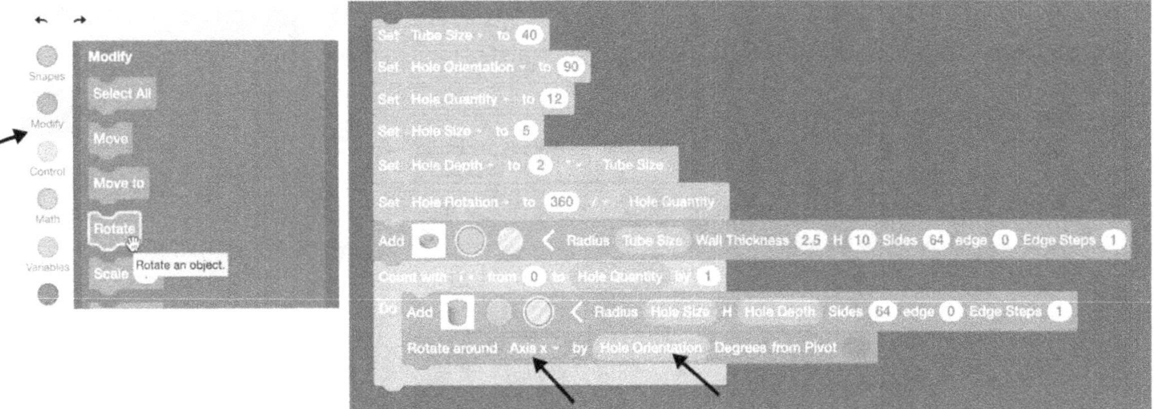

- From the **Modify** section, drag and drop the Rotate block below the Rotate block.
- Select **Axis z** from the axis drop-down available on the Rotate block.
- Drag and drop the **Arithmetic** block from the **Math** section into the Angle value box.

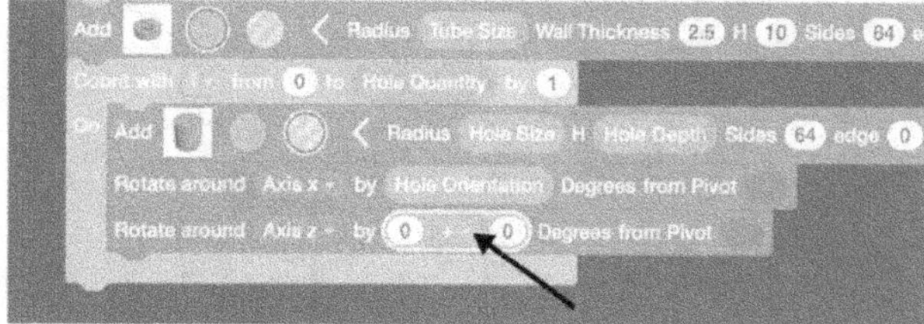

- Drag the **i** variable from the Variable section and drop it into the first value box of the Arithmetic block.
- Click the down arrow on the Arithmetic block and select *****.

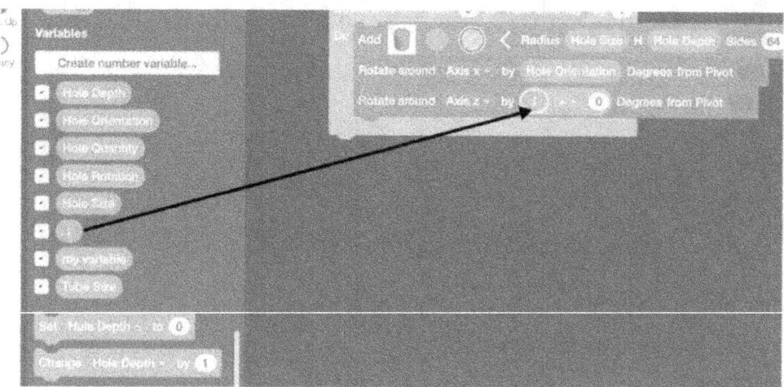 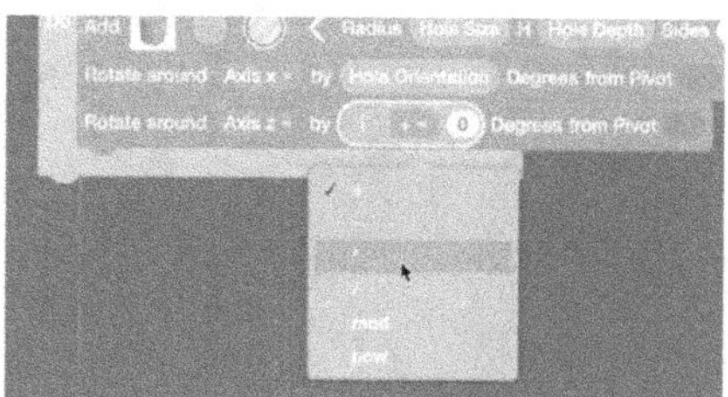

- Drag the **Hole Rotation** variable and drop it into the second value box.
- Change the **Hole Quantity** and **Hole Size** to **6** and **2**, respectively.
- Change the **Hole Rotation** value to **180/Hole Quantity**.

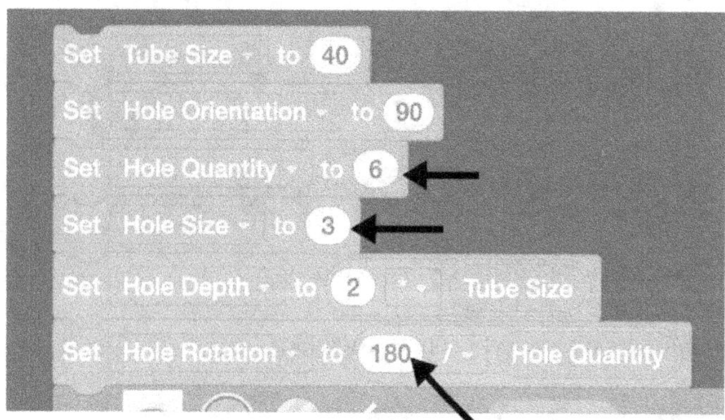

- Drag the **Create Group** block from the Modify section and place it at the bottom of the program

6. Using Markup Blocks

Now, you need to add comments to the code such that it is easy to understand.

- Click **Mark Up** and drag the **Comments** block. Next, place it above the variables.
- Change the comment to Bracelet Variables.

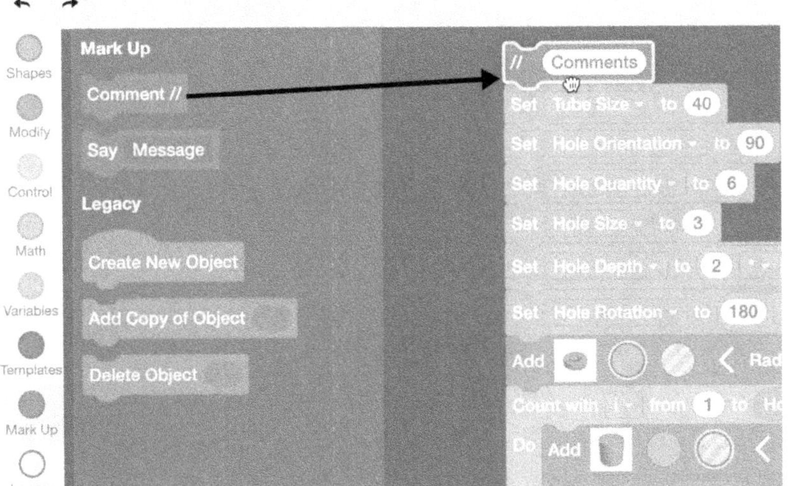
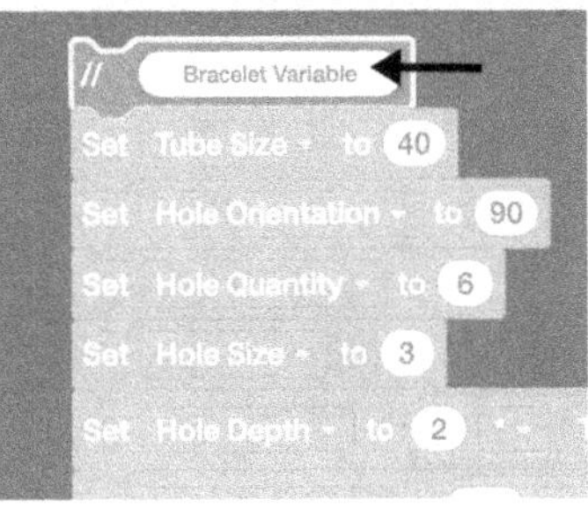

- Likewise, add comments to the blocks, as shown.

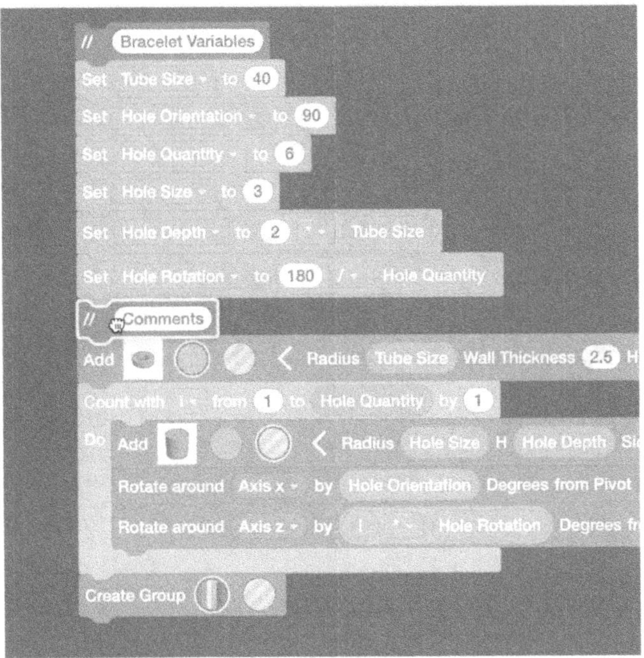
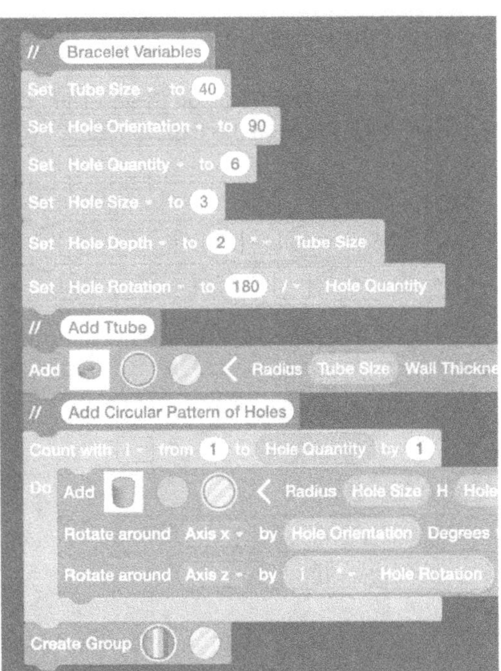

7. Testing and Previewing the Design

- Click the "**Run**" button and preview the bracelet design in the display area.

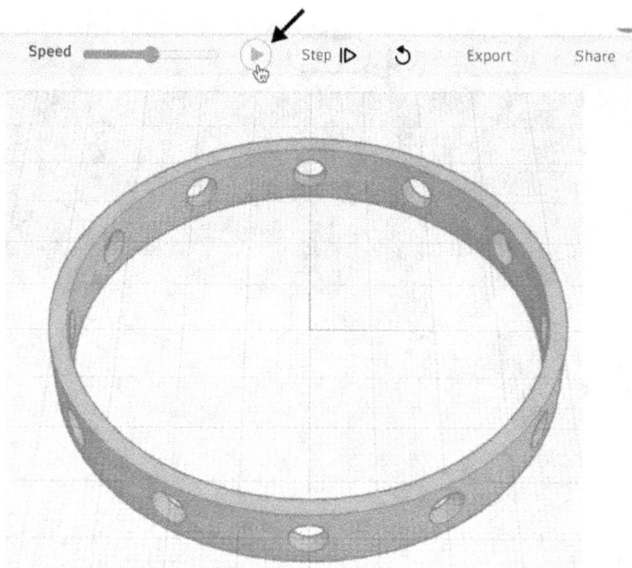

8. Exporting the Design

- Click the Export button on the top-right corner to export the design.
- Select the file from the Export dialog.